THE LITTLE FLOWERS OF SAINT FRANCIS

By ANONYMOUS

Translated by THOMAS OKEY

The Little Flowers of Saint Francis
By Anonymous
Translated by Thomas Okey

Print ISBN 13: 978-1-4209-6970-2
eBook ISBN 13: 978-1-4209-6971-9

This edition copyright © 2020. Digireads.com Publishing.

All rights reserved. No part of this publication may be reproduced, distributed, or transmitted in any form or by any means, including photocopying, recording, or other electronic or mechanical methods, without the prior written permission of the publisher, except in the case of brief quotations embodied in critical reviews and certain other noncommercial uses permitted by copyright law.

Cover Image: a detail of "St. Francis preaches to the birds", by Eugene Burnand, (1850-1921), c. 1919 (colour litho) / Bridgeman Images.

Please visit *www.digireads.com*

CONTENTS

THE LITTLE FLOWERS OF SAINT FRANCIS 5

THE CONSIDERATIONS OF THE HOLY STIGMATA 86

THE LIFE OF FRIAR JUNIPER 117

THE LIFE OF THE BLESSED FRIAR GILES 128

THE SAYINGS OF FRIAR GILES 134

The Little Flowers of Saint Francis

Chapter I

IN THE NAME OF OUR LORD JESUS CHRIST, THE CRUCIFIED, AND OF HIS MOTHER THE VIRGIN MARY. IN THIS BOOK ARE CONTAINED CERTAIN LITTLE FLOWERS, MIRACLES, AND DEVOUT EXAMPLES OF CHRIST'S POOR LITTLE ONE, ST. FRANCIS, AND OF SOME OF HIS COMPANIONS; TO THE PRAISE OF JESUS CHRIST. AMEN

It is first to be considered that the glorious St. Francis in all the acts of his life was conformable to Christ the Blessed. And that even as Christ, at the beginning of His mission, chose twelve Apostles who were to despise all worldly things and follow Him in poverty and in the other virtues, so St. Francis in the beginning chose for the foundation of his Order twelve companions who were possessed of naught save direst poverty. And even as one of the twelve Apostles of Christ, being reproved by God, went and hanged himself by the neck, so one of the twelve companions of St. Francis, whose name was Friar[1] John della Cappella, became a renegade and at last hanged himself by the neck. Now these things are a great warning to the elect, and matter for humility and fear when they consider that none is certain of persevering to the end in God's grace. And even as those holy Apostles were, above all, wondrous in their holiness and humility and filled with the Holy Ghost, so those most holy companions of St. Francis were men of such saintliness that, since the days of the Apostles, the world hath never beheld men so wondrously holy. For one among them was rapt, like St. Paul, up to the third heaven, and he was Friar Giles; another, to wit, Friar Philip, was touched on the lips by an angel with a coal of fire, even as the prophet Isaiah was; another, to wit, Friar Silvester, spake with God as one friend speaketh with another, after the manner of Moses; another by the purity of his mind soared as far as the light of the Divine Wisdom, even as did the Eagle, that is to say, John the Evangelist, and he was Friar Bernard, humblest of men, who was wont to expound the Holy Scriptures most profoundly; yet another was sanctified by God and canonised in heaven while yet he lived in the world, and he was Friar Rufus, a nobleman of Assisi. And thus were all distinguished by singular marks of holiness, as will be made clear hereafter.

---

[1] The Italian text distinguishes between *frate*—"friar" or "brother" in its religious sense—and *fratello*—"brother" in its ordinary sense.

Chapter II

OF FRIAR BERNARD OF QUINTAVALLE, THE FIRST COMPANION OF ST. FRANCIS

The first companion of St. Francis was Friar Bernard of Assisi, that was converted after this manner: St. Francis, while yet in the secular habit, albeit he had renounced the world, was wont to go about in meanest guise and so mortified by penance that by many he was held to be a fool, and was mocked and hunted as a madman and pelted with stones and filthy mire both by his kinsfolk and by strangers; but he, even as one deaf and dumb, went his way enduring every insult and injury patiently. Now Bernard of Assisi, who was one of the noblest and richest and wisest of that city, began to consider wisely concerning St. Francis and his exceeding contempt of this world and his long-suffering under injury; and that, albeit for two years he had been thus hated and despised by all men, yet did he ever seem more steadfast. And he began to ponder these things and to say within himself, "Of a surety this friar hath great grace from God." And he invited St. Francis to sup and lodge with him; and St. Francis accepted and supped and tarried the night. And then Bernard determined in his heart to contemplate his holiness: wherefore he had a bed made ready for him in his own chamber wherein by night a lamp ever burned. And St. Francis, to conceal his holiness, flung himself on his bed immediately he entered his chamber and feigned to sleep: and Bernard likewise, after a little while, lay down in his bed and began to snore loudly, as one wrapped in deepest slumber. Wherefore St. Francis, verily believing that Bernard slept, arose, in the stillness of the night, from his bed and knelt down to pray; lifting his eyes and hands to heaven he cried with great devotion and fervour, "My God, my God!" And so saying and weeping bitter tears, he prayed until morning, ever repeating, "My God, my God!" and naught else. And St. Francis said this, while contemplating and marvelling at the excellency of the Divine Majesty that had deigned to stoop down to this perishing world, and, through His poor little one, St. Francis, had resolved to bring healing salvation to his soul and to others. And therefore, illumined by the Holy Ghost or by the spirit of prophecy, he foresaw the great things that god was to work through him and his Order. And considering his own insufficiency and little worth he called on God Almighty and prayed that of His compassion He would supply, aid, and complete that which he of his own frailty could not achieve. Now Bernard, when he beheld these most devout acts of St. Francis by the light of the lamp, and had reverently considered the words he uttered, was moved and inspired by the Holy Ghost to change his manner of life; wherefore when morning was come he called St. Francis to him and spake thus, "Friar Francis, I have fully determined in my heart to forsake the world and obey thee in all things thou commandest me." When St. Francis heard this he rejoiced in spirit and said, "Bernard, this that you[2] tell is a work so great and so difficult that it behoves us to seek counsel of our Lord Jesus Christ and pray that it may please Him to reveal His will concerning this thing, and teach us how we may put it into execution. Therefore we will go together to the bishop's house, where a good priest dwells, and mass shall be said, and then we will remain in prayer until tierce, beseeching God that He will point out to us in three openings of the mass book the way it pleaseth Him we should choose." Bernard answered that this pleased him much. Whereupon they set forth and went to the bishop's house, and after they had heard mass and had remained in prayer until tierce, the priest, at the entreaty of St. Francis, took the book, and having made the sign of holy cross, opened it thrice in the name of our Lord Jesus Christ. And at the first opening he happened on those words that Christ in the gospel spake to the young man who asked concerning the perfect way, "If thou wilt be perfect, go and sell that thou hast and give to the poor and follow Me." In the second opening occurred those words that Christ spake to the Apostles when He sent them to preach, "Take nothing for your journey, neither staves nor scrip, neither shoes nor money," desiring by this to teach them that all trust for their livelihood should be placed in God, and all their mind intent on p reaching the holy gospel. In the third opening were found those words which Christ spake, "If any man will come after Me, let him take up his cross and follow Me." Then said St. Francis to Bernard, "Behold the counsel that Christ giveth us. Go, therefore, do faithfully what thou hast heard, and blessed be the name of our Lord Jesus Christ, who hath deigned to reveal to us the life evangelical." Hearing this, Bernard departed and sold all he had (for he was very rich), and with great joy distributed all to widows and orphans, to prisoners and hospitals and pilgrims; and in all these things St. Francis helped him faithfully and carefully. And one whose name was Silvester, when he saw that St. Francis gave and caused to be given so much money to the poor, was constrained by avarice, and said to St. Francis, "Thou didst not pay me fully for the stones thou boughtest of me to repair the church, and therefore now thou hast money, pay me." Then St. Francis, marvelling at his avarice, and as a true follower of the gospel desiring not to contend with him, thrust his hands in Bernard's bosom, and with hands full of money placed them in Silvester's bosom, saying, that if he would have more more should be given him. And

---

[2] *Voi* (you) instead of the more familiar *tu* (thou). The more reverent, *voi*, is used by Dante only in addressing spirits of great dignity, *e.g.* Brunetto Latino, Cacciaguida, and a very few others.

Silvester, satisfied with this, departed and returned home, but in the evening, pondering on what he had done that day and on the fervour of Bernard and the holiness of St. Francis, he reproved himself for his avarice. And that night following and two other nights he had from God this vision: he beheld a cross of gold issue from the mouth of St. Francis, the top whereof touched heaven, and the arms stretched from the east as far as the west. Because of this vision he gave up all he had for love of God, and became a friar minor, and such holiness and grace had he in the Order that he spake with God even as one friend with another, according as St. Francis proved and as will be related hereafter. Bernard likewise was so filled with God's grace that in contemplation he was often taken up to God. And St. Francis was wont to say of him that he was worthy of all reverence and had founded this Order, for he was the first who had forsaken the world, holding back nothing, but giving all to Christ's poor, and the first who began his evangelic poverty by offering himself naked to the arms of the Crucified, to whom be all praise and glory world without end. Amen.

Chapter III

HOW ST. FRANCIS, BY REASON OF AN EVIL THOUGHT HE CHERISHED AGAINST FRIAR BERNARD, COMMANDED THE SAID FRIAR THAT HE SHOULD TREAD THRICE ON HIS NECK AND MOUTH

St. Francis, the most devout servant of the Crucified, had grown almost blind by the rigour of his penance and incessant weeping, so that he saw but ill; and once on a time he departed from the place where he was, and went to a place where Friar Bernard was in order to speak with him of divine things. Being arrived there, he found that Friar Bernard was at prayer in the wood, wholly lifted up and united with God. Then St. Francis went forth into the wood and called him. "Come," said he, "and speak with this blind man." And Friar Bernard answered him not a word; for being a man great in contemplation, his soul was lifted up and raised to God. And forasmuch as Friar Bernard was possessed of singular grace in discoursing of God, even as St. Francis had proved many times, great was his desire to speak with him. After some while he called him a second and a third time in that same wise, and no time did Friar Bernard hear him: therefore he neither answered nor came to him; whereat St. Francis departed somewhat disconsolate, marvelling within himself and grieving that Friar Bernard, being called thrice, had not come to him. St. Francis turned away with these thoughts in his mind, and when he was gone some little distance he said to his companion, "Tarry for me here." And he went aside hard by into a solitary place and prostrated himself in prayer, beseeching God to reveal to him why Friar Bernard answered him not; and remaining thus in prayer there came to him a voice from God, saying, "O poor little one, wherefore art thou troubled? Ought a man to forsake God for His creature? When thou didst call, Friar Bernard was united with Me, and therefore could neither come to thee nor answer thee. Marvel thou not if he could not respond, for he was so lifted out of himself that of thy words he heard none." St. Francis, having heard these words from God, straightway returned with great haste towards Friar Bernard, in order to accuse himself humbly before him of the evil thoughts he had nursed concerning him. And Friar Bernard, beholding him come towards him, drew nigh and cast himself at his feet; and then St. Francis made him rise up, and with great humility related to him the thoughts he had had and the tribulation he had suffered concerning him, and how that God had answered his prayer. And thus he concluded, "I command thee by holy obedience that thou do whatsoever I command thee." Friar Bernard, fearing lest St. Francis might lay on him some excess of penance, as he was wont to do, desired with all sincerity to escape such obedience, and answered him thus, "I am ready to do your obedience if you will promise to do what I shall command you." And St. Francis gave him the promise. Then said Friar Bernard, "Say on, father; what would you that I do?" And St. Francis answered him, saying, "I command thee by holy obedience that, in order to punish the arrogance and rashness of my heart, thou shalt now, even as I lay me supine on the ground, set one foot on my neck and the other on my mouth, and so pass thrice from one side to the other, reviling and crying shame on me; and especially shalt thou say, 'Lie there, churl, son of Peter Bernadone! whence cometh such pride to thee, thou that art so vile a creature?'" Friar Bernard hearing this, albeit it was very hard to do, performed, in holy obedience, what St. Francis had commanded him, with all the gentleness he could. This done, St. Francis said, "Now command thou me what thou wouldest I should do, for I have promised thee holy obedience." Then said Friar Bernard, "I command thee by holy obedience, that every time we are together thou rebuke and correct me harshly for all my faults." Whereupon St. Francis marvelled greatly, for Friar Bernard was of such exceeding sanctity that he held him in great reverence and in no wise worthy of reproof. And thenceforth St. Francis was careful to avoid being much with him, because of the said obedience, lest it befell that he utter one word of reproof against him, that he knew to be of such great holiness. But when he desired to see him, or indeed to hear him speak of God, he made haste to leave him and depart from him, and a goodly thing it was to behold, what great charity and reverence and humility St. Francis, the father, used towards Bernard, his first-born son, when he spake with him. To the praise and glory of Christ Jesus and of the poor little Francis. Amen.

Chapter IV

HOW THE ANGEL OF GOD PUT A QUESTION TO FRIAR ELIAS, WARDEN OF THE FRIARY[3] IN THE VALE OF SPOLETO, AND BECAUSE FRIAR ELIAS ANSWERED HIM HAUGHTILY, DEPARTED AND WENT ALONG THE WAY TO ST. JAMES'S, WHERE HE FOUND FRIAR BERNARD AND TOLD HIM THE STORY

At the first beginning of the Order, when there were but few friars and their friaries were not yet established, St. Francis repaired for his devotions to St. James's of Compostella in Galicia, and took a few friars with him, one of whom was Friar Bernard. And as they journeyed thus together, he found a poor sick man in a village by the way. Filled with compassion, he said to Friar Bernard, "Son, I desire that thou remain here to tend this sick man"; and Friar Bernard humbly kneeling and bowing his head, reverently received the holy father's obedience and remained in that place: and St. Francis and the other companions went their way to St. James's. Arrived there, they passed the night in prayer in the church of St. James, where it was revealed to St. Francis that he was to establish many friaries throughout the world; for his Order was to spread and grow into a great multitude of friars: whereat, according to this revelation, St. Francis began to establish friaries in those lands. And as St. Francis was returning by the way he came, he found Friar Bernard, and the sick man with whom he had left him healed perfectly; whereupon St. Francis gave Friar Bernard leave to go the following year to St. James's. And St. Francis returned to the vale of Spoleto, and he and Friar Masseo and Friar Elias and others abode in a wilderness; and each took heed not to vex or disturb St. Francis in his prayers, because of the great reverence they bore him, and because they knew that God revealed great things to him in his prayers. It fell out one day, while St. Francis was in the wood at prayer, that a fair youth, apparelled as for a journey, came to the door of the friary and knocked so impatiently and loudly and for so long a time that the friars marvelled much at so unwonted a knocking. Friar Masseo went and opened the door, and said to the youth, "Whence comest thou, my son; it seemeth thou hast never been here before, so strangely hast thou knocked." The youth answered, "And how then ought one to knock?" Friar Masseo said, "Knock three times, one after the other, slowly; then tarry so long as the friar may say a paternoster and come to thee: and if

---

[3] *Luogo, luogo dei frati:* literally, "place of the friars." I have rendered this "friary" as well as the term *convento*, used by the Franciscans when in later times their poor hovels and caves were exchanged for edifices of brick and stone.

in this space of time he come not, knock once again." The youth answered, "I am in great haste, and therefore I knock thus loudly. I have to go a journey, and am come here to speak with Friar Francis; but he is now in the wood in contemplation, and I would not disturb him; but go and send Friar Elias to me, for I would ask him a question, and he is very wise." Friar Masseo goes and bids Friar Elias haste to that youth; and he takes offence and will not go. Whereat Friar Masseo knows not what to do, nor what answer to make to that youth; for if he said, "Friar Elias cannot come," he lied; if he said he was in evil humour, he feared to set a bad example. And while Friar Masseo was thus laggard in returning, the youth knocked yet again, even as before. Friar Masseo came back to the door and said to the youth, "Thou hast not observed my instructions in knocking." The youth answered, "Friar Elias will not come to me; but go thou and say to Friar Francis that I am come to speak with him; but since I would not disturb him in his prayers, bid him send Friar Elias to me." And then Friar Masseo went to St. Francis, that was praying in the wood with his face lifted up to heaven, and gave him the youth's message and Friar Elias's reply. And that youth was an angel of God in human form. Then St. Francis, changing neither his position nor lowering his face, said to Friar Masseo, "Depart and bid Friar Elias by obedience go to that youth." Now Friar Elias, when he heard the command of St. Francis, went in great fury to the door and flung it open with great violence and noise, saying to the youth, "What wouldst thou?" The youth answered, "Beware, friar, lest thou be angry as thou seemest, for anger hindereth much the soul and cloudeth the perception of truth." Friar Elias said, "Tell me, what wouldst thou of me?" The youth answered, "I ask thee if it be lawful for observers of the holy gospel to eat whatsoever is placed before them, according as Christ said to His disciples; and I likewise ask thee whether it be lawful for any man to command things contrary to evangelical liberty." Friar Elias answered proudly, "This know I well, but I will not answer thee: go thy ways." Said the youth, "I could answer this question better than thou." Then Friar Elias slammed the door in a great rage and departed. And then he began to ponder the said question and to doubt within himself, and he could not solve it; for he was vicar of the Order, and had ordered and made a rule outside the gospel and outside the Rule of St. Francis, to wit, that no friar of the Order should eat flesh: therefore the said question was aimed against him. Whereupon, unable to get clear with himself, he began to consider the youth's modesty, and that he had told him he could answer the question better than he, and Friar Elias returned to the door and opened it, to ask the youth concerning the aforesaid question. But he had already departed, for the pride of Friar Elias made him unworthy to speak with angels. This done, St. Francis, to whom all had been revealed by God, returned from the wood, and loudly and severely reproved Friar Elias, saying, "Thou dost ill, proud friar, that chasest away the holy angels from us that come to teach us. I tell thee, much do I fear lest thy pride make thee end thy days outside this Order." And so it befell thereafter even as St. Francis had said, for he died outside the Order. On that same day, at the very hour he departed, the angel appeared in that same form to Friar Bernard, who was walking along the bank of a great river, on his way back from St. James's, and gave him salutation in his own tongue, saying, "Hail, good friar, the peace of God be with thee!" And Friar Bernard marvelled greatly, and considering the comeliness of the youth and the salutation of peace in the mother tongue and his glad countenance, questioned him thus: "Whence comest thou, good youth?" The angel answered, "I come from such a place, where St. Francis dwells, and I went to speak with him, but could not, for he was in the wood contemplating divine things, and I would not disturb him. And in that same house dwell Friar Masseo and Friar Giles and Friar Elias; and Friar Masseo taught me how to knock at the door after the manner of a friar, but Friar Elias, because he would not answer a question I propounded to him, repented and desired thereafter to hear and see me; and he could not." Having spoken these words the angel said to Friar Bernard, "Wherefore dost thou not pass over yonder?" Friar Bernard answered, "Because I dread danger from the depth of the water I see." Said the angel, "Let us pass over together; fear not": and he takes his hand and in the twinkling of an eye places him on the other side of the river. Then Friar Bernard knew that he was the angel of God, and with great reverence and joy said in a loud voice, "O blessed angel of God, tell me, what is thy name?" The angel answered, "Wherefore askest thou my name, that is marvellous?" This said, the angel vanished, and left Friar Bernard much consoled, so much that he went all that journey with great joyfulness; and he marked the day and the hour of the angel's appearance. And reaching the friary, where St. Francis was with the aforesaid companions, he related to them all things in the order of their happening; and they knew of a surety that that same angel had appeared to them and to him on that very day and at that very hour.

Chapter V

HOW THE HOLY FRIAR BERNARD OF ASSISI WAS SENT BY ST. FRANCIS TO BOLOGNA, AND THERE ESTABLISHED A FRIARY

Forasmuch as St. Francis and his companions were called and chosen by God to bear the cross of Christ in their hearts and in their works, and to preach it with their tongues, they seemed and truly were, men crucified, so far as regarded their dress, the austerity of their lives, their acts, and their deeds; and therefore they desired rather to endure shame and reproach for love of Christ than worldly honour, or reverence, or praise from men. Yea, they rejoiced in contumely, and were afflicted by honour; they went about the world as pilgrims and strangers, bearing naught with them save Christ crucified. And because they were true branches of the true vine, which is Christ, they brought forth great and good fruit in the souls they won to God. It came to pass in the beginning of the Order that St. Francis sent Friar Bernard to Bologna, that he might bring forth fruit to God there, according to the grace God had given him. And Friar Bernard, having made the sign of holy cross, departed in holy obedience and came to Bologna. And when the children beheld him in a ragged and mean habit they mocked him and reviled him loudly as were he a fool. And Friar Bernard suffered all things patiently and joyfully for the love of Christ. Aye, and in order that he might be the more derided he set himself openly in the market-place of the city; and as he sat there many children and men gathered around him, and one plucked at his cowl from behind, and another in front; one cast dust at him, and another stones; one pushed him on this side, and another on that; but Friar Bernard, neither uttering complaint nor changing his position, abode there patient and glad: and for many days he returned to that same place, solely to endure the like things. And since patience is a work of perfection and proof of virtue, a wise doctor of laws, on beholding Friar Bernard's exceeding great constancy and virtue, and how he could not be provoked during many days by any hurt or insult, said within himself, "It is impossible but that this must be a holy man." And drawing nigh to him, spake to him thus, "Who art thou, and wherefore art thou come hither?" And for answer Friar Bernard put his hand in his bosom and drew forth the Rule of St. Francis and gave it him that he might read. And when he had read it and had considered its lofty perfection, he turned to the companions with greatest amazement and admiration, and said, "Verily this is the most exalted state of the religious life whereof I ever heard: therefore this man and his companions are the most saintly men in this world, and he who revileth him is the greatest of sinners; for he is worthy of highest honour since he is the true friend of God." Then said he to Friar Bernard, "If you would take a place wherein you might conveniently serve God, I fain would give it you for the salvation of my soul." Friar Bernard answered him, "Master, I believe this offer is an inspiration from our Lord Jesus Christ, and therefore willingly do I accept it for the honour of Christ." Then the said judge led Friar Bernard to his home with great love and joy: and he gave him the promised place, and furnished and completed it at his own cost: and thenceforth he became to him as a father, and was the diligent upholder of Friar Bernard and his companions. And Friar Bernard began to be so greatly honoured by all men, that any one who could touch or behold him held himself blessed. But he, as a true disciple of Christ and of the lowly Francis, fearing lest the honours of this world might hinder the peace and salvation of his soul, departed one day and returned to St. Francis, and spake to him thus, "The place has been taken in the city of Bologna; send friars thither to abide and maintain it, for I have no profit there; nay, I fear, by reason of the too great honour done to me, lest I lose more than I should gain." Then St. Francis, having heard all things in order that God had wrought there through Friar Bernard, gave thanks to God who thus began to spread abroad the poor little disciples of the cross: and then he sent some of his companions to Bologna and to Lombardy, who established many friaries in divers places.

Chapter VI

HOW ST. FRANCIS BLESSED THE HOLY FRIAR BERNARD AND APPOINTED HIM TO BE HIS VICAR WHEN HE SHOULD PASS FROM THIS LIFE

Friar Bernard was of such holiness that St. Francis bore him great reverence and ofttimes praised him. St. Francis being on a day devoutly at prayer, it was revealed to him of God that Friar Bernard, by divine permission, was to endure many and grievous assaults from devils, wherefore St. Francis, that had great compassion on the said Friar Bernard and loved him as a son, prayed many days in tears, commending him to Christ Jesus, and entreating God that victory over the devil might be vouchsafed to him. And one day while St. Francis was thus devoutly praying, God answered him, saying, "Francis, fear not; for all the temptations whereby Friar Bernard shall be assailed are permitted by God as an exercise of virtue and crown of merit; and at the last he shall gain the victory over all his enemies, for he is one of the ministers of the kingdom of heaven." At which answer St. Francis rejoiced greatly and gave thanks to God; and from that hour he bore greater love and reverence to Friar Bernard. And this he showed not only in his life, but also at his death, for when St. Francis came to die, after the manner of the holy patriarch Jacob, with his devout children standing around him, all sorrowing and weeping at the departure of so loving a father, he asked, "Where is my first-born? Come nigh to me, my son, that my soul may bless thee ere I die." Then Friar Bernard said secretly to Friar Elias, that was vicar of the Order, "Father, go to the right hand of the saint that he may bless thee." And Friar Elias drew nigh to his right hand, and St. Francis, that had lost his sight through excess of weeping, placed his right hand on Friar Elias's head, and said, "This is not the head of my first-born, Friar Bernard." Then Friar Bernard went to his left hand, and St. Francis moved his hands over in the form of a cross, and placed his right hand on Friar Bernard's head and his left on Friar Elias's head, and said to Friar Bernard, "God the Father and our Lord Jesus Christ bless thee with all spiritual and celestial blessings. Thou art the first-born, chosen in this holy Order to give evangelical example, and to follow Christ in evangelical poverty, for not only gavest thou thine own substance and didst distribute it wholly and freely to the poor for love of Christ, but thou didst offer thyself also to God in his Order, a sacrifice of sweetness. Blessed be thou therefore by our Lord Jesus Christ and by me, poor little one, His servant, with blessings everlasting, walking and standing, watching and sleeping, living and dying. Let him that blesseth thee be filled with blessings, and he who curseth thee go not unpunished. Be thou lord over thy brethren and let all the friars obey thy commands; whosoever thou wilt, let him be received into this Order; let no friar have lordship over thee, and be it lawful to thee to go and to abide wheresoever it may please thee." And after the death of St. Francis, the friars loved and revered Friar Bernard as a venerable father; and when he was nigh unto death, many friars came to him from divers parts of the earth, among whom was that angelic and divine Friar Giles; and he, beholding Friar Bernard, cried with great joy, "*Sursum corda, Friar Bernard, sursum corda!*" and Friar Bernard secretly bade a friar prepare for Friar Giles a place meet for contemplation; and this was done. Now Friar Bernard being come to the last hour of death, had himself raised up and spake to the friars that stood around him, saying, "Brethren, most dear, I will not say many words to you, but ye must consider that this religious state wherein I have lived, ye live; and such as I am now, ye shall be also, and this I know in my soul—that not for a thousand worlds such as this would I have renounced the service of our Lord Jesus Christ for that of any other lord, and I do now accuse me of all my offences, and confess my sins to Jesus my Saviour, and to you. I beseech you, dearest brothers mine, that ye love one another." And after these words and other good exhortations he lay back in his bed, and his countenance shone with exceeding great joy; whereat all the friars marvelled greatly; and in that joy his most holy soul departed from this present life, crowned with glory, to the blessed life of the angels.

Chapter VII

HOW ST. FRANCIS KEPT LENT ON AN ISLAND IN THE LAKE
OF PERUGIA, WHERE HE FASTED FORTY DAYS AND FORTY
NIGHTS, AND ATE NO MORE THAN HALF A LOAF

Forasmuch as St. Francis, the true servant of Christ, was in certain things well-nigh another Christ given to the world for the salvation of souls, it was the will of God the Father that in many of his acts he should be conformable and like unto His Son Jesus Christ, even as he showed to us in the venerable company of the twelve companions and in the wondrous mystery of the sacred stigmas, and in the continuous fast of the holy Lent, which he kept in this wise. St. Francis was once lodging on carnival day in the house of one of his devout followers on the shores of the lake of Perugia, and was inspired by God to go and pass that Lent on an island in the lake; wherefore St. Francis prayed his disciple to carry him in his little bark to an island, whereon no man dwelt, and this on the night of Ash Wednesday, to the end that none should perceive it. And he by the great love and devotion he bore to St. Francis satisfied diligently his desire, and carried him to the said island, St. Francis taking with him naught save two small loaves. And when he had reached the island, and his friend was about to depart and return to his home, St. Francis prayed him earnestly to reveal to no man where he was nor to come for him before Holy Thursday, and so the friend departed and St. Francis remained alone. And finding no house wherein he could take shelter, he crept into a very dense thicket of thorn and other bushes fashioned after the manner of a lair or a little hut: and in this place he betook himself to prayer and to the contemplation of divine things. And there he abode the whole of Lent, eating and drinking naught save the half of one of those small loaves, even as his devout friend perceived when he returned for him on Holy Thursday: for of the loaves he found one whole and the other half eaten. And it was believed that St. Francis ate this through reverence for the fasting of Jesus Christ, who fasted forty days and forty nights without taking any bodily food; for with this half-loaf he cast the venom of vainglory from him while following the example of Christ in the fast of forty days and forty nights. And God wrought many miracles thereafter in that same place where St. Francis had endured so marvellous an abstinence, because of his merits: wherefore folk began to build houses and to dwell there. And in brief time a fair town[4] was built there, and there also is the friary that is called of the island; and to this day the men and women of that town hold the place where St. Francis kept Lent in great devotion and reverence.

Chapter VIII

HOW ST. FRANCIS SET FORTH TO FRIAR LEO, AS THEY JOURNEYED TOGETHER, WHERE PERFECT JOY WAS TO BE FOUND

One winter's day, as St. Francis was going from Perugia with Friar Leo to St. Mary of the Angels, suffering sorely from the bitter cold, he called Friar Leo, that was going before him, and spake thus, "Friar Leo, albeit the friars minor in every land give good examples of holiness and

---

[4] *Castello.* See Petrocchi, *Nuovo dis. Universal de lingua ital. : piccolo paese con mura.*

edification, nevertheless write and note down diligently that perfect joy is not to be found therein." And St. Francis went his way a little farther, and called him a second time, saying, "O Friar Leo, even though the friar minor gave sight to the blind, made the crooked straight, cast out devils, made the deaf to hear, the lame to walk, and restored speech to the dumb, and, what is a yet greater thing, raised to life those who have lain four days in the grave; write perfect joy is not found there." And he journeyed on a little while, and cried aloud, "O Friar Leo, if the friar minor knew all tongues and all the sciences and all the Scriptures, so that he could foretell and reveal not only future things, but even the secrets of the conscience and of the soul; write—perfect joy is not there." Yet a little farther went St. Francis, and cried again aloud, "O Friar Leo, little sheep of god, even though the friar minor spake with the tongue of angels and knew the courses of the stars and the virtues of herbs, and were the hidden treasures of the earth revealed to him, and he knew the qualities of birds, and of fishes, and of all animals, and of man, and of trees, and stones, and roots, and waters—not there is perfect joy." And St. Francis went on again a little space, and cried aloud, "O Friar Leo, although the friar minor were skilled to preach so well that he should convert all the infidels to the faith of Christ; write— not there is perfect joy." And when this fashion of talk had endured two good miles, Friar Leo asked him in great wonder and said, "Father, prithee in God's name tell me where is perfect joy to be found?" And St. Francis answered him thus, "When we are come to St. Mary of the Angels, wet through with rain, frozen with cold, and foul with mire and tormented with hunger; and when we knock at the door, the doorkeeper cometh in a rage and saith, 'Who are ye?' and we say, 'We are two of your friars,' and he answers, 'Ye tell not true; ye are rather two knaves that go deceiving the world and stealing the alms of the poor; begone!' and he openeth not to us, and maketh us stay outside hungry and cold all night in the rain and snow; then if we endure patiently such cruelty, such abuse, and such insolent dismissal without complaint or murmuring, and believe humbly and charitably that that doorkeeper truly knows us, and that God maketh him to rail against us; O Friar Leo, write—there is perfect joy. And if we persevere in our knocking, and he issues forth and angrily drives us away, abusing us and smiting us on the cheek, saying, 'Go hence, ye vile thieves, get ye gone to the workhouse; here ye shall neither eat nor lodge'; if this we suffer patiently with love and gladness; write, O Friar Leo—this is perfect joy. And if, constrained by hunger and by cold, we knock once more and pray with many tears that he open to us for the love of God and let us but come inside, and he more insolently than ever crieth, 'These be impudent rogues, I will pay them out as they deserve'; and issues forth with a big knotted stick and seizes us by our cowls and flings us on the ground and rolls us in the snow, bruising every bone in our bodies with that heavy stick—if we, thinking on the agony of the blessed Christ, endure all these things patiently and joyously for love of Him; write, O Friar Leo, that here and in this perfect joy is found. And now, Friar Leo, hear the conclusion. Above all the grace and the gifts of the Holy Spirit that Christ giveth to His beloved is that of overcoming self, and for love of Him willingly to bear pain and buffetings and revilings and discomfort; for in none other of God's gifts, save these, may we glory, seeing they are not ours, but of God. Wherefore the Apostle saith, 'What hast thou that is not of God, and if thou hast received it of Him, wherefore dost thou glory as if thou hadst it of thyself?' But in the cross of tribulation and of affliction we may glory, because this is ours. Therefore the Apostle saith, 'I will not glory save in the cross of our Lord Jesus Christ.'"

Chapter IX

HOW ST. FRANCIS TAUGHT FRIAR LEO HOW TO ANSWER HIM, AND FRIAR LEO COULD NEVER SAY AUGHT SAVE THE CONTRARY OF THAT WHICH ST. FRANCIS BADE HIM ANSWER

In the early days of the Order, St. Francis and Friar Leo were once in a friary where no book could be found wherefrom the divine offices might be said, and when the hour of matins was come St. Francis said to Friar Leo, "Dearest, we have no breviary to say matins from; but in order that we may spend the time in praise of God, I will speak and thou shalt answer me as I teach thee, and beware lest thou change one of the words I teach thee. I will say thus, 'O Friar Francis, thou hast done so many evil deeds and committed so many sins in the world that thou art deserving of hell'; and thou, Friar Leo, shalt answer, 'Truly thou dost merit the deepest hell.'" Friar Leo said, with dove-like simplicity, "Willingly, father; do thou begin in God's name." Then St. Francis began to say, "O Friar Francis, thou hast done so many evil deeds and hast committed so many sins in the world that thou art deserving of hell." And Friar Leo answers, "God will perform so many good works through thee that thou shalt go to paradise." Saith St. Francis, "Say not so, Friar Leo, but when I say, 'O Friar Francis, thou hast committed so many iniquities against God that thou art worthy of being cursed by God,' do thou answer thus, 'Verily thou art worthy of being numbered among the accursed.'" And Friar Leo answers, "Willingly, father." Then St. Francis, with many tears and sighs and smitings of the breast, said with a loud voice, "O Lord God of heaven and earth, I have committed so many sins and iniquities against Thee that I am wholly worthy of being cursed by Thee." And Brother Leo answers, "O Friar Francis, God will do in such wise that among the blessed thou shalt be singularly blessed." St. Francis, marvelling that

Friar Leo ever answered contrary to that which he had charged him, rebuked him thus, saying, "Wherefore answerest thou not as I teach thee? I command thee by holy obedience that thou answer as I teach thee. I will say thus, 'O Friar Francis, little wretch, thinkest thou God will have mercy on thee, seeing thou hast committed so many sins against the Father of mercies and God of all consolations that thou art not worthy to find mercy?' And thou, Friar Leo, little sheep, shalt answer, 'In no wise art thou worthy of finding mercy.'" But when St. Francis said, "O Friar Francis, little wretch," *et cetera*, lo, Friar Leo answered, "God the Father, whose mercy is infinite, far exceeding thy sins, will show great mercy to thee, and will add likewise many graces thereto." At this answer St. Francis, sweetly angry and meekly perturbed, said to Friar Leo, "Wherefore hast thou had the presumption to act counter to obedience, and so many times hast answered the contrary of what I told thee and charged thee?" Father Leo answers, with deep humility and reverence, "God knoweth, my father; for I have purposed in my heart each time to answer as thou hast commanded me; but God maketh me to speak as it pleaseth Him, and not as it pleaseth me." Whereat St. Francis marvelled, and said to Friar Leo, "I pray thee most dearly, answer me this once as I have charged thee." Said Friar Leo, "Say on, in God's name, for of a surety this time I will answer as thou desirest." And St. Francis said, in tears, "O Friar Francis, little wretch, thinkest thou God will have mercy on thee?" *et cetera*. And Friar Leo answers, "Nay, rather great grace shalt thou receive of God, and He will exalt thee and glorify thee everlastingly, because he that humbleth himself shall be exalted; and naught else can I say, for God speaketh by my mouth." And so in this lowly disputation, with many tears and much spiritual consolation, they watched until the dawn.

Chapter X

HOW FRIAR MASSEO, HALF IN JEST, SAID TO ST. FRANCIS THAT THE WHOLE WORLD WAS FOLLOWING AFTER HIM; AND ST. FRANCIS ANSWERED THAT BY GOD'S GRACE IT WAS SO TO THE CONFUSION OF THE WORLD

While St. Francis was abiding at the friary of the Porziuncula with Friar Masseo of Marignano, a man of great holiness and discernment and grace in discoursing of God, and therefore much beloved of him, he was returning one day from prayer in the wood, and was already on the point of issuing therefrom, when Friar Masseo, desiring to prove his humility, made towards him and said, half jestingly, "Why after thee? Why after thee? Why after thee?" And St. Francis answered, "What meanest thou?" Said Friar Masseo, "I mean why doth all the world follow after thee, and why doth every man desire to see thee and to hear thee and to obey thee? Thou art not fair to look upon; thou art not a man of great parts; thou art not of noble birth. Whence cometh it, then, that all the world followeth after thee?" When St. Francis heard this he rejoiced exceedingly in spirit, and raising his face to heaven, remained for a great space with his soul uplifted to God. And then, returning to himself, he knelt down and gave praise and thanks to God. Then with great fervour of spirit he turned to Friar Masseo and said, "Wouldst thou know why after me? Wouldst thou know why after me? Wouldst thou know why after me? Know that this I have from those eyes of the most high God, that everywhere behold the righteous and the wicked, and forasmuch as those most holy eyes have beheld among sinners none more vile, more imperfect, nor a greater sinner than I, therefore since He hath found no viler creature on earth to accomplish the marvellous work He intendeth, He hath chosen me to confound the nobility, the majesty, the might, the beauty, and the wisdom of the world; in order to make manifest that every virtue and every good thing cometh from Him the Creator, and not from the creature, and that none may glory before Him: but that he that glories shall glory in the Lord, to whom belong all glory and all honour for ever and ever." Then Friar Masseo waxed sore afraid at this lowly answer given with great fervour, and knew of a surety that St. Francis was grounded in humility.

Chapter XI

HOW ST. FRANCIS MADE FRIAR MASSEO TURN ROUND AND ROUND
MANY TIMES, AND THEN WENT HIS WAY TO SIENA

On a day as St. Francis was journeying with Friar Masseo, the said Friar Masseo went a little in front of him; and when they reached a point where three ways met—one leading to Florence, another to Siena, and a third to Arezzo—Friar Masseo said, "Father, which road ought we to follow?" St. Francis answered, "That which God willeth." Said Friar Masseo, "And how shall we know the will of God?" St. Francis answered, "By the token I shall show thee: wherefore I command thee by the merit of holy obedience that at this parting of the ways, and on the spot where thou now standest, thou shalt turn round and round as children do, and shalt not cease turning until I bid thee." Then Friar Masseo began to turn round and round, and continued so long that by reason of the giddiness which is wont to be begotten by such turning, he fell many times to the ground; but, as St. Francis did not bid him stay, he rose up again, for faithfully he desired to obey him. At length, when he was turning lustily, St. Francis cried, "Stay; stir not!" And he stayed. Then St. Francis asked him, "Towards which part is thy face turned?" Friar Masseo answers, "Towards Siena." Said St. Francis, "That is the road God wills we should go." And as they walked by the way, Friar Masseo marvelled that St. Francis had made him turn around and around even as a child doth, in the presence of secular folk that were passing by: yet for very reverence he dared say naught thereof to the holy father. As they drew nigh to Siena the people of that city, hearing of the advent of the saint, made towards him; and in their devotion they carried the saint and his companion shoulder high as far as the bishop's house, so that they never touched ground with their feet. Now in that same hour certain men of Siena were fighting among themselves, and already two of them had been slain. When St. Francis came among them he preached with such great devotion and sanctity that he brought the whole of them to make peace and to dwell in great unity and concord together. Wherefore, when the bishop of Siena heard of the holy work that St. Francis had accomplished, he invited him to his house, and received him that day and that night also with the greatest honour. And the following morning St. Francis, who in all his works sought but the glory of God, arose betimes and with true humility departed with his companion without the knowledge of the bishop. Wherefore the said Friar Masseo went murmuring within himself by the way, and saying, "What is this that holy man hath done? Me he made to turn round and round as a child, and to the bishop who did him so much honour he said naught, not even a word of thanks": and it seemed to Friar Masseo that St. Francis had borne himself indiscreetly. But soon, by divine inspiration, Friar Masseo bethought him and reproved himself in his heart, and said, "Friar Masseo, thou art over-proud, thou that judgest the ways of God, and for thy indiscreet pride art worthy of hell. For yesterday Friar Francis wrought such holy works, that they could not have been more marvellous if the angel of God had done them. Wherefore if he should command thee to cast stones, thou shouldst obey him; for what he hath wrought in this city hath been by divine operation, even as is manifest in the good that followeth thereafter; because had he not made peace among those that were fighting, not only would many bodies have been slain by the knife (even as had already begun to come to pass), but many souls likewise would have been dragged to hell by the devil. Therefore art thou very foolish and proud, thou that murmurest at these things which manifestly proceed according to the will of God." Now all these things that this friar was saying in his heart were revealed by God to St. Francis, wherefore St. Francis drew nigh to him and said, "Hold fast to those things thou art now thinking, for they are good and profitable, and inspired by God; but thy first murmurings were blind and vain and proud, and instigated by the evil one." Then did Friar Masseo perceive clearly that St. Francis knew the secrets of his heart, and he understood that of a surety the Spirit of divine wisdom governed the holy father in all his works.

Chapter XII

HOW ST. FRANCIS APPOINTED FRIAR MASSEO TO BE
DOORKEEPER, ALMONER, AND COOK: THEN AT THE ENTREATIES
OF THE OTHER FRIARS REMOVED HIM

St. Francis, desiring to humble Friar Masseo in order that by reason of the many gifts and graces God had bestowed on him he should not be puffed up with vainglory, but by virtue of humility should increase from virtue to virtue, said to him on a day when he was dwelling with his first companions in a solitary place—those truly holy companions whereof Friar Masseo was one,—"O Friar Masseo, all these thy companions have the gift of contemplation and of prayer; but thou hast the gift of preaching the word of God to the satisfaction of the people. Therefore I desire that thou take upon thee the offices of doorkeeper, of almoner, and of cook, in order that thy companions may give themselves up to contemplation; and when the other friars are eating, thou shalt eat outside the door of the friary, so that thou mayst satisfy with some sweet words of God those who come to the convent, ere they knock; and so that no other friar than thou have need to go outside. And this do through the merit of holy obedience." Then Friar Masseo drew back his cowl and inclined his head and humbly received and fulfilled this command, and for many days he discharged the offices of doorkeeper, and almoner, and cook. Whereat the companions, even as men illumined by God, began to feel great remorse in their hearts, considering that Friar Masseo was a man of as great perfection as they were, or even greater; and yet on him was laid the whole burden of the convent, and not on them. Wherefore, moved by one desire, they went with one accord and entreated the holy father to be pleased to distribute those offices among them; for in no wise could they endure in their conscience that Friar Masseo should bear so many burdens. When St. Francis heard this he gave heed to their prayers and consented to their desire, and calling Friar Masseo he thus spake to him, "Friar Masseo, thy companions would have a share in the offices wherewith I have charged thee: it is therefore my will that the said offices be divided." Says Friar Masseo, with great humility and meekness, "Father, whatsoever thou layest upon me, either all or part, that I hold to be wholly done of God." Then St. Francis, beholding the love of them and the humility of Friar Masseo, preached a wondrous sermon touching most holy humility, admonishing them that the greater the gifts and graces that God bestows upon us, the greater ought our humility to be; for without humility no virtue is acceptable to God. And when he had made an end of his sermon he apportioned the offices among them with the great loving-kindness.

Chapter XIII

HOW ST. FRANCIS AND FRIAR MASSEO SET DOWN THE BREAD THEY HAD BEGGED ON A STONE BESIDE A SPRING, AND ST. FRANCIS GREATLY PRAISED POVERTY. THEN HE PRAYED UNTO GOD AND ST. PETER AND ST. PAUL THAT THEY WOULD INSPIRE HIM WITH THE LOVE OF HOLY POVERTY; AND HOW ST. PETER AND ST. PAUL APPEARED TO HIM

The wondrous servant and follower of Christ, to wit, St. Francis, to the end that he might conform himself to Christ perfectly in all things (who, according to the gospel, sent His disciples two by two unto all those cities and places whither He was to go), gathered together twelve companions and sent them forth after the example of Christ two by two to preach throughout the world. And St. Francis, that he might give them an example of true obedience, himself set forth first, after the example of Christ, who began to do before He began to teach. Wherefore, having assigned to his companions the other quarters of the world, he took Friar Masseo with him as his companion and went his way towards the land of France. And journeying one day they came to a city sore a-hungered, and went, according to the Rule, begging bread for love of God: and St. Francis took one street and Friar Masseo another. But forasmuch as St. Francis was a man of mean appearance and short of stature, and therefore looked down upon as a poor vile creature by those who knew him not, he collected naught save a few mouthfuls of dry crusts; but to Friar Masseo many large pieces of bread and even whole loaves were given, for he was fair and tall of body. And after they had begged their food, they met to eat together at a place outside the city where was a fair fountain, and beside it a fair broad stone, whereon each laid the alms he had collected. Now when St. Francis saw that the bread and loaves brought by Friar Masseo were finer and larger than his own, he showed forth joy exceeding great, and spake thus, "O Friar Masseo, we are not worthy of so great a treasure." And having repeated these words many times, Friar Masseo answered, "Dearest father, how can that be called a treasure where there is poverty so great and such lack of needful things? Here is neither cloth, nor knife, nor trencher, nor bowl, nor house, nor table, nor manservant, nor maid-servant." Then said St. Francis, "And this is what I hold to be a great treasure: where there is no dwelling made by human hands, but all is prepared for us by divine providence, even as is made manifest by the bread we have collected on this table of stone so fair and this fountain so clear. Therefore I desire that we pray unto God that He may make us love with all our hearts this noble treasure of holy poverty that hath God for its servitor." After these words they refreshed their bodies, and having made their prayer, rose up and journeyed on to France. And when they came to a church, St. Francis said to his companion, "Let us enter into this church to pray." And St. Francis goes behind the altar and kneels down in prayer. And as he prayed he was inspired by the divine presence with fervour so exceeding great that his whole soul was inflamed with love for holy poverty; in such wise that what with the hue of his face and the strange yawning of his mouth, it seemed as if flames of love were bursting from him. And coming thus aflame towards his companion, he spake thus to him, "Ah, ah, ah, Friar Masseo; give thyself to me." And this he said thrice; and the third time St. Francis lifted up Friar Masseo into the air with his breath, and cast him away from him the length of a tall spear; whereat Friar Masseo was filled with great amaze. And he afterwards related to his companions that when St. Francis thus lifted him up and cast him from him with his breath, he felt such great sweetness in his soul, and such deep consolation from the Holy Spirit, that never in his life had he felt the like. This done, St. Francis said, "Dearest companion, go we now to St. Peter and St. Paul and pray them to teach us and aid us to possess this boundless treasure of holiest poverty; for it is a treasure of such exceeding worth and so divine that we are unworthy to possess it in our vile vessels. Yea! this is that celestial virtue whereby all earthly and transitory things are trodden under foot and whereby every hindrance is removed from the soul that she may be freely conjoined with the eternal God. This is the virtue that maketh the soul, while yet on earth, have communion with the angels in heaven; that companioned Christ on the cross; with Christ was buried; with Christ rose again, and with Christ ascended into heaven. It is this virtue also that easeth the flight into heaven of those souls that love it; for it guards the armour of true humility and charity. Therefore let us pray unto the most holy Apostles of Christ, who were perfect lovers of this pearl evangelical, to obtain for us this grace from our Lord Jesus Christ: that He in His holy mercy may vouchsafe to us to grow worthy to be true lovers and followers and humble disciples of the most precious and most lovable gospel poverty." Thus discoursing, they came to Rome and entered St. Peter's church; and St. Francis set himself to pray in one corner of the church, and Friar Masseo in another. And as St. Francis remained in prayer a long while, with many tears and great devotion, the holy Apostles Peter and Paul appeared to him in great splendour, and said, "Forasmuch as thou askest and desirest to serve that which Christ and His holy Apostles served, our Lord Jesus Christ sendeth us to thee to announce that thy prayer is heard, and that God granteth to thee and to thy followers the perfect treasure of holiest poverty. And from Him also we say unto thee, that whosoever, following thy example, shall pursue this desire perfectly, he is assured of the blessedness of life eternal; and thou and all thy followers shall be blessed of God." These words said, they vanished, leaving St. Francis filled with consolation; who, rising from prayer, returned to his companion and asked him if God had revealed aught to him; and he answered, "Nay." Then St. Francis told him how the holy apostles had appeared to him, and what they had revealed. Whereupon each of them, filled with joy, purposed to return to the vale of Spoleto, and renounce the journey into France.

Chapter XIV

HOW, WHILE ST. FRANCIS AND HIS FRIARS WERE DISCOURSING OF GOD, HE APPEARED IN THEIR MIDST

In the early days of the Order, as St. Francis was communing with his companions and discoursing of Christ, he, in fervour of spirit, bade one of them open his lips in God's name and speak what the Holy Ghost would inspire him to say concerning God. This friar having fulfilled his behest and discoursed wondrously of God, St. Francis laid silence upon him, and gave a like command to another friar. He also having obeyed and spoken subtly of God, St. Francis in like manner laid silence upon him, and bade a third speak of God; and he likewise began to discourse so profoundly of the hidden things of God that St. Francis knew of a surety that he, together with the other two, had spoken by the Holy Ghost; and this was shown forth also by example and by a clear token; for while they were thus speaking the blessed Christ appeared in the midst of them in the similitude and form of a most fair youth, and blessed them and filled them with so much grace and sweetness that they all were rapt out of themselves, and lay as though dead and insensible to the things of this world. And when they returned to themselves, St. Francis said to them, "Brothers mine, most dear, give thanks to God, who hath willed to reveal the treasures of divine wisdom through the lips of the simple; for God is He that openeth the mouths of the dumb, and the tongues of the simple He maketh to speak great wisdom."

Chapter XV

HOW ST. CLARE ATE WITH ST. FRANCIS AND HIS FELLOW-FRIARS AT ST. MARY OF THE ANGELS

When St. Francis was at Assisi he visited St. Clare many times and gave her holy instruction, and she having great desire to eat once with him did entreat him thereof many times, but never would he grant her this consolation. Whereupon his companions, beholding St. Clare's desire, spake to St. Francis and said, "Father, it seemeth to us too severe a thing and not in accord with divine charity that thou grantest not the prayer of Sister Clare, that is a virgin so holy and so beloved of God, in so small a grace as to eat with thee; above all, when we consider that through thy preaching she forsook the pomps and riches of this world. Nay, had she asked even greater grace of thee thou shouldst grant it to her, thy spiritual plant." Then St. Francis answered, "Doth it seem good to you that I should grant her prayer?" His companions made answer, "Father, even so, for it is meet that thou grant her this grace and give her consolation." Then said St. Francis, "Since it seemeth good to you, even so it seemeth good to me. But that she may be the more consoled, I desire that this repast be made in St. Mary of the Angels; for long hath she been shut up in St. Damian's, and it will profit her to behold the friary of St. Mary, where her hair was shorn and she became the spouse of Jesus Christ: there will we break bread together in the name of God." And when the appointed day came, St. Clare came forth from the convent with one companion, and accompanied by the companions of St. Francis, journeyed to St. Mary of the Angels; and having devoutly saluted the Virgin Mary, before whose altar she had been shorn and veiled, the companions conducted her around to see the friary of St. Mary's until the hour of the repast was come. Meanwhile St. Francis made ready the table on the bare ground, as he was wont to do. And the hour for dinner being come, St. Francis and St. Clare, and one of the companions of St. Francis and the companion of St. Clare, seated themselves together; and all the other companions of St. Francis then humbly took their places at the table. And for the first dish St. Francis began to discourse of God so sweetly, so loftily, and so wondrously that a bounteous measure of divine grace descended upon them and they were all rapt in God. And being thus ravished, with eyes and hands lifted up to heaven, the men of Assisi and of Bettona, and the men of the country round about, beheld St. Mary of the Angels and the whole friary and the wood that was around about it brightly flaming; and it seemed as 'twere a great fire that was devouring the church and the friary and the wood together: wherefore the men of Assisi, verily believing that everything was in flames, ran down thither with great haste to quench the fire. But when they came to the friary and found nothing burning, they entered within and beheld St. Francis with St. Clare and all their companions seated around that humble table and rapt in the contemplation of God. Wherefore they understood that truly the fire had not been a material fire, but a divine fire which God had miraculously made to appear in order to show forth and signify the fire of divine love wherewith the souls of these holy friars and holy nuns did burn: and they departed with great consolation in their hearts and with holy edification. Then after a long space St. Francis and St. Clare, together with the companions, returned to themselves, and feeling well comforted with spiritual food, took little heed of corporeal food; and thus that blessed repast being ended, St.

Clare, well companioned, returned to St. Damian's. And when the sisters beheld her they had great joy, for they feared lest St. Francis had sent her to rule over some other convent, even as he had already sent Sister Agnes, her holy sister, to rule, as abbess, over the convent of Monticelli at Florence. For on a time St. Francis had said to St. Clare, "Make thee ready if it so be that I must needs send thee to another convent." And she, even as a daughter of holy obedience, he answered, "Father, behold I am ever ready to go withersoever thou wilt send me." Therefore the sisters rejoiced greatly when they had her back again, and thenceforth St. Clare abode there much consoled.

Chapter XVI

HOW ST. FRANCIS HAD COUNSEL FROM ST. CLARE AND FROM THE HOLY FRIAR SILVESTER, TO WIT, THAT HE WAS TO CONVERT MUCH PEOPLE: AND HOW HE STABLISHED THE THIRD ORDER AND PREACHED TO THE BIRDS AND MADE THE SWALLOWS HOLD THEIR PEACE

St. Francis, humble servant of God, a short time after his conversion, having gathered together many companions and received them into the Order, fell into great perplexity and doubt touching what it behoved him to do—whether to be wholly intent on prayer, or sometimes to preach. And greatly he desired to know the will of God touching these things. But since the holy humility wherewith he was filled suffered him not to lean overmuch on his own judgment, nor on his own prayers, he bethought him to seek the divine will through the prayers of others. Wherefore he called Friar Masseo to him and spake to him thus, "Go to Sister Clare and bid her from me that she and some of the most spiritual of her companions pray devoutly unto God, that He may be pleased to reveal to me which is the more excellent way: whether to give myself up to preaching or wholly to prayer; then go to Friar Silvester and bid him do the like." Now he had been in the world and was that same Friar Silvester that beheld a cross of gold issue from the mouth of St. Francis, the length whereof was high as heaven, and the breadth whereof reached to the uttermost parts of the earth. And this Friar Silvester was a man of such great devotion and holiness that whatsoever he asked of God he obtained, and the same was granted to him; and ofttimes he spake with God, wherefore great was the devotion of St. Francis to him. Friar Masseo went forth and gave his message first to St. Clare, as St. Francis had commanded, and then to Friar Silvester, who no sooner had heard the command than he straightway betook himself to prayer, and when he had received the divine answer, he returned to Friar Masseo and spake these words, "Thus saith the Lord God, 'Go to Friar Francis and say unto him that God hath not called him to this state for himself alone, but that he may bring forth fruit of souls and that many through him may be saved.'" Friar Masseo, having received this answer, returned to Sister Clare to learn what answer she had obtained of God; and she answered that she and her companions had received the selfsame response from God that Friar Silvester had. And Friar Masseo returned with this answer to St. Francis, who greeted him with greatest charity, washing his feet and setting meat before him. And St. Francis called Friar Masseo, after he had eaten, into the wood, and there knelt down before him, drew back his cowl, and making a cross with his arms, asked of him, "What doth my Lord Jesus Christ command?" Friar Masseo answers, "Thus to Friar Silvester and thus to Sister Clare and her sisterhood hath Christ answered and revealed His will: that thou go forth to preach throughout the world, for He hath not chosen thee for thyself alone, but also for the salvation of others." Then St. Francis, when he had heard these words and learned thereby the will of Christ, rose up and said with great fervour, "Let us then go forth in God's name." And with him he took Friar Masseo and Friar Agnolo, holy men both, and setting forth with great fervour of spirit and taking heed neither of road nor path, they came to a city called Saburniano. And St. Francis began to preach, first commanding the swallows to keep silence until his sermon were ended; and the swallows obeying him, he preached with such zeal that all the men and women of that city desired in their devotion to follow after him and forsake the city. But St. Francis suffered them not, saying, "Be not in haste to depart, for I will ordain what ye shall do for the salvation of your souls." And then he bethought him of the third Order which he stablished for the universal salvation of all people. And so, leaving them much comforted and well disposed to penitence, he departed thence and came to a place between Cannara and Bevagna. And journeying on in that same fervour of spirit, he lifted up his eyes and beheld some trees by the wayside whereon were an infinite multitude of birds; so that he marvelled and said to his companions, "Tarry here for me by the way and I will go and preach to my little sisters the birds." And he entered into the field and began to preach to the birds that were on the ground; and anon those that were on the trees flew down to hear him, and all stood still the while St. Francis made an end of his sermon; and even then they departed not until he had given them his blessing. And according as Friar Masseo and Friar James of Massa thereafter related, St. Francis went among them, touching them with the hem of his garment, and not one stirred. And the substance of the sermon St. Francis preached was this, "My little sisters the birds, much are ye beholden to God your Creator, and always and in every place ye ought to praise Him for that He hath given you a double and a triple vesture; He hath given you freedom to go into every place, and also did preserve the seed of you in the ark of Noe, in order that your kind might not perish from the earth. Again, ye are beholden to Him for the element of air which He hath appointed for you; moreover, ye sow not, neither do ye reap, and God feedeth you and giveth you the rivers and the fountains for your drink; He giveth you the mountains and the valleys for your refuge, and the tall trees wherein to build your nests, and forasmuch as ye can neither spin nor sew God clotheth you, you and your children: wherefore your Creator loveth you much, since He hath dealt so bounteously with you; and therefore beware, little sisters mine, of the sin of ingratitude, but ever strive to praise God." While St. Francis was uttering these words, all those birds began to open their beaks, and stretch their necks, and spread their wings, and reverently to bow their heads to the ground, showing by their gestures and songs that the holy father's words gave them greatest joy: and St. Francis was glad and rejoiced with them, and marvelled much at so great a multitude of birds and at their manifold loveliness, and at their attention and familiarity; for which things he devoutly praised the Creator in them. Finally, his sermon ended, St. Francis made the sign of holy cross over them and gave them leave to depart; and all those birds soared up into the air in one flock with wondrous songs, and then divided themselves into four parts after the form of the cross St. Francis had made over them; and one part flew towards the east; another towards the west; the third towards the south, and the fourth towards the north. And each flock sped forth singing wondrously, betokening thereby that even as St. Francis, standard-bearer of the cross of Christ, had preached to them and had made the sign of the cross over them, according to which they had divided themselves, singing, among the four quarters of the world, so the preaching of Christ's cross, renewed by St. Francis, was, through him and his friars, to be borne throughout the whole world; the which friars possessing nothing of their own in this world, after the manner of birds, committed their lives wholly to the providence of God.

Chapter XVII

HOW A LITTLE BOY FRIAR, WHILE ST. FRANCIS WAS PRAYING BY NIGHT, BEHELD CHRIST AND THE VIRGIN MARY AND MANY OTHER SAINTS DISCOURSING WITH HIM

A boy most pure and innocent was received into the Order, during the life of St. Francis, in a convent so small that the friars were of necessity constrained to sleep two in a bed. And St. Francis once came to the said convent, and at even, after compline, lay down to rest that he might rise up to pray in the night while the other friars slept, as he was wont to do. The said boy having set his heart on spying out diligently the ways of St. Francis, lay down to sleep beside St. Francis that he might understand his holiness, and chiefly what he did by night when he rose up; and in order that sleep might not beguile him, he tied his own cord to the cord of St. Francis, that he might feel when he stirred: and of this St. Francis perceived naught. But by night, during the first sleep, when all the friars were slumbering, St. Francis arose and found his cord thus tied; and he loosed it so gently that the boy felt it not, and went forth alone into the wood near the friary, and entered into a little cell there and betook himself to prayer. After some space the boy awoke, and finding his cord loosed, and St. Francis risen, he rose up likewise and went seeking him, and finding the door open which led to the wood, he thought St. Francis had gone thither, and he entered the wood. And coming nigh unto the place where St. Francis was praying, he began to hear much talking; and as he drew closer to see and understand what he heard, he beheld a wondrous light that encompassed St. Francis, wherein were Christ and the Virgin Mary, and St. John the Baptist, and the Evangelist, and an infinite multitude of angels that were speaking with St. Francis. Seeing and hearing this, the boy fell lifeless to the earth. And the mystery of that holy apparition being ended, St. Francis, as he returned to the house, stumbled with his foot against the boy, who lay as one dead, and in compassion lifted him up and carried him in his arms, even as the good shepherd doth his sheep. And then learning from him how he had beheld the said vision, St. Francis commanded him to tell it to no man, to wit, so long as he should live, and the boy increasing daily in the great grace of God and in devotion to St. Francis, became a valiant man in the Order, and after the death of St. Francis revealed the said vision to the friars.

Chapter XVIII

OF THE WONDROUS CHAPTER THAT ST. FRANCIS HELD
AT ST. MARY OF THE ANGELS, WHERE MORE THAN FIVE
THOUSAND FRIARS WERE ASSEMBLED

Francis, faithful servant of Christ, once held a Chapter-General at St. Mary of the Angels, where more than five thousand friars were gathered together. Now St. Dominic, head and founder of the Order of preaching friars, who was then journeying from Burgundy to Rome, came thither, and hearing of the congregation of the Chapter that St. Francis was holding in the plain of St. Mary of the Angels, he went with seven friars of his Order to see. And there was likewise at the said Chapter a cardinal who was most devoted to St. Francis, the which cardinal he had foretold should one day become pope:[5] even as it came to pass. This cardinal had journeyed diligently to Assisi from Perugia, where the papal court was, and every day he came to behold St. Francis and his friars, and sometimes sang the mass, and sometimes preached

---

[5] Cardinal Hugolin, who became Gregory IX.

the sermon to the friars in Chapter; and the said cardinal was filled with the greatest joy and devotion when he came to visit that holy assembly. And beholding the friars sitting on that plain, around St. Mary's, company by company, here forty, there a hundred, there eighty together, all engaged in discoursing of God, or at prayer, or in tears, or in works of charity, and all so silent and so meek that no sound nor discord was heard, and marvelling at so great and orderly a multitude, he said with great devotion and tears, "Verily this is the camp and the army of the knights of God." In so mighty a host was heard neither vain words nor jests, but wheresoever a company of friars was assembled together, there they prayed, or said the office, or bewailed their sins, or the sins of their benefactors, or discoursed of the salvation of souls. For shelter they made them little wicker cots of willow and of rush matting, divided into groups according to the friars of the divers provinces: and therefore that Chapter was called the Chapter of the wicker cots or of the mats. Their couch was the bare earth, with a little straw for some: their pillows were blocks of stone or of wood. For which cause so great was the devotion of whosoever heard or saw them, so great the fame of their sanctity, that many counts and barons, and knights and other noblemen, and many priests likewise, and cardinals and bishops, and abbots and other clerks, came from the papal court, which then was at Perugia, and from the vale of Spoleto, to behold that great assembly, so holy and so humble, and so many saintly men together, the like whereof the world had never known before. And chiefly they came to behold the head and most holy father of that saintly folk, who had snatched so fair a prey from the world, and had gathered together so fair and devout a flock to follow the footprints of the true Shepherd Jesus Christ. The Chapter-General then being assembled together, St. Francis, holy father of all and general minister, expounded the word of God in fervour of spirit and preached unto them in a loud voice whatsoever the Holy Spirit put into his mouth. And for the text of his sermon he took these words, "My children, great things have we promised unto God: things exceeding great hath God promised unto us, if we observe those we have promised unto Him: and of a surety do we await those things promised unto us. Brief is the joy of this world; the pain that cometh hereafter is everlasting: small is the pain of this life; but the glory of the life to come is infinite." And on these words he preached most devoutly, comforting the friars and moving them to obedience and to reverence of Holy Mother Church, to brotherly love and to pray to God for all men, to be patient under the adversities of this world, temperate in prosperity, observant of purity and angelic chastity, to live in peace and concord with God and with men and with their own conscience, and in the love and practice of most holy poverty. And then he spake and said, "I command you by the merit of holy obedience, all you that are here assembled, that none of you have care nor solicitude for what he shall eat nor what he shall drink, nor for aught necessary for the body, but give ye heed solely to prayer and to the praise of God: lay upon Him all solicitude for your body, for He hath special care of you." And all and sundry received this commandment with glad hearts and with joyful countenances: and the sermon of St. Francis being ended, all prostrated themselves in prayer. Whereat St. Dominic, that was present at all these things, marvelled mightily at the commandment of St. Francis and deemed it rash; for he knew not how so great a multitude could be governed while taking no thought or care for the things necessary to the body. But the chief Shepherd, Christ the blessed, being willed to show what care He hath for His sheep and His singular love for His poor ones, anon moved the hearts of the people of Perugia, of Spoleto, of Foligno, of Spello, and of Assisi, and of the other cities round about, to bring wherewithal to eat and to drink to that holy congregation. And lo, there came quickly from the aforesaid cities, men with sumpter mules and horses and carts, loaded with bread and wine, with beans and cheese and other good things to eat, according to the needs of Christ's poor ones. Besides this they brought napery and pitchers, and bowls and glasses, and other vessels needful for so great a multitude; and blessed he that could bring the heaviest load or serve most diligently, so that knights and barons also and other noblemen, who had come to look on, served them with great humility and devotion. Wherefore St. Dominic, beholding all these things and knowing of a truth that divine providence wrought in them, humbly owned that he had falsely judged St. Francis of rashness, and drawing nigh to him knelt down and humbly confessed his fault, and added, "Verily, God hath especial care of these His poor little ones, and I knew it not: henceforth I promise to observe holy gospel poverty, and in God's name do curse all the friars of my Order that shall dare to possess things of their own." And St. Dominic was much edified by the faith of the most holy St. Francis, and by the obedience and poverty of so great and well ordered an assembly, and by the divine providence and the rich abundance of all good things. Now in that same Chapter it was told St. Francis that many friars were wearing breastplates of iron[6]

---

[6] *Cuoretto*. The sense of this word is doubtful. A note to Cesari's text interprets "a kind of metal cilice in the form of a heart." The Upton fathers render "leather bands with sharp points;" Cardinal Manning has "small hearts of iron." Prof. Arnold in his admirable translation gives "shirts of mail." A shirt of mail was, however, an expensive harness in the Middle Ages, and a gathering of mendicant friars, 500 of whom were possessed of shirts of mail, is hardly credible. Petrocchi, *Nuovo diz. universale*, interprets, *specie di cilizio*, "a kind of cilice," and Johann Jörgensen, the Danish translator, has *Bodsskjorte*, "penitential shirt." A reference to the Latin original gives *loricam*, and since a well-known eleventh-century Italian hermit, S. Domenico Iorato, was thus called by reason of the iron cuirass he wore next his skin, I have small doubt that *cuoretto* should be rendered "breastplate." The friars could easily have begged old breast-plates for penitential purposes.

next their skins, and iron rings, whereby many grew sick even unto death and were hindered in their prayers. Whereat St. Francis, as a wise father, commanded by holy obedience that whosoever had these breastplates or iron rings should remove them and lay them before him, and thus did they; and there were numbered full five hundred breastplates, and many more rings, either for the arm or for the loins, so that they made a great heap; and St. Francis bade them be left there. After the Chapter was ended St. Francis heartened them all to good works, and taught them how they should escape without sin from this wicked world; then dismissed them with God's blessing and his own to their provinces, all consoled with spiritual joy.

Chapter XIX

HOW THE VINEYARD OF THE PARISH PRIEST OF RIETI, IN WHOSE HOUSE ST. FRANCIS PRAYED, WAS STRIPPED OF ITS GRAPES BY REASON OF THE MULTITUDES OF PEOPLE THAT CAME TO SEE HIM; AND HOW THAT VINEYARD BROUGHT FORTH MIRACULOUSLY MORE WINE THAN EVER BEFORE, ACCORDING TO THE PROMISE OF ST. FRANCIS. AND HOW GOD REVEALED TO ST. FRANCIS THAT PARADISE SHOULD BE HIS PORTION WHEN HE DEPARTED THIS LIFE

St. Francis being on a time sorely afflicted in his eyes, was invited by a letter from Cardinal Hugolin, protector of the Order, to come to Rieti, where excellent physicians for the eyes then dwelt, for he loved him tenderly. When St. Francis received the cardinal's letter he went first to St. Damian's, where St. Clare, the most devout spouse of Christ was, to give her some consolation; then he would go his way to the cardinal at Rieti. And the night after he came thither his eyes worsened so that he saw no light at all. Wherefore, being unable to depart, St. Clare made him a little cell of reeds wherein he might the better find repose. But St. Francis, what with the pain of his eyes and what with the multitude of mice that tormented him, could not rest a moment night or day. And after enduring that pain and tribulation many days, he began to bethink him and to understand that this was a divine scourge for his sins; and he began to thank God with all his heart and with his mouth, and then crying with a loud voice, said, "My Lord, worthy am I of all this and far worse. My Lord Jesus Christ, good Shepherd, that in Thy mercy hast laid upon us sinners divers corporeal pains and anguish, grant to me, Thy little sheep, such virtue and grace that for no sickness or anguish or suffering I may depart from Thee." And as he prayed there came to him a voice from heaven saying, "Francis, answer Me: If all the earth were gold, and all the sea and fountains and rivers were balm, and all the mountains and hills and rocks were precious stones, and thou shouldst find another treasure as much nobler than these things as gold is nobler than clay, and balm than water, and precious stones than mountains and rocks, and if that nobler treasure were given thee for thine infirmity, oughtest thou not to be right glad and right joyful?" St. Francis answers, "Lord, I am unworthy of so precious a treasure." And the voice of God said to him, "Rejoice, Francis, for that is the treasure of life eternal, which I have laid up for thee, and from this hour forth I do invest thee therewith: and this sickness and affliction is a pledge of that blessed treasure." Then St. Francis with exceeding great joy called his companion and said, "Go we to the cardinal." And first consoling St. Clare with holy words and humbly taking leave of her, he went his way towards Rieti. And when he drew nigh to the city, so great a multitude of people came forth to meet him that he would not enter therein, but went to a church that was perchance two miles distant therefrom. When the citizens heard that he was at the said church, they ran thither to behold him in such numbers that the vineyard of the said church was utterly despoiled, and all the grapes were plucked: whereat the priest, sorely grieved in his heart, repented that he had received St. Francis in his church. Now that priest's thoughts being revealed by God to St. Francis, he called him aside and said to him, "Dearest father, how many measures of wine doth this vineyard yield thee a year when the yield is highest?" He answered, "Twelve measures." Says St. Francis, "Prithee, father, suffer me patiently to sojourn here yet a few days, for I find much repose here; and for the love of God and of me, poor little one, let every man gather grapes from thy vineyard, and I promise thee, in the name of my Lord Jesus Christ, that every year thy vineyard shall yield thee twenty measures of wine." And St. Francis tarried there because of the great harvest of souls manifestly gathered from the folk that came thither; whereof many departed inebriated with divine love and forsook the world. The priest had faith in the promise of St. Francis, and surrendered the vineyard freely to those that came thither: and the vineyard was all wasted and stripped, so that scarce a bunch of grapes remained. Marvellous to tell, the vintage season comes, and lo, the priest gathers the few bunches that were left and casts them into the wine-press and treads them, and, according to the promise of St. Francis, he harvested twenty measures of excellent wine. In this miracle was manifestly seen that, since by the merits of St. Francis the vineyard, stripped of its grapes, gave forth abundance of wine, so Christian folk, barren of virtue through sin, ofttimes abounded in good fruit of penitence through the merits and teaching of St. Francis.

Chapter XX

TOUCHING A MOST BEAUTIFUL VISION THAT A YOUNG
FRIAR SAW, WHO SO HATED HIS HABIT THAT HE WAS
MINDED TO CAST IT OFF AND FORSAKE THE ORDER

A youth of very noble birth and gently nurtured entered the Order of St. Francis; and after some days, at the instigation of the devil, began to hold the habit he wore in such abomination that it seemed to him of vilest sackcloth. The sleeves thereof he held in horror; he hated the cowl, and the length and coarseness thereof seemed to him an intolerable burden. And his dislike of the Order increasing also, he finally determined to quit the habit and return to the world. Now he was already wonted, even as he had been taught by his master, to kneel down with great reverence and draw off his cowl and cross his arms on his breast and prostrate himself whensoever he passed before the altar of the friary, where the body of Christ was reserved. Now it befell on the night when he was minded to depart and leave the Order, that it behoved him to pass before the altar of the convent: and passing there he knelt down as was his wont and did reverence. And suddenly he was rapt in spirit, and a wondrous vision was shown him by God; for he beheld, as it were, a countless multitude of saints pass before him, after the manner of a procession, two by two, clad in most fair and precious raiment; and the countenances and hands of them shone like the sun; and they paced to the chants and music of angels. And amid these saints were two more nobly arrayed and adorned than all the others; and they were encompassed with such brightness that he who beheld them was filled with great amaze; and well-nigh at the end of the procession he beheld one adorned so gloriously that he seemed a new-made knight, more honoured than the others. This youth, beholding the said vision, marvelled greatly, and knew not what that procession betokened, yet dared not ask, and remained dazed with the sweetness thereof. And, nevertheless, when all the procession was passed, he took courage and ran after the last of them, and asked, saying, "O beloved, prithee of your courtesy tell me who be they so marvellously arrayed that walk in this venerable procession?" They answered, "Know, my son, that we are all friars minor, who now are coming from the glory of paradise." Then asked he thus, "Who be those two that shine more brightly than the others?" They answered, "Those are St. Francis and St. Anthony; and he the last of all whom thou sawest thus honoured is a holy friar that newly died, whom we are leading in triumph to the glory of paradise, for that he hath fought valiantly against temptation and persevered unto the end; and these fair garments of fine cloth we wear, are given to us by God in lieu of the coarse tunics we wore in the

Order; and the glorious brightness that thou beholdest is given to us by God for the humility and patience, and for the holy poverty and obedience and chastity we kept even to the last. Therefore, my son, be it not hard to thee to wear the sackcloth of the Order, that is so fruitful, because, if clothed in the sackcloth of St. Francis, thou for love of Christ despise the world and mortify thy flesh and valiantly fight against the devil, thou, with us, shalt have a like raiment and exceeding brightness of glory." These words said, the youth returned to himself, and heartened by this vision, cast away from him all temptation, and confessed his fault before the warden and the friars; and thenceforth he desired the bitterness of penitence and the coarseness of the habit, and ended his life in the Order in great sanctity.

Chapter XXI

OF THE MOST HOLY MIRACLE THAT ST. FRANCIS WROUGHT
WHEN HE CONVERTED THE FIERCE WOLF OF GUBBIO

in the days when St. Francis abode in the city of Gubbio, a huge wolf, terrible and fierce, appeared in the neighbourhood, and not only devoured animals but men also; in such wise that all citizens went in great fear of their lives, because ofttimes the wolf came close to the city. And when they went abroad, all men armed themselves as were they going forth to battle; and even so none who chanced on the wolf alone could defend himself; and at last it came to such a pass that for fear of this wolf no man durst leave the city walls. Wherefore St. Francis had great compassion for the men of that city, and purposed to issue forth against that wolf, albeit the citizens, with one accord, counselled him not to go. But he, making the sign of holy cross, and putting all his trust in God, set forth from the city with his companions; but they, fearing to go farther, St. Francis went his way alone towards the place where the wolf was. And lo! the said wolf, in the sight of much folk that had come to behold the miracle, leapt towards St. Francis with gaping jaws; and St. Francis, drawing nigh, made to him the sign of most holy cross and called him, speaking thus, "Come hither, friar wolf; I command thee in the name of Christ that thou do hurt neither to me nor to any man." Marvellous to tell! no sooner had St. Francis made the sign of holy cross than the terrible wolf closed his jaws and stayed his course; no sooner was the command uttered than he came, gentle as a lamb, and laid himself at the feet of St. Francis. Then St. Francis speaks to him thus, "Friar wolf, thou workest much evil in these parts, and hast wrought grievous ill, destroying and slaying God's creatures without His leave; and not only hast thou slain and devoured the beasts of the field, but thou hast dared to destroy and slay men made in the image of God; wherefore thou art worthy of the gallows as a most wicked thief and murderer: all folk cry out and murmur against thee, and all this city is at enmity with thee. But, friar wolf, fain would I make peace with them and thee, so that thou injure them no more; and they shall forgive thee all thy past offences, and neither man nor dog shall pursue thee more." Now when St. Francis had spoken these words, the wolf, moving his body and his tail and his ears, and bowing his head, made signs that he accepted what had been said, and would abide thereby. Then said St. Francis, "Friar wolf, since it pleaseth thee to make and observe this peace, I promise to obtain for thee, so long as thou livest, a continual sustenance from the men of this city, so that thou shalt no more suffer hunger, for well I ween that thou hast wrought all this evil to satisfy thy hunger. But after I have won this favour for thee, friar wolf, I desire that thou promise me to do hurt neither to man nor beast. Dost thou promise me this?" And the wolf bowed his head and gave clear token that he promised these things. And St. Francis said, "Friar wolf, I desire that thou pledge thy faith to me to keep this promise, that I may have full trust in thee." And when St. Francis held forth his hand to receive this pledge, the wolf lifted up his right paw and gently laid it in the hand of St. Francis, giving him thereby such token of good faith as he could. Then said St. Francis, "Friar wolf, I command thee in the name of Jesus Christ to come with me; fear naught, and we will go and confirm this peace in the name of God." And the wolf, obedient, set forth by his side even as a pet lamb; wherefore, when the men of the city beheld this, they marvelled greatly. And anon this miracle was noised about the whole city, and all the folk, great and small, men and women, old and young, flocked to the market-place to see the wolf with St. Francis. And when all people were gathered together there, St. Francis stood forth and preached to them, saying, among other things, how that for their sins God had suffered such calamities to befall them, and how much more perilous were the flames of hell which the damned must endure everlastingly than was the ravening of a wolf that could only slay the body; and how much more to be feared were the jaws of hell, since that for fear of the mouth of a small beast such multitudes went in fear and trembling. "Turn ye, then, dearest children, to God, and do fitting penance for your sins, and so shall God free you from the wolf in this world and from eternal fire in the world to come." And having made an end of his sermon, St. Francis said, "Hark ye, my brethren, friar wolf, here before you, hath promised and pledged his faith to me never to injure you in anything whatsoever, if you will promise to provide him daily sustenance; and here stand I, a bondsman for him, that he will steadfastly observe this pact of peace." Then the people with one voice promised to feed him all his days. And St. Francis, before all the people, said to the wolf, "And thou, friar wolf, dost promise to observe the conditions of this peace before all this people, and that thou wilt injure neither man nor beast nor any living creature?" And the wolf knelt down and bowed his head, and with gentle movements of tail and body and ears, showed by all possible tokens his will to observe every pact of peace. Says St. Francis, "I desire, friar wolf, that even as thou didst pledge thy faith to me without the city gates to hold fast to thy promise, so here, before all this people, thou shalt renew thy pledge, and promise thou wilt never play me, thy bondsman, false." Then the wolf, lifting up his right paw, placed it in the hand of St. Francis. Whereat, what with this act and the others aforesaid, there was such marvel and rejoicing among all the people—not only at the strangeness of the miracle, but because of the peace made with the wolf—that they all began to cry aloud to heaven, praising and blessing God, who had sent St. Francis to them, by whose merits they had been freed from the cruel wolf. And the said wolf lived two years in Gubbio, and was wont to enter like a tame creature into the houses from door to door, doing hurt to no one and none doing hurt to him. And he was kindly fed by the people; and as he went about the city never a dog barked at him. At last, after two years, friar wolf died of old age; whereat the citizens grieved much, for when they beheld him going thus tamely about the city, they remembered better the virtues and holiness of St. Francis.

Chapter XXII

HOW ST. FRANCIS TAMED THE WILD TURTLE DOVES

A certain youth one day, having snared many turtle doves, was taking them to market when St. Francis met him. And St. Francis, who ever had singular compassion for gentle creatures, gazed upon those doves with a pitying eye, and said to the youth, "O good youth, prithee give them to me, lest birds so gentle, that chaste, humble, and faithful souls are compared to them in the scriptures, fall into the hands of cruel men who would kill them." Straightway the youth, inspired by God, gave them all to St. Francis, who received them into his bosom and began to speak sweetly to them, "O my little sisters, ye simple doves, innocent and chaste, wherefore suffer yourselves to be caught? Now will I rescue you from death, and make nests for you, that ye may be fruitful and multiply, according to the commandments of our Creator." And St. Francis went and made nests for them all; and they took to the nests and began to lay eggs and rear their young before the eyes of the friars; and thus they abode tamely and grew familiar with St. Francis and the other friars, as if they had been chickens ever fed by their hands: nor did they depart until St. Francis gave them leave with his blessing. And he said to the youth that had given them to him, "Son, thou shalt yet be a friar in this Order and serve Jesus Christ in grace." And so it befell, for the said youth became a friar and lived in the Order with great holiness.

Chapter XXIII

HOW ST. FRANCIS DELIVERED A SINFUL FRIAR FROM THE POWER OF THE DEVIL

It fell out on a time as St. Francis was at prayer in the friary of the Porziuncula, that he beheld by divine revelation the whole house surrounded and besieged by devils in the similitude of a mighty army. But they could not enter within because those friars were of such holiness that no evil spirit could come nigh them. And as the enemy lay in wait, one of the friars on a day quarrelled with another, and thought in his heart how he might accuse him and be avenged. Wherefore, while he nursed this evil thought, the devil saw the way open and entered into the friary and sat on the friar's shoulder. But the compassionate and vigilant shepherd that ever watched over his flock, seeing the wolf had entered the fold to devour his lamb, let that friar be called to him, and commanded him straightway to reveal the venom of hatred he had conceived towards his neighbour, whereby he had fallen into the power of the enemy of mankind. The friar, affrighted when he perceived that the holy father had thus read his heart, revealed all the venom and malice he had borne in his breast, and confessed his sin and humbly craved mercy and penance. This done, and his penance being accepted, he was assoiled of his sin, and straightway the devil departed in the presence of St. Francis. And the friar, thus delivered from the power of the cruel fiend through the loving-kindness of the good shepherd, gave thanks to God, and returned chastened and admonished to the fold of the holy pastor, and ever after lived in great sanctity.

Chapter XXIV

HOW ST. FRANCIS CONVERTED THE SOLDAN OF BABYLON TO THE TRUE FAITH

St. Francis, stirred by zeal for the faith of Christ and by the desire of martyrdom, voyaged on a time over the seas with twelve of is holiest companions, to fare straight to the Soldan of Babylon;[7] and when they came to the land of the Saracens, where the passes were guarded by certain men so cruel that never a Christian who journeyed that way escaped death at their hands, by the grace of God they escaped, and were not slain; but seized and beaten, they were led in bonds before the Soldan. And standing before him, St. Francis, taught by the Holy

---

[7] Old Cairo.

Ghost, preached the faith of Christ so divinely that for his faith's sake he even would have entered the fire. Whereat the Soldan began to feel great devotion towards him, as much for the constancy of his faith as for his contempt of the world (for albeit he was very poor, he would accept no gift), and also for the fervour of martyrdom he beheld in him. From that time forth the Soldan heard him gladly, and entreated him many times to come back, granting to him and to his companions freedom to preach wheresoever it might please them; and he gave them also a token, so that no man should do them hurt. Having therefore received this licence, St. Francis sent forth those chosen companions, two by two, in divers parts, to preach the faith of Christ to the Saracens. And himself, with one of them, chose a way, and journeying on he came to an inn to rest. And therein was a woman, most fair in body but foul in soul, who, accursed one, did tempt him to sin. And St. Francis, saying he consented thereto, she led him into a chamber. Said St. Francis, "Come with me." And he led her to a fierce fire that was kindled in that chamber, and in fervour of spirit stripped himself naked and cast himself beside that fire on the burning hearth; and he invited her to go and strip and lie with him on that bed, downy and fair. And when St. Francis had lain thus for a great space, with a joyous face, being neither burned nor even singed, that woman, affrighted and pierced to the heart, not only repented of her sin and of her evil intent, but likewise was wholly converted to the faith of Christ; and she waxed so in holiness that many souls were saved through her in those lands.

At last, when St. Francis saw he could gather no more fruit in those parts, he prepared by divine admonition to return to the faithful with all his companions; and having assembled them together, he went back to the Soldan and took leave of him. Then said the Soldan to him, "Friar Francis, fain would I convert me to the faith of Christ, but I fear to do so now, for if this people heard thereof they would surely slay thee and me and all thy companions; and forasmuch as thou canst yet work much good, and as I have certain affairs of great moment to despatch, I will not be the cause of thy death and of mine. But teach me how I may be saved; lo, I am ready to do whatsoever thou layest upon me." Then said St. Francis, "My lord, now must I depart from you, but after I am returned to mine own country and by the grace of God have ascended to heaven, after my death, as it may please God, I will send thee two of my friars, at whose hands thou shalt receive the holy baptism of Christ and be saved, even as my Lord Jesus Christ hath revealed to me. And do thou meanwhile get thee free from all hindrance, so that when the grace of God shall come upon thee thou shalt find thyself well disposed to faith and devotion." Thus he promised and thus he did. This said, St. Francis returned with that venerable college of his holy companions, and after some years he gave up his soul to God by the death of the body. And the Soldan, being fallen sick, awaits the promise of St.

Francis, and stations guards at certain of the passes, and commands them that if two friars appear in the habit of St. Francis, they shall straightway be led before him. At that very hour St. Francis appeared to two friars, and bade them tarry not, but hasten to the Soldan and compass his salvation, according as he had promised. And anon the friars set forth, and having crossed the pass, were led by the said guards before the Soldan. And when the Soldan beheld them he was filled with great joy, and said, "Now do I truly perceive that God hath sent his servants to me for my salvation, according to the promise St. Francis made to me by divine inspiration." And when he had received instruction from those friars in the faith of Christ and holy baptism, he, being born again in Christ, died of that sickness, and his soul was saved through the merits and the prayers of St. Francis.

Chapter XXV

HOW ST. FRANCIS MIRACULOUSLY HEALED A LEPER, BODY AND SOUL, AND WHAT THAT SOUL SAID TO HIM ON HER WAY TO HEAVEN

St. Francis, true disciple of Christ, while he lived in this miserable life, strove with all his might to follow Christ, the perfect Master; wherefore it befell many times, by divine power, that the souls of those, whose bodies he healed, were also healed at the selfsame hour, even as we read of Christ. And he not only served lepers gladly, but had also ordained that the friars of his Order, as they went about the world, should serve lepers for love of Christ, who for our sakes was willing to be accounted a leper. Now it befell on a time, in a friary nigh unto where St. Francis then was dwelling, that the friars were serving lepers and other sick folk in a lazar-house, among whom was a leper, so froward, so intolerable, and so insolent, that all believed of a surety he was possessed of the devil; and so in sooth it was, for he reviled so shamefully with words, and beleaboured whosoever was tending him, and, what is worse, did foully blaspheme the blessed Christ and His most holy Mother the Virgin Mary, so that in no wise could one be found willing or able to serve him. And albeit the friars strove to bear patiently the injuries and insults heaped upon themselves, in order to increase the merit of their patience, nevertheless, their consciences were unable to endure those uttered against the Christ and His Mother: so they resolved to forsake the said leper, but would not until they had signified all things in due order to St. Francis, who was then dwelling in a friary hard by. And when they had signified these things to him, St. Francis came to this perverse leper, and drawing nigh, gave him salutation, saying, "God give thee peace, my dearest brother." The leper answers, "What peace can I have from God, who hath taken peace from me and all good things, and hath made me all rotten and stinking?" And St. Francis said, "My son, have patience, for the infirmities of the body are given to us by God in this world for the salvation of souls; inasmuch as they are of great merit when they are endured patiently." The sick man answers, "And how can I bear patiently this continual pain that afflicts me day and night? And not only am I afflicted by my sickness, but the friars thou gavest to serve me do even worse, and serve me not as they ought." Then St. Francis, knowing by divine revelation that this leper was possessed of the evil spirit, went aside and betook himself to prayer, and devoutly prayed God for him. His prayer ended, he returns to the leper and bespeaks him thus, "My son, I will serve thee, even I, since thou art not content with the others." And the leper answers, "So be it; but what canst thou do more than the others?" St. Francis answers, "Whatsoever thou wilt, that will I do." Says the leper, "I will that thou wash me all over, for I stink so foully that I cannot abide myself." Then St. Francis made quickly water boil, with many sweet-smelling herbs therein; then did strip the leper and began to wash him with his own hands, while another friar poured water over him. And by miracle divine, wherever St. Francis touched him with his holy hands the leprosy departed, and the flesh became perfectly whole. And even as the flesh began to heal, the soul began to heal also; whereupon the leper, seeing the leprosy on the way to leave him, began to have great compunction and repentance for his sins; and bitterly he began to weep; so that while the body was outwardly cleansed of the leprosy by the washing with water, the soul within was cleansed of sin by amendment and tears. And being wholly healed, as well in body as in soul, he humbly confessed his sins, and weeping, said with a loud voice, "Woe unto me, who am worthy of hell for the insults and injuries I have put upon the friars in word and deed, and for my perversity and blasphemies against God." Wherefore a fortnight long he persevered in bitter weeping for his sins and in craving mercy of God, confessing himself unto the priest with a whole heart. And when St. Francis beheld so clear a miracle that God had wrought by his hands, he gave thanks to God, and departing thence, journeyed into a very far country; for through humility he desired to flee all vainglory, and in all his works sought the honour and glory of God, and not his own. Then as it pleased God, the said leper, being healed in body and soul, fell sick of another infirmity a fortnight after his repentance; and, armed with the sacraments of the church, died a holy death. And his soul, on her way to paradise, appeared in the air to St. Francis, who was at prayer in a wood, and said to him, "Knowest thou me?" "Who art thou?" said St. Francis. "I am the leper whom the blessed Christ healed through thy merits, and this day am going to life everlasting; wherefore I render thanks to God and to thee. Blessed be thy soul and thy body; blessed thy holy words and deeds, because through thee many souls shall be saved in the world: and know that not a day passeth in the world but that the holy angels and the other saints give thanks to God for the holy fruits that thou and thy Order bring forth in divers parts of the world. Therefore be comforted, and give thanks to God and abide with His blessing." These words said, the soul passed into heaven, and St. Francis remained much comforted.

Chapter XXVI

HOW ST. FRANCIS CONVERTED THREE MURDEROUS ROBBERS THAT BECAME FRIARS; AND OF THE MOST NOBLE VISION THAT ONE OF THEM BEHELD WHO WAS A MOST HOLY FRIAR

St. Francis on a time was journeying through the wilderness of Borgo San Sepolcro, and as he passed by a stronghold, called Monte Casale, a noble and delicate youth came to him and said, "Father, fain would I become one of your friars." St. Francis answers, "Son, thou art but a delicate youth and of noble birth, peradventure thou couldst not endure our poverty and our hardships." And the youth said, "Father, are ye not men as I am? Since ye then endure these things, even so can I by the grace of Jesus Christ." St. Francis, well pleased with this answer, gave him his blessing, and anon received him into the Order, and gave him for name Friar Angel. And this youth waxed so in grace that short time after St. Francis made him warden of the friary called of Monte Casale. Now in those days three famous robbers who infested that country and wrought much evil therein, came to the said friary and besought the said warden, Friar Angel, to give them food to eat; and the warden answered them in this wise, rebuking them harshly, "Ye robbers and cruel manslayers, are ye not ashamed to steal the fruit of others' labours, but, frontless and insolent, would seek likewise to devour the alms bestowed on God's servants? Ye are not worthy even to walk this earth, for ye reverence neither man nor the God that created you; get ye gone, then, and be seen here no more." Whereat they, perturbed, departed in great fury. And lo, St. Francis appeared outside the friary, his wallet filled with bread, and carrying a small vessel of wine, that he and his companion had begged. And when the warden related to him how he had driven the robbers away, St. Francis chid him severely, saying he had borne himself cruelly, since sinners were better drawn to God by gentleness than by cruel reproof. "Wherefore our Master, Jesus Christ, whose gospel we have promised to observe, saith, that the whole need not a physician, but they that are sick, and that He had not come to call the just but sinners to repentance; and therefore many times He ate with them. Forasmuch as thou hast done contrary to charity and contrary to Christ's holy gospel, I command thee by holy obedience that thou straightway take this wallet of bread that I have begged and this vessel of wine, and go diligently after them over hill and valley until thou find them, and give them all this bread and wine from me: then kneel thee down before them and confess humbly thy fault of cruelty, and entreat them for my sake to work evil no more, but to fear God and offend Him no more; and say that if they will do this I promise to provide for all their needs, and give them continually enough to eat and to drink. And when thou hast done this, return humbly hither." While the said warden went to do this bidding, St. Francis betook himself to prayer, and besought God that He would soften the hearts of those robbers and convert them to repentance. The obedient warden overtakes them and gives them the bread and wine, and does and says what St. Francis had commanded him. And it pleased God that those robbers, as they ate of the alms of St. Francis, began to say to one another, "Woe unto us, wretched and hapless! what hard torments await us in hell! For we go about not only robbing our neighbours, beating and wounding them, but do slay them likewise; and so many evil deeds and wicked works notwithstanding, we have neither remorse of conscience nor fear of God; and lo, this holy friar hath come to us, and for a few words wherewith he justly rebuked our wickedness, hath humbly confessed to us his fault; and moreover, hath brought us bread and wine and promise so bounteous from the holy father: verily these are God's holy friars that merit His paradise, and we are children of eternal wrath that deserve the pains of hell, and each day do increase our doom; yea, we know not whether for the sins we have committed to this day we may return to the mercy of God." These and the like words being spoken by one of them, the others said, "Of a surety thou speakest sooth, but look ye, what must we do?" "Go we," said one, "to St. Francis, and if he give us hope that we may find mercy from God for our sins, let us do whatsoever he command us, and so may we deliver our souls from the torments of hell." Now this counsel was pleasing to the others, and thus all three being in accord, they came in haste to St. Francis and spake to him thus, "Father, we for our many wicked sins believe we cannot return to the mercy of God; but if thou have some hope that God in His mercy will receive us, lo, we are ready to do thy bidding and to do penance with thee." Then St. Francis received them with loving-kindness and comforted them with many examples, and made them confident of God's mercy, promising he would surely obtain it for them from God. He told them that the mercy of God was infinite, and that, according to the gospel, even if our sins were infinite, His mercy was yet greater than our sins; and that the Apostle St. Paul hath said, "Christ the blessed came into the world to save sinners." Hearing these words and the like teachings, the said three robbers renounced the devil and all his works, and St. Francis received them into the Order, and they began to do great penance. And two of them lived but a brief space after their conversion and went to paradise; but the third lived on, and, pondering on his sins, gave himself up to do such penance during fifteen unbroken years that, besides the common lenten fasts which he kept with the other friars, he fasted three days of the week on bread and water; he went ever barefoot, with naught on his back but a single tunic, nor ever slept after matins. In the meantime St. Francis passed from this miserable life; and this friar through many years continued his penance, when lo, one night after matins, so sore a temptation to sleep came upon him, that in no wise could he resist it, nor watch as he was wont to do. At length, unable to overcome his drowsiness, or to pray, he lay on his bed to sleep. No sooner had he laid down his head than he was rapt and led in spirit to the top of a very high mountain over a steep place, and on this side and on that were broken and jagged rocks and monstrous crags that jutted forth from the rocks; wherefore this steep place was frightful to behold. And the angel that was leading this friar pushed him and flung him down that steep place; and as he fell he was dashed from rock to rock and from crag to crag until he fell to the bottom of the abyss, his limbs all broken and shattered to pieces, according as it seemed to him. And lying thus mangled on the ground, he that led him said, "Rise up, for it behoves thee to go a yet greater journey." The friar answered, "Methinks thou art a most foolish and cruel man; for thou seest I am well-nigh dead of my fall, which has dashed me to pieces, and thou yet biddest me rise up." And the angel drew nigh and, touching him, made all his members whole again and healed his wounds. And then he showed him a great plain, full of sharp and pointed stones and thorns and briars, and told him he must needs run across all this plain and pass over it with naked feet until he came to the end; there he would behold a fiery furnace wherein he must enter. And the friar having passed over all the plain with great pain and anguish, the angel said to him, "Enter yon furnace, for this it behoves thee now to do." He answers, "Alas! how cruel a guide art thou, that seest I am nigh unto death, because of this horrible plain; and now for repose thou biddest me enter this fiery furnace." And as he gazed, he beheld many devils around the furnace with iron forks in their hands, wherewith, seeing him slow to enter, they thrust him into the furnace. Having entered the furnace, he gazed around and beheld one that had been his boon companion, who was all a-burning; and he asked of him, "O hapless comrade, how camest thou here?" And he answered and said, "Go a little farther and thou shalt find my wife, thy gossip; she will tell thee the cause of our damnation." And as the friar passed on, lo, the said gossip appeared, all aflame and enclosed in a fiery measure of corn; and he asked her, saying, "O gossip, hapless and wretched, why art thou in so cruel a torment?" And she answered, "Because at the time of the great famine that St. Francis had foretold, my husband and I gave false measure of corn and wheat; therefore do I burn in this measure." These words said, the angel who was leading the friar thrust him out of the furnace and said to him, "Make thee ready for a horrible journey thou hast to take." And he, lamenting, said, "O guide most cruel, that hast no compassion on me, thou seest I am well-nigh all burned in this furnace, and yet wouldst lead me on a perilous and horrible journey." And the angel touched him, and made him whole and strong. Then he led him to a bridge, which could not be crossed without great peril, for it was very frail and narrow and slippery and without a rail at the sides; and beneath it flowed a terrible river, filled with serpents and dragons and scorpions, that it gave forth a great stench. And the angel said to him, "Pass over this bridge; at any cost thou must pass over." And the friar answers, "And how shall I cross without falling into this perilous river?" Says the angel, "Follow after me, and set thy foot where thou seest me place mine; so shalt thou pass over well." This friar passes behind the angel as he had shown him, until he reached the middle of the bridge, and as he stood thus on the crown of the bridge the angel flew away, and departing from him, went to the top of a most high mountain far away beyond the bridge. And the friar considered well the place whither the angel had flown; but, left without a guide and gazing below him, he beheld those terrible beasts with their heads out of the water and with open jaws ready to devour him if peradventure he should fall; and he trembled so that in no wise knew he what to do, nor what to say; for he could neither turn back nor go forward. Wherefore, beholding himself in such great tribulation, and that he had no other refuge save in God, he stooped down and clasped the bridge, and with his whole heart and in tears he commended himself to God, and prayed that of His most holy mercy he would succour him. His prayer ended, himseemed to put forth wings, whereat with great joy he waited until they grew, that he might fly beyond the bridge whither the angel had flown. But after a while, by the great desire he had to pass beyond this bridge, he set himself to fly, and because his wings were not yet fully grown, he fell upon the bridge and his wings dropped from him; whereat he clasped the bridge again, and commended himself as before to God. And his prayer ended, again himseemed to put forth wings; but, as before, he waited not until they had fully grown, and setting himself to fly before the time, he fell again on the bridge, and his wings dropped. Wherefore, seeing these things, and that he had fallen, through his untimely haste to fly, he began to say within himself, "Of a surety, if I put forth wings a third time, I will wait until they be so great that I may fly without falling again." And pondering these things, lo, himseemed yet a third time to put forth wings; and waiting a great space, until they were well grown, himseemed with the first and second and third putting forth of wings that he had waited full a hundred and fifty years or more. At length he lifted him up this third time, and with all his might took wing and flew on high as far as the place whither the angel had flown. And knocking at the door of the palace wherein the angel was, the doorkeeper asked of him, "Who art thou that comest here?" He answered, "I am a friar minor." Says the doorkeeper, "Tarry a while, for I will bring St. Francis hither, to see if he know thee." As he went his way to St. Francis, this friar began to gaze on the marvellous walls of the palace; and lo, these walls appeared translucent and of such exceeding brightness that he beheld clearly the choirs of the saints and all that was doing within. And standing thus amazed at this vision, lo, St. Francis cometh, and Friar Bernard, and Friar Giles; and after these, so great a multitude of sainted men and women that had followed the example of his life, that they seemed well-nigh countless; and St. Francis came forth and said to the doorkeeper, "Let him enter, for he is one of my friars." And no sooner had he entered therein than he felt such great consolation and such sweetness that he forgot all the tribulations he had suffered, even as if they had not been. And then St. Francis led him in and showed him many marvellous things, and thus bespake him, "Son, needs must thou return to the world and abide there seven days, wherein thou shalt make thee ready diligently and with great devotion; for after these seven days I will come for thee, and then shalt thou enter with me this abode of the blessed." Now St. Francis was arrayed in a wondrous garment, adorned with fairest stars, and his five stigmas were like unto five beauteous stars, of such exceeding splendour that the whole palace was illumined with their beams. And Friar Bernard's head was crowned with fairest stars, and Friar Giles was aureoled with wondrous light; and many other friars he knew among them that in the world he had never seen. Then taking leave of St. Francis he returned, albeit with laggard steps, to the world again. And when he awoke and returned to himself and came to his wits again, the friars were chanting prime; so that he had been in that vision but from matins to prime, albeit it had seemed to him that he had remained therein many years. And having related to the warden all this vision in due order, he began, within seven days, to sicken of a fever; and on the eighth day St. Francis came for him, according to his promise, with a great multitude of glorious saints, and led his soul to life everlasting in the realms of the blessed.

Chapter XXVII

HOW ST. FRANCIS CONVERTED TWO SCHOLARS AT
BOLOGNA THAT BECAME FRIARS, AND THEN DELIVERED
ONE OF THEM FROM A GREAT TEMPTATION

Once on a time when St. Francis came to the city of Bologna all of the people of the city ran forth to behold him, and so great was the press that the folk could with great difficulty reach the market-place; and the whole place being filled with men and women and scholars, lo,

St. Francis stood up on high in the midst of them and began to preach what the Holy Ghost taught him. And so wondrously he preached that he seemed to speak with the voice of an angel rather than of a man; his celestial words seemed to pierce the hearts of those that heard them, even as sharp arrows, so that during his sermon a great multitude of men and women were converted to repentance. Among whom were two students of noble birth from the Marches of Ancona, the one named Pellegrino, the other Rinieri: and being touched in their hearts by divine inspiration through the said sermon, they came to St. Francis saying they desired wholly to forsake the world and be numbered among his friars. Then St. Francis, knowing by divine revelation that they were sent of God and were to lead a holy life in the Order, and considering their great fervour, received them joyfully, saying, "Thou, Pellegrino, keep the way of humility in the Order, and do thou, Friar Rinieri, serve the friars;" and thus it was: for Friar Pellegrino would never go forth as a priest but as a lay brother, albeit he was a great clerk and learned in the canon law. And by reason of this humility he attained to great perfection of virtue; in such wise that Friar Bernard, first-born of St. Francis, said of him, that he was one of the most perfect friars in this world. Finally, the said Friar Pellegrino passed from his blessed life, full of virtue, and wrought many miracles before his death and after. And the said Friar Rinieri, devoutly living in great holiness and humility, faithfully served the friars, and was much beloved of St. Francis. Being afterwards chosen minister of the province of the Marches of Ancona, he ruled it a long time with great peace and discretion. After a while God suffered a sore temptation to arise in his soul; whereat, in anguish and tribulation, he afflicted himself mightily with fastings and scourgings, with tears and prayers, both day and night. Nevertheless, he could not banish that temptation, but ofttimes was in great despair because he deemed himself forsaken by God. In this great despair he resolved, as a last remedy, to go to St. Francis, thinking thus within himself, "If St. Francis meet me with a kindly countenance, and show me affection, as he is wont to do, I believe that God will yet have compassion on me: but if not it shall be a token that I am forsaken of God." Thereupon he set forth and went to St. Francis , who at that time lay grievously sick in the bishop's palace at Assisi; and God revealed to him all the manner of that temptation, and of the state of the said Friar Rinieri, and his coming. And straightway St. Francis calls Friar Leo and Friar Masseo, and says to them, "Go ye quickly and meet my most dear son, Friar Rinieri, and embrace him for me and salute him, and say unto him that among all the friars that are in the world, him I love with singular love." They go forth and find Friar Rinieri by the way and embrace him, saying unto him what St. Francis had charged them to say. Whereupon such great consolation and sweetness filled his soul that he was well-nigh beside himself with joy, and giving thanks to God with all his heart he journeyed on and reached the place where St. Francis lay sick. And albeit St. Francis was grievously sick, nevertheless, when he heard Friar Rinieri coming, he rose up from is bed and went towards him and embraced him most sweetly and spake to him thus, "Friar Rinieri, dearest son, thee I love above all the friars in this world; thee I love with singular love": and these words said, he made the sign of most holy cross on his brow and there did kiss him. Then he said to him, "Son most dear, God hath suffered this sore temptation to befall thee for thy great gain of merit: but if thou desire this gain no longer, have it not." Marvellous to tell! no sooner had St. Francis uttered these words than all temptation departed from him, even as if he ne'er had felt it in his life: and he remained fully comforted.

Chapter XXVIII

OF THE DIVINE ECSTASY THAT CAME TO FRIAR BERNARD WHEREBY HE REMAINED FROM MORN TO NOON INSENSIBLE TO OUTWARD THINGS

How large a measure of grace God oft bestowed on poor followers of the gospel that forsook the world for love of Christ was shown forth in Friar Bernard of Quintavalle, who, after having put on the habit of St. Francis, was rapt many times in God through contemplation of celestial things. Among others, it befell on a time that when he was in church hearing mass, and with his whole mind lifted up to God, he became so absorbed and rapt in God that he perceived not when the body of Christ was elevated, nor knelt down, nor drew off his cowl as the other friars did: but without moving his eyes, stood with fixed gaze, insensible to outward things from morn till noon. And after noon, returning to himself, he went about the friary crying with a voice of wonder, "O friars, O friars, O friars, there is no man in this country, were he ever so great or so noble, but if he were promised a beautiful palace filled with gold would not find it easy to carry a sack full of dung in order to win that treasure so noble." To this celestial treasure, promised to those that love God, the aforesaid Friar Bernard had his mind so lifted up that for full fifteen years he ever went with his mind and his countenance raised to heaven; during which time he never satisfied his hunger at table, albeit he ate a little of that which was placed before him: for he was wont to say that perfect abstinence did not consist in foregoing that which a man did not relish, but that true abstinence lay in using temperance in those things that were of pleasant savour in the mouth; and thereby he attained to such degree of clearness and light of understanding that even great doctors had recourse to him for the solution of the knottiest questions and of difficult passages in the Scriptures, and he resolved all their difficulties.

And forasmuch as his mind was wholly loosed and detached from earthly things, he, like the swallows, soared high by contemplation: wherefore, sometimes twenty days, sometimes thirty, he dwelt alone on the tops of the highest mountains, contemplating divine things. For which cause Friar Giles was wont to say of him, that on no other man was this gift bestowed as it was on Friar Bernard; to wit, that he should feed flying, as the swallows did. And for this excellent grace that he had from God, St. Francis willingly and oft spake with him, both day and night; so that sometimes they were found together in the wood, rapt in God, the whole night long, whither they had both withdrawn to discourse of God.

Chapter XXIX

HOW THE DEVIL IN THE FORM OF THE CRUCIFIED APPEARED MANY TIMES TO FRIAR RUFFINO AND TOLD HIM HE WAS LOSING THE GOOD HE WAS PRACTISING BECAUSE HE WAS NOT OF THE ELECT. WHEREAT ST. FRANCIS, KNOWING THIS BY REVELATION FROM GOD, MADE FRIAR RUFFINO WARE OF THE ERRORS WHERETO HE HAD GIVEN CREDENCE

Friar Ruffino, one of the noblest gentlemen of the city of Assisi, and the companion of St. Francis, a man of great holiness, was once mightily assailed and tempted in soul touching predestination; whereby he became full of sadness and melancholy; for the devil put it into his heart that he was damned, and not among those predestined to eternal life; and that he was losing all his work in the Order. And this temptation lasting many days, he, for very shame, did not reveal it to St. Francis; nevertheless he ceased not to pray nor to observe the usual fasts: whereat the enemy began to heap trial upon trial upon him, and ever and above the battle within did likewise assail him outwardly with false visions. Wherefore he appeared to him once in the form of the Crucified, and said to him, "O Friar Ruffino, wherefore afflict thyself with penance and prayer, seeing thou art not among those predestined to life eternal? Believe me, for I know whom I have elected and predestined, and heed not the son of Peter Bernadone if he tell thee contrary; and moreover, question him not concerning this matter, for neither he nor any man knoweth; none save Me, that am the Son of God, therefore believe that of a surety thou art numbered among the damned; and the son of Peter Bernadone, thy father, and his father also are damned, and whosoever followeth him is beguiled." These words said, Friar Ruffino began to be so overcast by the prince of darkness that already he lost all the faith and love he had had for St. Francis, and cared not to tell him aught of his condition. But that which Friar Ruffino told not the holy father was revealed to him by the Holy Spirit; whereat St. Francis, beholding in spirit the great peril of the said friar, sent Friar Masseo for him; to whom Friar Ruffino answered, murmuring, "What have I to do with Friar Francis?" Then Friar Masseo, filled with divine wisdom, and knowing the wiles of the devil, said, "O Friar Ruffino, knowest thou not that St. Francis is like unto an angel of God that hath illumined so many souls in this world and from whom we have received the grace of God? Therefore I desire that thou, by all means, come with me to him, for clearly do I perceive thou art beguiled by the devil." This said, lo, Friar Ruffino set forth and went to St. Francis; and St. Francis beholding him coming from afar, began to cry, "O naughty Friar Ruffino, to whom hast thou given credence?" And when Friar Ruffino was come to him, St. Francis related all the temptation he had suffered from the devil in due order, both within and without, and showed to him clearly that he who had appeared to him was the devil and not Christ, and that in no wise should he consent unto his suggestions; but that "whenever the devil saith again to thee: 'Thou art damned,' answer him thus: 'Open thy mouth and I will drop my dung therein.' And let this be a token to thee that he is the devil and not Christ; and when thou hast thus answered he will forthwith flee from thee. By this token also shalt thou know that it was the devil: for that he hardened thy heart against all good, which thing is his own proper office; but the blessed Christ never hardeneth the heart of the man of faith, rather doth He soften it according as He speaketh by the mouth of the prophet: 'I will take away the stony heart out of their flesh, and will give them an heart of flesh.'" Then Friar Ruffino, seeing that St. Francis had told him all the circumstance of his temptation, was melted by his words, and began to weep bitterly and to give praise to St. Francis, humbly confessing his fault in that he had hidden his temptation from him. And thus he remained fully consoled and comforted by the holy father's admonitions and wholly changed for the better. Then at the last St. Francis said to him, "Go, my son, confess thee, and cease not the exercise of thy wonted prayers, and know of a surety that this temptation shall be of great profit and consolation to thee, and in brief time shalt thou prove it." Friar Ruffino returns to his cell in the wood, and being at prayer with many tears, lo, the enemy comes in the form of Christ, according to outward similitude, and saith to him, "O Friar Ruffino, did I not tell thee thou shouldst not believe the son of Peter Bernadone, and shouldst not weary thee in tears and prayers, seeing thou art damned? What doth it profit thee to afflict thyself while thou art yet alive, seeing that when thou diest thou shalt be damned?" And anon Friar Ruffino answered the devil and said, "Open thy mouth and I will drop my dung therein." Whereupon the devil straightway departed in great wrath, and with such tempest and ruin of stones from Mount Subasio hard by, that the thunder of the falling rocks endured a great space; and so mightily did they smite one against the other as they rolled down that they kindled horrible sparks of fire through the vale below: and at the terrible noise they made, St. Francis and his companions issued forth from the friary in great amaze to behold what strange thing had befallen; and to this very day that mighty ruin of rocks may be seen. Then did Friar Ruffino manifestly perceive that he who had beguiled him was the devil, and returning to St. Francis flung himself again on the ground and confessed his fault. And St. Francis comforted him with sweet words, and sent him forth all consoled to his cell; wherein, while he remained in devoutest prayers, the blessed Christ appeared to him and kindled his whole soul with divine love, and said, "Well didst thou, My son, to believe in Friar Francis; for he who afflicted thee was the devil; but I am Christ thy Master, and to make thee full sure I give thee this token: that while thou livest thou shalt feel neither sadness nor melancholy." This said, Christ departed, leaving him in such gladness and sweetness of spirit and elevation of mind, that day and night he was absorbed and rapt in God. And thenceforth was he so confirmed in grace and in certainty of salvation that he became wholly changed into another man, and would have remained both day and night in prayer and in contemplation of divine things, if the friars had suffered him. Wherefore St. Francis said of him, that Friar Ruffino was canonised by Christ in this life, and that save in his presence he would not hesitate to call him Saint Ruffino, albeit he still was living on the earth.

Chapter XXX

OF THE FAIR SERMON THAT ST. FRANCIS AND
FRIAR RUFFINO PREACHED AT ASSISI

The said Friar Ruffino was by his continual contemplation so absorbed in God that he grew dumb and almost insensible to outward things, and spake very seldom, and, moreover, had no longer grace, nor courage, nor eloquence in preaching. None the less St. Francis on a time bade him go to Assisi and preach to the people what God should inspire him to say. Whereat Friar Ruffino answered and said, "Reverend father, prithee forgive me and send me not, for thou knowest I lack the gift of preaching, and am simple and unlearned." Then said St. Francis, "Forasmuch as thou hast not obeyed quickly, I command thee by holy obedience that thou go to Assisi naked, and clothed only in thy breeches, and enter into a church and preach to the people." At his command Friar Ruffino strips himself and goes forth to Assisi and enters a church; and having made his reverence to the altar ascends the pulpit and begins to preach. Whereat the children and the men of Assisi began to laugh and said, "Now look ye, these friars do such penance that they grow foolish and lose their wits." Meanwhile, St. Francis, bethinking him of the ready obedience of Friar Ruffino, that was one of the noblest gentlemen of Assisi, and of the hard command he had laid upon him, began to upbraid himself, saying, "Whence, O son of Peter Bernadone, thou sorry churl, whence such great presumption that thou commandest Friar Ruffino, one of the noblest gentlemen of Assisi, to go and preach to the people like a crazy man? By God's grace thou shalt prove in thyself what thou commandest others to do." And straightway in fervour of spirit he stripped himself in like manner and set forth for Assisi; and with him he took Friar Leo, who carried his and Friar Ruffino's habits. And the men of Assisi, beholding him in like plight, mocked him, deeming that he and Friar Ruffino were crazy from excess of penance. St. Francis enters the church, where Friar Ruffino was preaching thus, "O dearest brethren, flee from the world and forsake sin, make restoration to others if ye would escape from hell; keep God's commandments and love God and your neighbour if ye would go to heaven; do penance if ye would possess the kingdom of heaven." Then St. Francis mounted the pulpit and began to preach so wondrously of the contempt of the world, of holy penance, of voluntary poverty, and of the desire for the heavenly kingdom, and of the nakedness and shame of the passion of our Lord Jesus Christ, that all they that were present at the sermon, men and women, in great multitudes, began to weep bitterly with wondrous devotion and contrition of heart; and not only there, but throughout the whole of Assisi, was such bewailing of the passion of Christ that the like had never been known before. And the people being thus edified and consoled by this act of St. Francis and of Friar Ruffino, St. Francis clothed himself and Friar Ruffino again; and thus re-clad they returned to the friary of the Porziuncula, praising and glorifying God, who had given them the grace to vanquish themselves by contempt of self, and to edify Christ's little sheep by good example, and to show forth how much the world is to be despised. And on that day the devotion of the people towards them increased so greatly that he who could touch the hem of their garments deemed himself blessed.

Chapter XXXI

HOW ST. FRANCIS KNEW THE SECRETS OF THE CONSCIENCES OF HIS FRIARS IN ALL THINGS

Even AS our Lord Jesus Christ saith in the gospel, "I know My sheep, and Mine own know Me," etc., so the blessed father St. Francis, like a good shepherd, knew all the merits and the virtues of his companions by divine revelation, and likewise their failings: by which means he knew how to provide the best remedy for each, to wit, by humbling the proud, exalting the humble, reproving vice, and praising virtue, even as may be read in the wondrous revelations he had, touching his first household. Among which it is found that St. Francis being on a time with his household in a friary discoursing of God, and Friar Ruffino not being with them during that discourse, but in the wood absorbed in contemplation, lo, while they continued in their discourse of God, Friar Ruffino came forth from the wood and passed by somewhat afar from them. Then St. Francis, beholding him, turned to his companions and asked of them, saying, "Tell me, who think ye is the saintliest soul God hath in this world?" And they answered him, saying, they believed it was his own; and St. Francis said to them, "Dearest friars, I am of myself the most unworthy and vilest of men that God hath in this world; but, behold yon Friar Ruffino, that now cometh forth from the wood! God hath revealed to me that his soul is one of the three saintliest souls in this world: and truly I say unto you, that I would not doubt to call him St. Ruffino even while he yet liveth, for his soul is confirmed in grace, and sanctified and canonised in heaven by our Lord Jesus Christ." But these words St. Francis never spoke in the presence of the said Friar Ruffino. Likewise, how that St. Francis knew the failings of his friars is clearly manifest in Friar Elias, whom many times he chid for his pride; and in Friar John della Cappella, to whom he foretold that he was to hang himself by the neck; and in that friar whom the devil held fast by the throat when he was corrected for his disobedience; and in many other friars whose secret failings and virtues he clearly knew by revelation from Christ.

Chapter XXXII

HOW FRIAR MASSEO CRAVED FROM CHRIST THE VIRTUE OF HUMILITY

The first companions of St. Francis strove with all their might to be poor in earthly things and rich in virtue, whereby they attained to true celestial and eternal riches. It befell one day that while they were gathered together discoursing of God, a friar among them spake thus by way of example, "One there was, a great friend of God, that had much grace both for the active and for the contemplative life, and withal he was of such exceeding humility that he deemed himself the greatest of sinners. And this humility confirmed and sanctified him in grace and made him increase continually in virtue and in divine gifts, and never suffered him to fall into sin." Now Friar Masseo, hearing such wondrous things of humility, and knowing it to be a treasure of life eternal, began to be so kindled with love, and with desire for this virtue of humility, that in great fervour of spirit he lifted up his face to heaven and made a vow and steadfast aim never to rejoice again in this world until he felt the said virtue perfectly in his soul: and thenceforth he remained well-nigh continually secluded in his cell, mortifying himself with fasts, vigils, prayer, and bitter tears before God to obtain that virtue from Him, failing which he deemed himself worthy of hell—the virtue wherewith that friend of God of whom he had heard was so bounteously dowered. And Friar Masseo, being thus for many days filled with this desire, it fell out on a day that he entered the wood, and in fervour of spirit roamed about giving forth tears, sighs, and cries, and craving this virtue from God with fervent desire: and since God willingly granteth the prayers of humble and contrite hearts, there came a voice from heaven to Friar Masseo, as he thus strove, and called him twice, "Friar Masseo, Friar Masseo!" And he, knowing in spirit that it was the voice of Christ, answered thus, "My Lord." And Christ said to him, "What wouldst thou give to possess the grace thou askest?" Friar Masseo answered, "Lord, I would give the eyes out of my head." And Christ said to him, "And I will that thou have this grace and thine eyes also." This said, the voice vanished, and Friar Masseo remained filled with such grace of the yearned-for virtue of humility, and of the light of God, that from thenceforth he was ever blithe of heart. And many times he made a joyous sound like the cooing of a dove, "Coo, coo, coo." And with glad countenance and jocund heart he dwelt thus in contemplation; and withal, being grown most humble, he deemed himself the least of men in the world. Being asked by Friar James of Falterone wherefore he changed not his note in these his jubilations, he answered with great joyfulness, that when we find full contentment in one song there is no need to change the tune.

Chapter XXXIII

HOW ST. CLARE, BY COMMAND OF THE POPE, BLESSED THE BREAD THAT LAY ON THE TABLE, WHEREUPON THE SIGN OF THE HOLY CROSS APPEARED ON EVERY LOAF

St. Clare, most devout disciple of the cross of Christ and noble plant of St. Francis, was so filled with holiness that not only bishops and cardinals but the pope also, with great affection, desired to behold and to hear her, and ofttimes visited her in person. Among other times, the holy father once went to her convent to hear her discourse of divine and celestial things: and being thus together, holding divers discourses, St. Clare had the table laid and set loaves of bread thereon that the holy father might bless them. Whereupon, the spiritual discourse being ended, St. Clare knelt down with great reverence and besought him to be pleased to bless the bread placed on the table. The holy father answers, "Sister Clare, most faithful one, I desire that thou bless this bread, and make over it the sign of the most holy cross of Christ, to which thou hast wholly devoted thyself." And St. Clare saith, "Most holy father, pardon me, for I should merit too great reproof if, in the presence of the vicar of Christ, I, that am a poor, vile woman, should presume to give such benediction." And the pope gives answer, "To the end that this be not imputed to thy presumption, but to the merit of obedience, I command thee, by holy obedience, that thou make the sign of the most holy cross over this bread, and bless it in the name of God." Then St. Clare, even as a true daughter of obedience, devoutly blessed the bread with the sign of the most holy cross. Marvellous to tell! forthwith on all those loaves the sign of the cross appeared figured most beautifully. Then, of those loaves, a part was eaten and a part preserved, in token of the miracle. And the holy father, when he saw this miracle, partook of the said bread and departed, thanking God and leaving his blessing with St. Clare. In that time Sister Ortolana, mother of St. Clare, abode in the convent, and Sister Agnes, her own sister, both of them, together with St. Clare, full of virtue and of the Holy Spirit, and with many other nuns, to whom St. Francis sent many sick persons; and they, with their prayers and with the sign of the most holy cross, restored health to all of them.

Chapter XXXIV

HOW ST. LOUIS, KING OF FRANCE, WENT IN PERSON, IN THE GUISE OF A PILGRIM, TO PERUGIA TO VISIT THE SAINTLY FRIAR GILES

St. Louis, King of France, went on a pilgrimage to visit the holy places throughout the world, and hearing of the far-famed holiness of Friar Giles, who had been one of the first companions of St. Francis, purposed and set his heart wholly on visiting him in person: for which thing he came to Perugia, where the said friar then dwelt. And coming to the door of the friary as a poor unknown pilgrim, with but few companions, he asked with great importunity for Friar Giles, telling not the doorkeeper who he was. So the doorkeeper goes to Friar Giles and says, "There is a pilgrim at the door that asketh for you." And God inspired and revealed to him that this was the King of France. Whereat, anon he comes forth from his cell with great fervour and runs to the door; and asking naught, and never having seen each other before, they knelt down with great devotion, and embraced each other, and kissed with such affection as if for a long space they had been great friends together; yet, through all this, neither one nor the other spake, but they remained silently locked in each other's arms with those outward signs of loving charity. And after they had remained thus a great space, saying no word each to other, they both departed: St. Louis went his way and Friar Giles returned to his cell. Now as the king was setting forth, a friar asked of one of the king's companions who he might be that had so long embraced Friar Giles, and answer was made that he was Louis, King of France, who had come to see Friar Giles. And when the friar told this to the others they waxed mightily afflicted that Friar

Giles had spoken no word with the king, and, making complaint, they cried, "O Friar Giles, wherefore hast thou been so churlish as to speak no word to so great and saintly a king, that hath come from France to see thee and to hear some good word from thee?" Friar Giles answered, "Dearest friars, marvel not thereat, for neither I to him nor he to me could utter one word; since, no sooner had we embraced together, than the light of wisdom revealed and manifested his heart to me and mine to him, and thus, by divine power, as we looked in each other's breasts, we knew better what I would say to him and he to me than if we had spoken with our mouths; and greater consolation had we than if we had sought to explain with our lips what we felt in our hearts. For, because of the defect of human speech, that cannot express clearly the mysteries and secrets of God, words would have left us disconsolate rather than consoled; know, therefore, that the king departed from me marvellously glad and consoled in spirit."

Chapter XXXV

HOW ST. CLARE, BEING SICK, WAS MIRACULOUSLY BORNE ON CHRISTMAS EVE TO THE CHURCH OF ST. FRANCIS, AND THERE HEARD THE OFFICE

St. Clare, being on a time grievously sick, so that she could in no wise go to say the office in church with the other nuns, and seeing that when the feast of the Nativity of Christ came all the others went to matins, while she remained in bed, grew ill at ease that she could not go with them and enjoy that spiritual consolation. But Jesus Christ, her spouse, not willing to leave her thus disconsolate, caused her to be miraculously borne to the church of St. Francis and to be present at the whole office of matins, and at the midnight mass; and moreover, she received the holy communion, and then was borne back to her bed. When the nuns returned to St. Clare, after the office at St. Damian's was over, they spake to her thus, "O Sister Clare, our mother, what great consolation have we had on this holy feast of the Nativity; would now it had pleased God that you had been with us!" And St. Clare answered, "Thanks and praise do I render to our blessed Lord Jesus Christ, my sisters, and dearest daughters, for at all the solemn offices of this most holy night, yea, and at even greater festivals have I been present with great consolation of soul, than ye have seen, for by the solicitude of my father, St. Francis, and by the grace of Jesus Christ, have I been present in the church of my venerable father, St. Francis; and with my bodily and spiritual ears have I heard all the office and the music of the organs that were played there, and in that same church have I partaken of the most holy communion. Wherefore rejoice ye that such grace hath been vouchsafed to me and praise our Lord Jesus

Christ."

Chapter XXXVI

HOW ST. FRANCIS INTERPRETED A FAIR VISION THAT FRIAR LEO HAD SEEN

On a time when St. Francis lay grievously sick and Friar Leo was tending him, the said friar, being in prayer by the side of St. Francis, was rapt in ecstasy and led in spirit to a mighty torrent, wide and raging. And as he stood gazing on those who were crossing it, he beheld certain friars, bearing burdens, enter into this stream that anon were overthrown by the fierce buffetings of the waves and drowned; some reached as far as a third of the way across; others as far as the middle; yet others reached nigh over unto the shore. But all of them, by reason of the fury of the waters and the heavy burdens they bore on their backs, fell at last and were drowned. Friar Leo, beholding this, had compassion on them exceeding great, and straightway, as he stood thus, lo, there comes a great multitude of friars, bearing no burdens or load of any kind, in whom shone forth the light of holy poverty: and they entered this stream and passed over to the other side without peril: and when he had seen this, Friar Leo returned to himself. Then St. Francis, feeling in spirit that Friar Leo had seen a vision, called him to himself and asked touching the vision he had seen. And as soon as the aforesaid Friar Leo had told his vision in due order, St. Francis said, "What thou hast seen is true. The mighty stream is this world; the friars that were drowned therein are they that followed not the teachings of the gospel, and especially in regard to most high poverty; but they that passed over without peril are those friars that seek after no earthly or carnal thing, nor possess aught in this world; but, temperate in food and clothing, are glad, following Christ naked on the cross, and bear joyously and willingly the burden and sweet yoke of Christ and of most holy obedience. Therefore they pass with ease from this temporal life to life eternal."

Chapter XXXVII

HOW JESUS CHRIST THE BLESSED, AT THE PRAYER OF ST. FRANCIS, CAUSED A RICH AND NOBLE KNIGHT TO BE CONVERTED AND BECOME A FRIAR; WHICH KNIGHT HAD DONE GREAT HONOUR AND HAD MADE MANY GIFTS UNTO ST. FRANCIS

St. Francis, servant of Christ, coming late at eve to the house of a great and potent nobleman, was received and entertained by him, both he and his companion, as had they been angels of God, with the greatest courtesy and devotion; wherefore St. Francis loved him much, considering that on entering the house he had embraced him and kissed him affectionately; then had washed his feet and wiped them and humbly kissed them; and had kindled a great fire and made ready the table with much good food; and while he ate, did serve him zealously with joyful countenance. Now when St. Francis and his companion had eaten, this nobleman said, "Lo, my father, I proffer myself and my goods to you; how many times soever you have need of tunic or cloak or aught else, buy them and I will pay for you; nay, look you, I am ready to provide for all your needs, for by God's grace I am able so to do, inasmuch as I have abundance of all worldly goods; therefore, for love of God, that hath bestowed them on me, I willingly do good to His poor." St. Francis, beholding such great courtesy and loving-kindness in him, and his bounteous offerings, conceived for him love so great that when he afterwards departed from him he spake thus to his companion as they journeyed together, "Verily this noble gentleman, that is so grateful and thankful to God and so kind and courteous to his neighbour and to the poor, would be a good companion for our Order. Know, dearest friar, that courtesy is one of the attributes of God, who of His courtesy giveth His sun and His rain to the just and to the unjust: and courtesy is sister to charity, that quencheth hatred and kindleth love. And since I have found in this good man such divine virtue, fain would I have him for companion: therefore I will that one day we return to him, if haply God may touch his heart and bend his will to accompany us in the service of God. Meanwhile, pray we unto God that He may set this desire in his heart and give him grace to attain thereto." Marvellous to tell! a few days after St. Francis had made this prayer, God put these desires into this nobleman's heart, and St. Francis said to his companion, "Let us go, my brother, to the abode of that courteous gentleman, for I have a certain hope in God that, with the same bounty he hath shown in temporal things, he will give himself also, and will be our companion." And they went. And coming nigh unto his house, St. Francis said to his companion, "Tarry a while for me; I desire first to pray to God that He may prosper our way, and that it may please Jesus Christ to grant unto us, poor and weak men, the noble prey we think to snatch from the world by virtue of His most holy Passion." This said, he went forth to pray in a place where he might be seen of that same courteous gentleman. Now, as it pleased God, he, looking hither and thither, had perceived St. Francis most devoutly in prayer before Jesus Christ, who with great splendour had appeared to him and stood before him during the said prayer; and as he thus gazed he beheld St. Francis lifted up a great space bodily from the earth. Whereat he was so touched by God and inspired to forsake the world that he straightway came forth from his mansion and ran in fervour of spirit towards St. Francis, and coming to him, who still remained in prayer, knelt down at his feet, and with great instance and devotion prayed that it might please him to receive him and do penance with him together. Then St. Francis, seeing his prayer was heard of God, and that what he himself desired, that noble gentleman was craving with much importunity, lifted himself up, and in fervour and gladness of heart embraced and kissed him, devoutly giving thanks to God, who had increased his company by so great a knight. And that gentleman said to St. Francis, "What dost thou command me to do, my father? Lo, I am ready to do thy bidding and give all I possess to the poor, and thus disburdened of all worldly things to follow Christ with thee." Thus did he, according to the counsel of St. Francis, for he distributed all his goods among the poor, and entered the Order and lived in great penitence and holiness of life and godly conversation.

Chapter XXXVIII

HOW ST. FRANCIS KNEW IN SPIRIT THAT FRIAR ELIAS WAS DAMNED AND WAS TO DIE OUTSIDE THE ORDER: WHEREFORE, AT THE PRAYER OF FRIAR ELIAS, HE BESOUGHT CHRIST FOR HIM AND WAS HEARD

On a time when St. Francis and Friar Elias were dwelling in a friary together, it was revealed by God to St. Francis that Friar Elias was damned, and was to become a renegade and in the end, die outside the Order. Whereat St. Francis conceived so great a displeasure towards him that he never spake nor held converse with him; and if it befell that Friar Elias came towards him at any time, he turned aside and went another way that he might not encounter him; whereby Friar Elias began to perceive and comprehend that St. Francis was displeased with him. And desiring one day to know the cause thereof, he accosted St. Francis and would speak with him; and as St. Francis turned from him he gently held him back by force, and began to entreat him earnestly to be pleased to signify to him the reason why he thus shunned his company and forbore to speak with him. And St. Francis answered, "The cause is this: It hath been revealed to me by God that thou, for thy sins, shalt become a renegade and shalt die outside the Order; and God hath likewise revealed to me that thou art damned." Hearing these words, Friar Elias spake thus, "My reverend father, I pray thee for the love of Jesus Christ, that for this cause thou shun me not, nor cast me from thee; but as a good shepherd, after the example of Christ, thou seek out and receive again the sheep that will perish except thou aid him, and that thou wilt pray to God for me, if haply He may revoke the sentence of my damnation; for it is written that God will remit the sentence, if the sinner amend his ways; and I have such great faith in thy prayers, that if I were in the midst of hell, and thou didst pray to God for me, I should feel some refreshment: wherefore yet again I beseech thee that thou commend me, a sinner, unto God, who came to save sinners, that He may receive me to His mercy-seat." This, Friar Elias said with great devotion and tears; whereat St. Francis, even as a compassionate father, promised he would pray for him. And praying most devoutly to God for him, he understood by revelation that his prayer was heard of God in so far as concerned the revocation of the sentence of damnation passed on Friar Elias, and that at the last his soul should not be damned; but that of a surety he would forsake the Order and, outside the Order, would die. And so it came to pass. For when Frederick, King of Sicily, rebelled against the church and was excommunicated by the pope, he and whosoever gave him aid or counsel, the said Friar Elias, that was reputed one of the wisest men in the world, being entreated by the said King Frederick, went over to him, and became a rebel to the church and a renegade from the Order. Wherefore he was banned by the pope and stripped of the habit of St. Francis. And being thus excommunicate, behold he fell grievously sick; and his brother, a lay friar who had remained in the Order, and was a man of good and honest life, went to visit him, and among other things spake to him thus, "Dearest brother mine, it grieveth me sorely that thou art excommunicate and cast out of thine Order and even so shall die: but if thou seest any way or means whereby I may deliver thee from this peril, willingly will I undertake any toil for thee." Friar Elias answered, "Brother mine, no other way do I see but that thou repair to the pope and beseech him, for the love of God and of St. Francis His servant, at whose teachings I forsook the world, that he absolve me from his ban and restore to me the habit of the Order." And his brother answered that willingly would he labour for his salvation: and departing from him he went to the footstool of the holy father and humbly besought him that he would grant this grace to his brother, for love of Christ and of St. Francis His servant. And as it pleased God, the pope consented that he should return; and that if he found Friar Elias yet living, he should absolve him in his name from the ban and restore the habit to him. Whereat he departed joyfully, and returned in great haste to Friar Elias, and, finding him alive, but well-nigh at the point of death, absolved him from the ban; and Friar Elias, putting on the habit again, passed from this life, and his soul was saved by the merits of St. Francis and by his prayers, wherein Friar Elias had placed hope so great.

Chapter XXXIX

OF THE MARVELLOUS SERMON THAT ST. ANTHONY OF PADUA,
A FRIAR MINOR, PREACHED IN THE CONSISTORY

That wondrous vessel of the Holy Spirit, St. Anthony of Padua, one of the chosen disciples and companions of St. Francis, he that St. Francis called his vicar, was once preaching in the consistory before the pope and the cardinals, in which consistory were men of divers nations, to wit, French, Germans, Sclavonians, and English, and divers other tongues throughout the world. Inflamed by the Holy Spirit, he expounded the word of God so effectually, so devoutly, so subtly, so sweetly, so clearly, and so wisely, that all they that were in the consistory, albeit they were of divers nations, clearly understood all his words distinctly, even as though he had spoken to each one of them in his native tongue; and all were filled with wonder, for it seemed that that miracle of old were renewed when the Apostles, on the day of Pentecost, spake, by the power of the Holy Spirit, in every tongue. And marvelling, they said one to another, "Is not he that preacheth a Spaniard? How then hear we all the tongue of our native land in his speech?" The pope likewise, considering and marvelling at the depth of his words, said, "Verily this friar is the ark of the covenant and the treasury of divine scriptures."

Chapter XL

OF THE MIRACLE THAT GOD WROUGHT, WHEN ST. ANTHONY,
BEING AT RIMINI, PREACHED TO THE FISHES IN THE SEA

Christ the blessed, being pleased to show forth the great holiness of His most faithful servant, St. Anthony, and with what devotion his preaching and his holy doctrine were to be heard, one time, among others, rebuked the folly of infidel heretics by means of creatures without reason, to wit, the fishes; even as in days gone by, in the Old Testament, He rebuked the ignorance of Balaam by the mouth of an ass. Wherefore it befell, on a time when St. Anthony was at Rimini, where was a great multitude of heretics whom he desired to lead to the light of the true faith and to the paths of virtue, that he preached for many days and disputed with them concerning the faith of Christ and of the Holy Scriptures: yet they not only consented not unto his words, but even hardened their hearts and stubbornly refused to hear him. Wherefore St. Anthony, by divine inspiration, went one day to the bank of the river, hard by the seashore, and standing there on the bank of the river, between it and the sea, began to speak to the fishes after the manner of a preacher sent by God, "Hear the word of God, ye fishes of the sea and of the river, since the miscreant heretics scorn to hear it." And when he had thus spoken, anon there came towards the bank such a multitude of fishes, great and small, and middling, that never before in those seas, nor in that river, had so great a multitude been seen; and all held their heads out of the water in great peace and gentleness and perfect order, and remained intent on the lips of St. Anthony: for in front of him and nearest to the bank were the lesser fishes; and beyond them were those of middling size; and then behind, where the water was deepest, were the greater fishes. The fishes being then mustered in such order and array, St. Anthony began to preach to them solemnly, and spake thus, "Ye fishes, my brothers, much are ye bound, according to your power, to thank God our Creator, who hath given you so noble an element for your habitation; for at your pleasure have ye waters, sweet and salt, and He hath given you many places of refuge to shelter you from the tempests; He hath likewise given you a pure and clear element, and food whereby ye can live. God, your Creator, bountiful and kind, when He created you, commanded you to increase and multiply, and gave you His blessing; then, in the universal deluge and when all other animals were perishing, you alone did God preserve from harm. Moreover, He hath given you fins that ye may fare withersoever it may please you. To you was it granted, by commandment of God, to preserve Jonah the prophet, and after the third day to cast him forth on dry land, safe and whole. Ye did offer the tribute money to Christ our Lord, to Him, poor little one, that had not wherewithal to pay. Ye, by a rare mystery, were the food of the eternal King, Christ Jesus, before the resurrection and after. For all those things much are ye held to praise and bless God, that hath given you blessings so manifold and so great; yea, more even than to any other of His creatures." At these and the like words and admonitions from St. Anthony, the fishes began to open their mouths and bow their heads, and by these and other tokens of reverence, according to their fashion and power, they gave praise to God. Then St. Anthony, beholding in the fishes such great reverence towards God their Creator, rejoiced in spirit, and said with a loud voice, "Blessed be God eternal, since the fishes in the waters honour Him more than do heretic men; and creatures without reason hear His word better than infidel men." And the longer St. Anthony preached, the greater the multitude of fishes increased, and none departed from the place he had taken. And the people of the city began to run to behold this miracle, among whom the aforesaid heretics were also drawn thither; and when they beheld a miracle so marvellous and manifest, they were pricked in their hearts, and cast themselves all at the feet of St. Anthony to hear his words. Then St. Anthony began to preach the catholic faith, and so nobly did he expound the faith that he converted all those heretics, and they turned to the true faith of Christ; and all the faithful were comforted and filled with joy exceeding great, and were strengthened in the faith. This done, St. Anthony dismissed the fishes, with God's blessing, and all they departed with wondrous signs of gladness, and the people likewise. And then St. Anthony sojourned in Rimini many days, preaching and gathering much spiritual fruit of souls.

Chapter XLI

HOW THE VENERABLE FRIAR SIMON DELIVERED A FRIAR FROM A GREAT TEMPTATION WHO FOR THIS CAUSE HAD DESIRED TO LEAVE THE ORDER

In the early days of the Order of St. Francis, and while the saint was yet alive, a youth of Assisi came to the Order that was called Friar Simon, whom God adorned and endowed with such grace and such contemplation and elevation of mind that all his life he was a mirror of holiness, even as I heard from those that were with him a long time. Very seldom was he seen outside his cell, and if at any time he was seen with the friars, he was ever discoursing of God. He had never been through the schools, yet so profoundly and so loftily spake he of God, and of the love of Christ, that his words seemed supernatural; wherefore one evening being gone into the wood with Friar James of Massa to speak of God, they spent all the night in that discourse; and when the dawn came it seemed to them they had been together but for a very brief space of time, as the said Friar James related to me. And the said Friar Simon received the divine and loving illuminations of God to such a degree of pleasantness and sweetness that ofttimes when he felt them coming he lay down on his bed; for the gentle sweetness of the Holy Spirit required of him, not only rest of soul, but also of body, and in divine visitations, such as these, he was many times rapt in God and became insensible to corporeal things. Wherefore on a time when he was thus rapt in God and insensible to the world, and burning inwardly with divine love, so that he felt naught of outward things with his bodily senses, a friar, desiring to have experience thereof and prove if it were verily as it seemed to be, went and took a coal of fire and laid it on his naked foot. And Friar Simon felt naught, nor made it any scar on the foot, albeit it remained there a great space, so great that it went out of itself. The said Friar Simon, when he sat down at table, before he partook of bodily food was wont to take to himself and give to others spiritual food, discoursing of God. By his devout speech a young man of San Severino was once converted, that in the world was a most vain and worldly youth, and of noble blood and very delicate of body; and Friar Simon receiving this youth into the Order, put aside his worldly vestments and kept them near himself, and he abode with Friar Simon to be instructed by him in the observances of the Order. Whereat the devil, that ever seeketh to thwart every good thing, set within him so mighty a thorn and temptation of the flesh that in no wise could he resist; wherefore he repaired to Friar Simon and said to him, "Restore to me my clothes that I brought from the world, for I can no longer endure the temptation of the flesh." And Friar Simon, having great compassion on him, spake to him thus, "Sit thou here, my son, a while with me." And he began to discourse to him of God, in such wise that all temptation left him; then after a time the temptation returned, and he asked for his clothes again, and Friar Simon drave it forth again by discoursing of God. This being done many times, at last the said temptation assailed him so mightily one night, even more than it was wont to do, that for naught in this world was he able to resist it; and he went to Friar Simon and demanded from him yet again all his worldly clothes, for in no wise could he longer remain. Then Friar Simon, according as he was wont to do, made him sit beside him; and as he discoursed to him of God, the youth leaned his head on Friar Simon's bosom for very woe and sadness. Then Friar Simon, of his great compassion, lifted up his eyes to heaven and made supplication to God; and as he prayed most devoutly for him, the youth was rapt in God and Friar Simon's prayers were heard: wherefore the youth returning to himself was wholly delivered from that temptation, even as though had he never felt it: yea, the fire of temptation was changed to the fire of the Holy Spirit, forasmuch as he had sat beside that burning coal, Friar Simon, who was all inflamed with the love of God and of his neighbour, in such wise that on a time, when a malefactor was taken that was to have both his eyes plucked out, the said youth for very pity went boldly up to the governor, and in full council and with many tears and devout prayers entreated that one of his own eyes might be plucked out, and one of the malefactor's, in order that the wretch might not be deprived of both. But the governor and his council, beholding the great fervour and charity of the friar, pardoned both of them. One day as Friar Simon was in the wood at prayer, feeling great consolation in his soul, a flock of rooks began to do him much annoy by their cawing: whereat he commanded them in the name of Jesus to depart and return no more; and the said birds departing thence were no more seen nor heard, neither in the wood nor in all the country round about. And the miracle was manifest over all the custody of Fermo wherein the said friary stood.

Chapter XLII

OF THE FAIR MIRACLES GOD WROUGHT THROUGH HIS HOLY FRIARS, BENTIVOGLIA, FRIAR PETER OF MONTICELLO, AND FRIAR CONRAD OF OFFIDA; AND HOW FRIAR BENTIVOGLIA CARRIED A LEPER FIFTEEN MILES IN A VERY BRIEF TIME; AND HOW THE OTHER FRIAR SPAKE WITH ST. MICHAEL, AND HOW TO THE THIRD CAME THE VIRGIN MARY AND LAID HER SON IN HIS ARMS

The province of the Marches of Ancona was adorned of old, after the manner of the starry firmament, with holy and exemplary friars who, like the shining lights of heaven, have adorned and illumined the Order of St. Francis and the world by their example and doctrine. Among others there was, in the early days, Friar Lucido Antico, that was truly lucent by his holiness and burning with divine charity, whose glorious tongue, informed of the Holy Spirit, brought forth marvellous fruit by his preaching. Another was Friar Bentivoglia of San Severino, who was seen by Friar Masseo to be lifted up in the air for a great space while he was at prayer in the wood; for which miracle the devout Friar Masseo, being then a parish priest, left his parish and became a friar minor; and he was of holiness so great that he wrought many miracles during his life and after his death, and his body lies at Murro. The aforesaid Friar Bentivoglia, when he sojourned alone at Ponte della Trave, tending and serving a leper, was commanded by his superior to depart thence and go to another friary that was fifteen miles away; and not being willing to forsake the leper, he laid hold of him, and with great fervour of charity lifted him on to his shoulder and carried him between dawn and sunrise the whole of those fifteen miles as far as the place whither he was sent, that was called Monte Sancino: which distance, even had he been an eagle, he could not have flown in so short a time; and in all that country was much wonder and amazement at this divine miracle. Another was Friar Peter of Monticello, who was seen by Friar Servodio of Urbino, then warden of the old friary of Ancona, to be lifted bodily up from the ground full five or six cubits, as far as the foot of the crucifix before which he was in prayer. And this Friar Peter, while keeping the forty days' fast of St. Michael the Archangel with great devotion, and being in church at prayer on the last day of that fast, was heard by a young friar speaking with St. Michael the Archangel, for he had hidden himself under the high altar to behold somewhat of his sanctity; and the words he spake were these. Said St. Michael, "Friar Peter, thou hast faithfully travailed for me, and in many ways hast afflicted thy body: lo, I am come to comfort thee, and that thou mayest ask whatsoever grace thou desirest I will promise to obtain it of God." Friar Peter answered, "Most holy prince of the host of heaven, and faithful zealot of divine love and compassionate protector of souls, this grace do I ask of thee: that thou obtain from God the pardon of my sins." St. Michael answered, "Ask some other grace, for this shall I obtain for thee right easily." But Friar Peter asking naught else, the archangel made an end, saying, "For the faith and devotion thou hast in me I will obtain this grace for thee and many others." And their discourse being ended, that endured a great space, the archangel Michael departed, leaving him comforted exceedingly. In the days of this holy Friar Peter lived the holy Friar Conrad of Offida, who, dwelling with him together at the friary of Forano in the custody of Ancona, went forth one day into the wood for divine contemplation; and Friar Peter secretly followed after him to see what should befall him. And Friar Conrad betook himself to prayer and most devoutly besought the Virgin Mary, of her great compassion, that she would obtain this grace from her blessed Son: to wit, that he might feel a little of that sweetness that St. Simeon felt on the day of Purification when he bore Jesus the blessed Saviour in his arms. And his prayer ended, the merciful Virgin Mary granted it. And lo, the Queen of Heaven appeared with resplendent clarity of light, with her blessed Son in her arms, and drawing nigh to Friar Conrad, laid her blessed Son in his arms, who, receiving Him, devoutly embraced and kissed Him, then clasping Him to his breast, was wholly melted and dissolved in love divine and unspeakable consolation: and Friar Peter likewise, who secretly beheld all these things, felt great sweetness and consolation in his soul. And when the Virgin Mary had departed from Friar Conrad, Friar Peter returned in haste to the friary that he might not be seen of him. But thereafter when Friar Conrad returned, all joyous and glad, Friar Peter said to him, "O celestial soul, great consolation hast thou had this day." Said Friar Conrad, "What sayest thou, Friar Peter? How knowest thou what I may have had?" "Full well I know, full well I know," said Friar Peter, "that the Virgin Mary with her blessed Son hath visited thee." Then Friar Conrad, who with true humility desired that this grace of God should be hidden, besought him to speak no word of these things. And so great thenceforth was the love between these two friars that they seemed to be of one heart and one mind in all things. And the said Friar Conrad on a time in the friary of Siruolo delivered a woman possessed of a devil by praying for her the whole night through, and being seen of her mother on the morrow, he fled lest he might be found and honoured by the people.

Chapter XLIII

HOW FRIAR CONRAD OF OFFIDA CONVERTED A YOUNG FRIAR THAT WAS A STUMBLING-BLOCK TO THE OTHER FRIARS. AND HOW AFTER THE SAID YOUNG FRIAR DIED HE APPEARED TO THE SAID FRIAR CONRAD AND ENTREATED HIM TO PRAY FOR HIM; AND HOW HE DELIVERED HIM BY HIS PRAYERS FROM THE MOST GRIEVOUS PAINS OF PURGATORY

The said Friar Conrad of Offida, wondrous zealot of gospel poverty and of the Rule of St. Francis, was of so religious a life, and of such great merit before god, that Christ the blessed honoured him in his life and after his death with many miracles, among which, being come on a time to the friary of Offida as a guest, the friars prayed him for love of God and of his charity to admonish a young friar that was in the settlement, who bore himself so childishly, so disorderly and dissolutely, that he disturbed both old and young of that community during the divine offices, and cared little or naught for the observances of the Rule. Whereupon Friar Conrad, in compassion for that youth, and at the prayers of the friars, called the said youth apart one day, and in fervour of charity spake to him words of admonition, so effectual and so divine, that by the operation of divine grace he straightway became changed from a child to an old man in manners, and grew so obedient and benign and diligent and devout, and thereafter so peaceful and obedient, and so studious of every virtuous thing, that even as at first the whole community were perturbed because of him, so now all were content with him, and comforted, and greatly loved him. And it came to pass, as it pleased God, that some time after this conversion, the said youth died, whereat the said friars mourned; and a few days after his death, his soul appeared to Friar Conrad, while he was devoutly praying before the altar of the said friary, and saluted him devoutly as a father; and Friar Conrad asked him, "Who art thou?" And he answered and said, "I am the soul of that young friar that died these latter days." And Friar Conrad said, "O my dearest son, how is it with thee?" He answered, "By God's grace, and your teaching, 'tis well; for I am not damned, but for certain of my sins, whereof I lacked time to purge me sufficiently, I suffer grievous pains in purgatory; but I pray thee, father, that as of thy compassion thou didst succour me while I lived, so may it please thee to succour me now in my pains, and say some paternosters for me; for thy prayers are very acceptable before God." Then Friar Conrad consented kindly to his prayers and recited the paternoster, with the *requiem æternum*, once for him. Said that soul, "O dearest father, what great good and what great refreshment do I feel! Now, prithee recite it once again." And Friar Conrad recited it, and when it was repeated again, that soul said, "Holy father, when thou prayest for me I feel all my pains lightened, wherefore I beseech thee that thou cease not thy prayers for me." Then Friar Conrad, beholding his prayers availed that soul so much, said a hundred paternosters for her. And when they were recited, that soul said, "I thank thee, dearest father, in God's name, for the charity thou hast had for me: for by thy prayers am I freed from all the pains of purgatory, and am on my way to the kingdom of heaven." This said, the soul departed. Then Friar Conrad, to give joy and comfort to the friars, related to them all this vision in order; and thus the soul of that youth went to paradise through the merits of Friar Conrad.

Chapter XLIV

HOW THE MOTHER OF CHRIST AND ST. JOHN THE EVANGELIST APPEARED TO FRIAR PETER AND TOLD HIM WHICH OF THEM SUFFERED GREATEST PAIN AT THE PASSION OF CHRIST

In the days when the aforesaid Friar Conrad and Friar Peter abode together at the friary of Forano, in the district of Ancona—those two friars that were bright twin stars in the province of the Marches, and two most godly men—forasmuch as they seemed of one heart and one mind, they, in their love and charity, bound themselves together in this covenant: That they would reveal to each other in charity every consolation that God in His mercy bestowed on them. This covenant being made between them, it befell on a day when Friar Peter was at prayer and pondering most devoutly on the Passion of Christ, and how that the most blessed Mother of Christ, and John the Evangelist, the most beloved disciple, and St. Francis, were all painted at the foot of the cross, crucified in dolour of soul with Christ, a desire came upon him to know which of those three had suffered greatest sorrow in the Passion of Christ—the Mother that had begotten Him, or the disciple that had slept on His breast, or St. Francis, crucified with the wounds of Christ. And being thus absorbed in meditation, the Virgin Mary appeared to him, with St. John the Evangelist and St. Francis, clothed in noblest raiment of beatific glory; but St. Francis seemed arrayed in a fairer garment than St. John. And Peter being sore afraid at this vision, St. John comforted him and said to him, "Fear not, dearest brother, for we are come to console thee in thy doubt. Know then that the Mother of Christ and I sorrowed above all other creatures at the Passion of Christ; but after us St. Francis felt greater sorrow than any other: therefore thou seest him in such glory." And Friar Peter asked, "O holiest Apostle of Christ, wherefore doth the raiment of St. Francis seem fairer than thine?" St. John answered, "The reason is this: that in the world he wore viler garments than I." These words said, St. John gave Friar Peter a glorious robe that he bore in his hand, and said to him, "Take this robe which I have brought to give thee." And when St. John was about to clothe him with it, Friar Peter fell dazed to the ground and began to cry, "Friar Conrad, dearest Friar Conrad, succour me quickly; come and behold marvellous things." And at these holy words the saintly vision vanished. Then when Friar Conrad came he told him all things in order, and they gave thanks to God.

Chapter XLV

OF THE CONVERSION, LIFE, MIRACLES, AND DEATH OF THE HOLY FRIAR JOHN OF LA PENNA

One night, in the province of the Marches, a child, exceeding fair, appeared to Friar John of La Penna, when he was yet a lad in the world, and called him, saying, "John, go to the church of St. Stephen, where one of my friars minor is preaching; believe in his teaching and give heed to his words, for I have sent him thither; this done, thou shalt take a long journey and thou shalt come to me." Whereat, anon he rose up, and felt a great change in his soul, and going to St. Stephen's, he found a great multitude of men and women that were assembled there to hear the sermon. And he that was to preach there was a friar, called Friar Philip, who was one of the first friars that had come to the Marches of Ancona; and as yet few friaries were established in the Marches. Up climbs this Friar Philip to preach, and preaches most devoutly, and not in words of human wisdom; but by virtue of the spirit of Christ he announced the kingdom of life eternal. The sermon ended, the lad went to the said Friar Philip and said to him, "Father, if it please you to receive me into the Order, fain would I do penance and serve our Lord Jesus Christ." Friar Philip, beholding and knowing the wondrous innocence of the said lad and his ready will to serve God, spake to him thus, "Thou shalt come to me on such a day at Ricanati, and I will have thee received." Now the provincial Chapter was to be held in that city, wherefore the lad, being very guileless, thought this was the great journey he was to make, according to the revelation he had had, and then was to go to paradise; and this he thought to do straightway after he was received into the Order. Therefore he went and was received: and then, seeing his thought was not fulfilled, and hearing the minister say in the Chapter that whosoever would go to the province of Provence, through the merit of holy obedience, he would freely give him leave, there came to him a great desire to go thither, believing in his heart that that was the great journey he must take ere he went to paradise. But he was ashamed to say so, and confided at last in the aforesaid Friar Philip, that had had him received into the Order, and gently prayed him to obtain that grace for him, to wit, that he should go to the province of Provence. Then Friar Philip, beholding his innocency and his holy intent, obtained leave for him to go; whereupon Friar John set forth on his way with great joy, believing that, the journey accomplished, he would go to paradise. But it pleased God that he should remain in the said province five-and-twenty years in this expectancy and desire, a pattern of sanctity and walking in great godliness; and increasing ever in virtue and in the favour of God, and of the people, he was greatly loved by the friars and by the world. And Friar John, being one day devoutly in prayer, weeping and lamenting that his desire was not fulfilled and that his earthly pilgrimage was too prolonged, the blessed Christ appeared to him, at sight of whom his soul was all melted, and said to him, "My son, Friar John, ask of Me what thou wilt." And he answered, "My Lord, I know not what to ask of Thee save Thyself, for naught else do I desire; this alone I pray— that Thou forgive me all my sins, and give me grace to behold Thee once again when I may have a greater need of Thee." Said Christ, "Thy prayer is granted." After these words He departed, and Friar John remained all comforted. At last the friars of the Marches, hearing of the fame of his holiness, wrought so with the general of the Order that he bade him by obedience return to the Marches; and when Friar John received this command, joyously he set forth on his way, thinking that this journey being accomplished he should go to heaven, according to the promise of Christ. But when he was a returned to the province of the Marches, he abode there yet thirty years, and none of his kinsfolk knew him: and every day he waited for the mercy of God and that He should fulfil the promise made to him. And during these years he filled the office of warden many times with great discretion, and through him God wrought many miracles. Now among other gifts he had of God was the spirit of prophecy. Wherefore, on a time when he was gone forth from the friary, one, his novice, was assailed by the devil and tempted so mightily that he consented to the temptation, and purposed within himself to leave the Order as soon as Friar John had returned. But this temptation and purpose being known to Friar John by the spirit of prophecy, he straightway returned to the friary and called the said novice to him and bade him confess: and before he confessed he related all the temptation to him in order, even as God had revealed it to him, and ended thus, "Son, forasmuch as thou didst wait for me, and wouldst not depart without my blessing, God hath granted thee this grace—that thou shalt never issue forth from this Order, but by divine grace shalt die in the Order." Then the said novice was strengthened in his good will, and remaining in the Order, became a holy friar. And all these things Friar Hugolin related to me. The said Friar John, that was a man of joyful and tranquil mind, spake but rarely, and was given to great meditation and devotion: and above all, after matins he never returned to his cell, but remained in church at prayer until the day broke. And he, being at prayer one night after matins, the angel of God appeared to him and said, "Friar John, thy journey is accomplished for which thou hast waited so long: therefore I announce to thee in God's name that thou mayst ask whatsoever grace thou desirest. And likewise I announce to thee that thou mayst choose which thou wilt—either one day in purgatory or seven days' pain on earth." And Friar John, choosing rather seven days' pain on earth, anon fell sick of divers infirmities; for a violent fever took him, and gout in his hands and feet, and colic, and many other ills; but what wrought him greatest pain was, that a devil stood before him, holding in his hand a great scroll, whereon were written all the sins he had ever done or thought, and spake to him thus, "For those sins that thou hast done, either in thought, or word, or deed, thou art damned to the lowest depths of hell." And he remembered naught of good that he had ever done, nor that he was in the Order, nor ever had been therein; but he believed he was thus damned, even as the devil told him. Wherefore, when he was asked how it went with him, he answered, "Ill, for I am damned." The friars, seeing this, sent for an aged friar, whose name was Friar Matthew of Monte Rubbiano, that was a holy man and dear friend of this Friar John: and the said Friar Matthew, being come to him on the seventh day of his tribulation, gave him salutation and asked how it was with him. He answered, that it fared ill with him because he was damned. Then said Friar Matthew, "Rememberest thou not that many times thou hast confessed to me, and I have wholly absolved thee of thy sins? Rememberest thou likewise that thou hast ever served God in this holy Order many years? Moreover, rememberest thou not that God's mercy exceedeth all the sins of this world, and that Christ, our blessed Saviour, paid an infinite price to redeem us? Therefore be of good hope, for a surety thou art saved"; and with these words, forasmuch as the term of his purgation was accomplished, temptation vanished and consolation came. And with great gladness Friar John said to Friar Matthew, "Because thou art weary and the hour is late, I pray thee, go to rest." And Friar Matthew would not leave him; but at last, at his urgent prayers, he departed from him and went to rest; and Friar John remained alone with the friar that tended him. And lo, Christ the blessed came, in great splendour and in fragrance of exceeding sweetness, even as He had promised to appear to him again when he should have greater need, and healed him perfectly from all his infirmities. Then Friar John, with clasped hands giving thanks to God that he had accomplished the great journey of this present miserable life with so good an end, commended his soul to the hands of Christ and rendered it up to God, passing from this mortal life to life eternal with Christ the blessed, that he so long a time had desired and waited to behold. And the said Friar John is laid to rest in the friary of La Penna di San Giovanni.

Chapter XLVI

HOW FRIAR PACIFICO, BEING AT PRAYER, BEHELD THE SOUL OF FRIAR UMILE, HIS BROTHER, ASCENDING TO HEAVEN

In the said province of the Marches there lived two brothers in the Order, after the death of St. Francis, the one called Friar Umile, the other Friar Pacifico, and they were men of the greatest holiness and perfection. And one, to wit, Friar Umile, was in the friary of Soffiano, and there died; the other belonged to the community of another friary in a far country. It pleased God, that as Friar Pacifico was at prayer one day, in a solitary place, he was rapt in ecstasy and saw the soul of his brother, Friar Umile, which but then had left his body, ascending straight to heaven without any let or hindrance. It befell that after many years this Friar Pacifico, who was left on earth, went to the community of the said friary of Soffiano, where his brother had died; and in those days the friars, at the petition of the lords of Bruforte, moved from the said friary to another; and among other things, they translated the relics of the holy friars that had died there. And Friar Pacifico, coming to the sepulchre of Friar Umile, took away his bones and washed them with good wine and then wrapped them in a white napkin, and with great reverence and devotion kissed them, weeping. Whereat the other friars marvelled and held it no good example, for he, being a man of great holiness, did seem, out of carnal and worldly affection, to weep for his brother, and show forth more devotion for his relics than for those of the other friars that had been of no less sanctity than Friar Umile, and were as much worthy of reverence as his. And Friar Pacifico, knowing the friars to be thinking badly of him, satisfied them humbly, and said to them, "My brethren, most dear, marvel not if I have done this to the bones of my brother and have done it not to the others, because, blessed be God, carnal affection hath not urged me to this, as ye believe, for when my brother passed from this life, I was at prayer in a desert place far away from him, and I beheld his soul ascend by a straight way into heaven: therefore am I sure that his bones are holy and ought to be in paradise. And if God had vouchsafed to me such certainty of the other friars, that selfsame reverence would I have shown to their bones." Wherefore the friars, seeing his holy and devout intent, were much edified by him, and praised God that worketh such wondrous things for His holy friars.

Chapter XLVII

TOUCHING THAT HOLY FRIAR TO WHOM THE MOTHER OF CHRIST APPEARED WHEN HE LAY SICK AND BROUGHT HIM THREE BOXES OF ELECTUARY

In the aforesaid friary of Soffiano there was of old a friar minor of such great holiness and grace that he seemed wholly divine, and ofttimes was rapt in God. This friar, being on a time wholly lifted up and ravished in God, for he had notably the grace of contemplation, certain birds of divers kinds came to him and settled themselves tamely upon his shoulders, upon his head, and in his arms, and in his hands, and sang wondrously. Now this friar loved solitude and spake but seldom; yet, when aught was asked of him, he answered so graciously and so wisely that he seemed an angel rather than a man; and he excelled in prayer and in contemplation, and the friars held him in great reverence. The friar, having run the course of his virtuous life, according to divine disposition, fell sick unto death, so that he could take naught; and withal he would receive no carnal medicine, but all his trust was in the heavenly physician, Jesus Christ the blessed, and in his blessed Mother, by whom, through divine clemency, he was held worthy to be mercifully visited and healed. Wherefore, lying on a time in his bed, and preparing for death with all his heart, the glorious Virgin Mary, Mother of Christ, appeared to him in wondrous splendour, with a great multitude of angels and holy virgins, and drew nigh to his bed; and he, gazing at her, took great comfort and joy, both of soul and body; and he began to make humble supplication that she would pray her beloved Son to deliver him, through His merits, from the prison of this miserable flesh. And persevering in this supplication, with many tears, the Virgin Mary answered him, calling him by name, and said, "Fear not, my son, for thy prayer is heard, and I am come to comfort thee a while ere thou depart from this life." Beside the Virgin Mary were three holy virgins that bore three boxes in their hands of an electuary of surpassing fragrance and sweetness. Then the glorious Virgin took one of these boxes and opened it, and the whole house was filled with fragrance; then, taking of that electuary with a spoon, she gave it to the sick friar. And no sooner had the sick man savoured it than he felt such comfort and such sweetness that it seemed as though his soul could not remain in his body. Wherefore he began to say, "No more, O most holy and blessed Virgin Mother; O blessed physician and saviour of human kind, no more, for I cannot endure such sweetness." But the compassionate Mother and kind, again and again offering of that electuary to the sick man and making him partake thereof, emptied the whole box. Then the first box being void, the blessed Virgin takes the second and puts the spoon therein to give him thereof, whereat he, complaining, saith, "O most blessed Mother of God, if my soul is wellnigh all melted with the ardour and sweetness of the first electuary, how shall I endure the second? I pray thee, O thou blessed above all the other saints and above all the angels, that thou wilt give me no more." The glorious Virgin Mary makes answer, "Taste, my son, taste yet a little of this second box," and giving him a little thereof, she said to him, "This day, son, thou hast enough to satisfy thee; be of good cheer, for soon will I come for thee and lead thee to the kingdom of my Son, that thou hast ever sought after and desired." This said, and taking leave of him, she departed, and he remained so comforted and consoled, through the sweetness of this confection, that for many days he lived on, sated and strong, without any corporeal food. And some days thereafter, while blithely speaking with the friars, he passed from this miserable life in great jubilation and gladness.

Chapter XLVIII

HOW FRIAR JAMES OF LA MASSA SAW IN A VISION ALL THE FRIARS MINOR IN THE WORLD IN THE SIMILITUDE OF A TREE, AND KNEW THE VIRTUES AND THE MERITS AND THE SINS OF EACH ONE OF THEM

Friar James of La Massa, to whom God opened the door of His mysteries and gave perfect knowledge and understanding of the divine scripture and of future things, was of such sanctity that Friar Giles of Assisi, and Friar Mark of Montino, and Friar Juniper and Friar Lucido, said of him, that they knew no one in the world greater in the sight of God than this Friar James. I had great desire to behold him; for on praying Friar John, the companion of the said Friar Giles, to expound to me certain spiritual things, he answered, "If thou wouldst be well informed in matters of the spiritual life, strive to speak with Friar James of La Massa (for Friar Giles was fain to be instructed by him), and to his words naught can be added nor taken away; for his mind hath penetrated the mysteries of heaven, and his words are words of the Holy Ghost, and there is no man on earth that I have so great a desire to see." This Friar James, when Friar John of Parma took up his office as minister of the Order, was rapt in God while at prayer, and remained thus rapt in ecstasy three days, bereft of all bodily senses, and was so insensible that the friars doubted lest he were truly dead: and in this ecstasy it was revealed to him by God what things were to come to pass in our Order. Wherefore, when Friar Giles said those words, my desire to hear him and to speak with him increased within me. And when it pleased God that I should have opportunity to speak with him, I besought him thus, "If this that I have heard tell of thee be true, prithee keep it not hidden from me. I have heard that when thou remained well-nigh dead for three days, God revealed to thee, among other things, what should come to pass in this our Order; for this was related to me by Friar Matthew, minister of the Marches, to whom thou didst reveal it by obedience." Then Friar James confessed to him, with great humility, that what Friar Matthew said was true. And his words, to wit, the words of Friar Matthew, minister of the Marches, were these, "I know a friar to whom God hath revealed what shall hereafter come to pass in our Order; for Friar James of La Massa hath made known to me and said, that after many things God revealed to him touching the state of the Church Militant, he beheld in a vision a tree, fair and very great, whose roots were of gold, and whose fruits were men, and all they were friars minor; and the chief branches thereof were marked out according to the number of the provinces of the Order, and each branch had as many friars as there were in the province marked on that branch. And so he knew the numbers of all the friars in the Order, and of each province, and likewise their names, and the ages and the conditions and the high offices and the dignities and the graces of all, and their sins. And he beheld Friar John of Parma in the highest place on the mid-most branch of this tree; and on the top of the branches that were round about this branch were the ministers of all the provinces. And thereafter he beheld Christ seated on a pure white throne exceeding great, whereunto Christ called St. Francis and gave him a cup, full of the spirit of life, and sent him forth, saying, "Go and visit thy friars and give them to drink of this cup of the spirit of life; for the spirit of Satan shall rise up against them and shall smite them, and many of them shall fall and not rise again." And Christ gave two angels to St. Francis to bear him company. And then St. Francis came and held forth the cup of life to his friars: and he began to hold it forth first to Friar John of Parma, who, taking it, drank it all devoutly and in great haste; and forthwith he became all bright and shining as the sun. And after him St. Francis held it forth to all the others in due order, and few were they among these that took it and drank it all with meet reverence and devotion. They that took it devoutly and drank it all became straightway bright and shining as the sun; and they that poured it away, and took it not with devotion, became black or dark and misshapen and horrible to behold: and they that drank a part and threw a part away became in part bright and shining, in part dark and shadowy, more or less, according to the measure of their drinking or pouring away the cup. But, resplendent above all the others, was the aforesaid Friar John, that most completely had drunk of the cup of life, whereby he had most deeply fathomed the abyss of the infinite light divine; and therein he had foreseen the adversity and storms that were to rise up against the said tree, and buffet it and make the branches thereof to shake. Wherefore the said Friar John descended from the top of the branch whereon he was, and climbed down all the branches and hid himself beneath them against the knotted bole of the tree, and there remained deep in thought. And a friar that had drunken part of the cup and part had poured away, climbed up that branch and to that place whence Friar John had descended. And while he stood in that place the nails of his fingers became of steel, sharp and cutting as razors; whereat he came down from that place whither he had climbed, and with rage and fury would have flung himself against Friar John to do him hurt. But Friar John, beholding this, cried aloud and commended himself to Christ that was seated on the throne: and Christ, at his cries, called St. Francis to him and gave him a sharp flintstone, and said to him, "Go, and with this stone cut the nails of that friar, wherewith he would fain rend Friar John, so that they may do him no hurt." Then St. Francis came and did as Christ had commanded him. This done, there arose a storm of wind and smote against the tree so mightily that the friars fell to the ground; and first fell they that had poured out all the cup of the spirit of life, and were carried away by devils into places of darkness and torment. But Friar John, together with those others that had drunk all the cup, were translated by angels into a place of eternal life and light and beatific splendour. And the aforesaid Friar James, that beheld the vision, discerned and understood particularly and distinctly all he saw touching the names and conditions and state of each one, and that clearly. And so mightily did that storm prevail against the tree that it fell: and the wind bore it away. And then, no sooner had the storm ceased, than from the root of this tree, which was all of gold, another tree sprung up all of gold, that put forth golden leaves and flowers and fruit. Touching which tree and the growth and the deep roots thereof, the beauty and fragrance and virtue, 'twere fitter to keep silence than to tell thereof at this season.

Chapter XLIX

HOW CHRIST APPEARED TO FRIAR JOHN OF LA VERNA

Among the other wise and holy friars and sons of St. Francis who, according as Solomon saith, are the glory of their father, there lived in our time in the province of the Marches the venerable and holy Friar John of Fermo; and he, for that he sojourned a long time in the holy place of La Verna and there passed from this life, was likewise called Friar John of La Verna; and he was a man of great and singular holiness of life. This Friar John, while yet a boy in the world, desired with all his heart to follow the ways of penance, that ever preserveth the purity of the body and of the soul. Wherefore, when he was quite a little child, he began to wear a breastplate of mail[8] and iron rings on his naked flesh, and to practise great abstinence; and above all, when he abode with the canons of St. Peter's at Fermo, who fared sumptuously, he eschewed all carnal delights, and mortified his body with great and severe fastings; but his companions, being much set against these things, took from him his breastplate and thwarted his abstinence in divers ways; wherefore he purposed, being inspired of God, to forsake the world and those that loved worldly things and cast himself wholly into the arms of the Crucified with the habit of the crucified St. Francis; and this he did. And being thus received into the Order while yet a boy, and committed to the care of the master of the novices, he became so spiritual and devout, that hearing the master once discoursing of God, his heart was melted as wax before a fire; and with such exceeding sweetness of grace was he kindled by divine love, that unable to remain still and endure such great sweetness, he arose, and as one inebriated with spiritual things, ran hither and thither, now in the garden, now in the wood, now in the church, according as the fire and spur of the spirit drave him. Then in process of time this angelic man, by divine grace, so continually increased from virtue to virtue, and in celestial gifts and divine exaltation and rapture, that at one time his soul was lifted up to the splendours of the cherubim, at another to the flaming seraphim, yet another to the joys of the blessed; yea, even to the loving and ineffable embraces of Christ. And notably, on a time, his heart was so mightily kindled by the flames of love divine, that this flame endured full three years, in which time he received wondrous consolations and divine visitations, and ofttimes was he rapt in God; and for a brief space, in the said time, he seemed all aflame and burning with the love of Christ; and this was on the holy mount of La Verna. But forasmuch as God hath singular care of His children, and giveth them according to divers seasons, now consolation, now tribulation, now prosperity, now adversity, even as He seeth their need, either to strengthen them in humility, or to kindle within them greater desire for celestial things; now it pleased divine goodness to withdraw, after three years, from the said Friar John this ray and this flame of divine love, and to deprive him of all spiritual consolation. Whereat Friar John remained bereft of the light and the love of God, and all disconsolate and afflicted and sorrowing. Wherefore, in this anguish of heart, he wandered about the wood, running to and fro, calling with a loud voice and with tears and sighs on the beloved spouse of his soul, who had withdrawn and departed from him, and without whose presence his soul found neither peace nor rest. But in no place nor in any wise could he find the sweet Jesus again, nor taste again, as he was wont to do, of those sweetest spiritual saviours of the love of Christ. And the like tribulation he

---

[8] *See* note, p. 30.

endured many days, wherein he persevered continually in tears and sighs, and in supplication to God, that of His pity He would restore to him the beloved spouse of his soul. At the last, when it had pleased God to prove his patience enough and fan the flame of his desire, one day, as Friar John was wandering about the said wood, thus afflicted and tormented, he sat him down a-wearied and leaned against a beech tree, and with his face all bathed in tears gazed towards heaven; and behold, Jesus Christ appeared suddenly nigh to him, in the path whereby this Friar John had come, but spake no word. And Friar John, beholding Him and knowing full well that it was the Christ, straightway flung himself at His feet, and with piteous tears entreated Him most humbly and said, "Help me, my Lord, for without Thee, O my sweetest Saviour, I wander in darkness and in tears; without Thee, most gentle Lamb, I dwell in anguish and in torments and in fear; without Thee, Son of God, most high, I remain in shame and confusion; without Thee I am stripped of all good, and blind, for Thou art Christ Jesus, true light of souls; without Thee I am lost and damned, for Thou art the Life of souls and Life of life; without Thee I am barren and withered, for Thou art the fountain of every good gift and of every grace; without Thee I am wholly disconsolate, for Thou art Jesus our Redeemer, our love and our desire, the Bread of consolation and the Wine that rejoiceth the hearts of the angels and of all the saints. Let Thy light shine upon me, most gracious Master, and most compassionate Shepherd, for I am Thy little sheep, unworthy tho' I be." But because the desires of holy men, which God delayeth to grant, kindle them to yet greater love and merit, the blessed Christ departed without hearing him, without uttering one word, and went away by the said path. Then Friar John rose up and ran after Him, and again fell at His feet, and with holy importunity held Him back and entreated Him, with devoutest tears, saying, "O Jesus Christ, most sweet, have mercy on me in my tribulation; hear me by the multitude of Thy mercies, and by the truth of Thy salvation restore to me the joy of Thy countenance and of Thy pitying eye, for all the earth is full of Thy mercy." And again Christ departed and spake him no word, nor gave aught of consolation, and did after the way of a mother with her child, when she maketh him to yearn for the breast, and causeth him to follow after her weeping, that he may take it the more willingly. Whereupon Friar John, yet again, with greater fervour and desire, followed Christ, and no sooner had he come up to Him than the blessed Christ turned round to him, and looked upon him with joyful and gracious countenance; then, opening His most holy and most merciful arms, He embraced him very sweetly, and as He thus opened His arms, Friar John beheld rays of shining light coming from the Saviour's most holy breast, that illumined all the wood, and himself likewise, in soul and body. Then Friar John kneeled down at the feet of Christ; and the blessed Jesus, even as He did to the Magdalen, graciously held forth His foot that he might kiss it; and Friar John, taking it with highest reverence, bathed it with so many tears that he verily seemed to be a second Magdalen, and devoutly said, "I pray Thee, my Lord, that Thou regard not my sins, but by Thy most holy Passion, and by the shedding of Thy most holy and precious blood, Thou mayest make my soul to live again in the grace of Thy love, forasmuch as this is Thy commandment: that we love Thee with all our hearts and all our affections, which commandment none can keep without Thy aid. Help me, then, most beloved Son of God, that I may love Thee with all my heart and with all my might." And Friar John, standing as he thus spake at the feet of Christ, was heard of Him, and he regained the former state of grace, to wit, the flame of divine love, and he felt himself all consoled and renewed; and when he knew that the gift of divine grace was restored to him, he began to give thanks to Christ the blessed and to kiss His feet devoutly. And then, rising up to gaze on the face of Christ, Jesus Christ stretched forth and offered him His most holy hands to kiss. And when Friar John had kissed them, he drew nigh and leaned on Christ's bosom and embraced Him and kissed Him, and Christ likewise embraced and kissed him. And in these embraces and kisses Friar John perceived such divine fragrance, that if all the sweet-smelling graces and all the most fragrant things in the world had been gathered together, they would have seemed but a stink compared with that fragrance; and thereby was Friar John ravished and consoled and illumined; and that fragrance endured in his soul many months. And thenceforward there issued from his mouth, that had drunk at the fountain of divine wisdom in the sacred breast of the Saviour, words so wondrous and so heavenly, that they changed all hearts and brought forth great fruit in the souls of those that heard him. And in the pathway of the wood, whereon the blessed feet of Christ had trod, and for a good space round about, Friar John perceived that same fragrance and beheld that splendour for a long time thereafter, whensoever he went thither. And Friar John, coming to himself after that rapture and after the bodily presence of Christ had vanished, remained so illumined in his soul and in the abyss of the divine nature, that albeit he was not a learned man, by reason of human study, nevertheless, he solved wondrously and made plain the most subtle and lofty questions touching the divine Trinity and the profound mysteries of the Holy Scriptures. And many times thereafter, when speaking before the pope and the cardinals and the king, and barons and masters and doctors, he set them all in great amaze at the lofty words and most profound judgments he uttered.

Chapter L

HOW FRIAR JOHN OF LA VERNA, WHILE SAYING MASS ON ALL SOULS' DAY, BEHELD MANY SOULS SET FREE FROM PURGATORY

On a time when Friar John was saying mass, the day after All Saints, for the souls of all the dead, according as the church hath ordained, he offered up with such great affection and charity and with such pitying compassion that most high sacrament (which, by reason of its efficacy, the souls of the dead desire above all other benefits we can bestow upon them), that he seemed all melted with the sweetness of pity and of brotherly love. Wherefore, as he devoutly elevated the body of Christ in that mass and offered it up to God the Father, and prayed that, for love of His beloved Son, Jesus Christ, who was nailed on the cross to redeem souls, He would be pleased to deliver from the pains of purgatory the souls of the dead by Him created and redeemed, he straightway beheld a multitude of souls, well-nigh infinite, come forth from purgatory, after the manner of countless sparks issuing from a fiery furnace; and he beheld them ascend to heaven through the merits of Christ's Passion, that each day is offered up for the living and the dead in that most sacred Host which is worthy to be worshipped world without end.

Chapter LI

OF THE HOLY FRIAR JAMES OF FALTERONE, AND HOW AFTER HIS DEATH HE APPEARED TO FRIAR JOHN OF LA VERNA

At the time when Friar James of Falterone, a man of great holiness, lay grievously sick at the friary of Moliano in the custody of Fermo, Friar John of La Verna, who then abode in the friary of La Massa, heard of his sickness; and, for that he loved him as a dear father, he betook himself to pray for him, devoutly beseeching God with all his heart that if it were good for his soul He would restore him to health of body. And while thus devoutly praying he was rapt in ecstasy, and beheld in the air, above his cell in the wood, a great host of angels and saints, of such dazzling splendour that the whole country round about was illumined thereby; and in the midst of these angels he beheld this sick Friar James, for whom he was praying, all resplendent in pure white robes. He saw likewise among them the blessed father, St. Francis, adorned with the sacred stigmas of Christ and with much glory. And he beheld also and knew the saintly Friar Lucido, and the aged Friar Matthew of Monte Rubbiano, and many other friars that in this life he had never seen nor known. And as Friar John was thus gazing, with great delight, on that blessed company of saints, it was revealed to him that of a surety the soul of that sick friar was saved, and that he was to die of that sickness; but that he was not to ascend straightway after his death to paradise, for that it behoved him to purge himself a while in purgatory. At this revelation Friar John felt such exceeding joy because of the salvation of his soul, that he grieved not for the death of the body, but with great sweetness of spirit called him within himself, saying, "Friar James, sweet father mine; Friar James, sweet brother; Friar James, faithfullest servant and friend of God; Friar James, companion of the angels and consort of the blessed!" and in this certitude and joy he came to himself again. And anon he departed from that place and went to visit the said Friar James at Moliano, and finding the sickness so heavily upon him that scarce could he speak, he announced to him the death of the body and the salvation and glory of his soul, according to the certitude he had had by divine revelation. Whereat Friar James rejoiced gladly in spirit and in countenance, and received him with great gladness, and with jocund mien gave thanks to him for the good tidings he had brought, commending himself devoutly to him. Then Friar John besought him dearly that he would return to him after his death and speak to him of his state: and Friar James promised this, if God so pleased. These words said, the hour of his passing away drew nigh, and Friar James began to recite devoutly that verse from the Psalms: *In pace in idipsum dormiam et requiescam*, which is to say, "I will both lay me down in peace and sleep." This verse said, he passed from this life with glad and joyful countenance. And after he was buried, Friar John returned to the friary of La Massa and waited for the promise of Friar James, that he would return to him on the day he had said. But while he was at prayer on that day, Christ appeared to him with a great company of angels and saints, and among them Friar James was not: whereupon Friar John, marvelling greatly, commended him devoutly to Christ. Then on the day following, as Friar John was praying in the wood, Friar James appeared to him accompanied by the angels, all glorious and all glad; and Friar John said to him, "O dearest father, wherefore hast thou not returned to me the day that thou didst promise?" Friar James answered, "Because I had need of some purgation; but in that same hour when Christ appeared to thee, and thou didst commend me to Him, Christ heard thee and delivered me from all pain. And then I appeared to the holy lay Friar James of La Massa, that was serving mass, and saw the consecrated Host, when the priest elevated it, converted and changed into the form of a living child most fair; and I said to him, 'This day do I go with that child to the realm of life eternal, whither none can go without him.'" These words said, Friar James vanished and went to heaven with all that blessed company of angels; and Friar John remained much comforted. And the said Friar James of Falterone died on the vigil of St. James the Apostle, in the month of July, in the aforesaid friary of Moliano, wherein, through his merits, divine goodness wrought many miracles after his death.

Chapter LII

OF THE VISION OF FRIAR JOHN OF LA VERNA WHEREIN HE KNEW ALL THE ORDER OF THE HOLY TRINITY

The aforesaid Friar John of La Verna, for that he had wholly smothered all worldly and temporal joys and consolations, and in God had placed all his joys and all his hopes, the divine goodness gave him wondrous consolations and revelations, and, above all, in the solemn festivals of Christ; wherefore on a time when the feast of the Nativity was drawing nigh, whereon he had the expectancy of certain consolation from God in the sweet humanity of Christ, the Holy Spirit set in his mind such exceeding great love and fervour for the charity of Christ whereby He had abased Himself to take our humanity upon Him, that it verily seemed to him as were his soul ravished from his body, and that it burned like a furnace. And being unable to endure this burning, and being in sore distress of soul, he cried out with a loud voice; for by the power of the Holy Spirit and by the exceeding fervour of his love he could not withhold his cry. And at the hour when that consuming fervour came upon him, there came withal so strong and sure a hope of his salvation, that in no wise could he believe that, had he then died, he would need to pass through the pains of purgatory; and this love endured within him full six months, albeit that excessive fervour possessed him not continuously, but came upon him only at certain hours of the day, and then in these times he received wondrous visitations and consolations from God. And ofttimes was he rapt in ecstasy, even as that friar saw who first wrote down these things; among which, one night, he was so lifted up and rapt in God that he beheld in Him, the Creator, all created things in heaven and on earth, and all their perfections and degrees and their several orders. And then he perceived clearly how every created thing was related to its Creator, and how God is above, is within, is without, is beside all created things. Thereafter he perceived one God in three Persons, and three Persons in one God, and the infinite love that made the Son of God become flesh in obedience to the Father. And at the last he perceived, in that vision, how that no other way was there whereby the soul might ascend to God and have eternal life save through the blessed Christ, that is the Way, the Truth, and the Life of the soul.

Chapter LIII

HOW FRIAR JOHN OF LA VERNA, WHILE SAYING MASS, FELL DOWN AS ONE DEAD

On a time, as the friars that were present were wont to tell, a wondrous case befell the said Friar John in the aforesaid friary of Moliano; for, on the first night after the octave of St. Lawrence, and within the octave of the Assumption of Our Lady, having said matins in church with the other friars, and the unction of divine grace falling upon him, he went forth into the garden to mediate on the Passion of Christ and to prepare himself, with all devotion, to celebrate the mass that it was his turn to sing that morning. And while he was meditating on the words of the consecration of the body of Christ, to wit, while he was considering the infinite love of Christ, and that He had been willing to redeem us, not only with His precious blood, but likewise to leave us His most worthy body and blood for food of souls, the love of sweet Jesus began so to wax within him, and with such great fervour and tenderness, that his soul could no longer endure such sweetness; and he cried out with a loud voice, and as one inebriate in spirit, ceased not to repeat to himself, *Hoc est corpus meum:* for as he spake these words he seemed to behold the blessed Christ, with the Virgin Mother and a multitude of angels; and he was illumined by the Holy Spirit in all the deep and lofty mysteries of that most high sacrament. And when the dawn was come, he went into the church, with that same fervour of spirit, and with that same absorption, and believing he was neither heard nor seen of men, went on repeating those words; but there was a certain friar at prayer in the choir that saw and heard all. And, unable to contain himself in that fervour of spirit by reason of the abundance of grace divine, he cried out with a loud voice, and so continued until the hour of mass was come. Wherefore he went to vest himself for the altar. And when he began the mass, the farther he proceeded the more the love of Christ and that fervour of devotion increased within him, whereby an ineffable sense of God's presence was given to him, which he could neither comprehend nor thereafter express with his lips. Wherefore, fearing lest that fervour and sense of God's presence should so wax within him that he must needs leave the altar, he fell into great perplexity, and knew not what he should do—whether to go on with the mass, or stay and wait. But, forasmuch as at other times a like case had befallen him, and the Lord had so far tempered that fervour that he had needed not to leave the altar, he trusted He might do the like this time; so he set himself with fear and trembling to go forward with the mass: and when he came as far as the preface of Our Lady, the divine illumination of the gracious sweetness of the love of God began so to increase within him, that coming to the *Qui pridie*, scarce could he endure such ravishing sweetness. At last, when he came to the act of consecration, and had said the first half of the words over the Host, to wit, *Hoc est*, in no wise could he go farther, but only repeated those selfsame words, to wit, *Hoc est enim*. And the cause wherefore he could go no farther was, that he felt and beheld the presence of Christ, with a multitude of angels, whose majesty he could not endure. And he saw that Christ entered not into the Host, or, in sooth, that the Host would not become changed into the body of Christ, except he uttered the other half of the words, to wit, *corpus meum*. Whereupon, while he stood thus perplexed and could proceed no farther, the warden and the other friars, and many lay folk likewise that were in the church hearing mass, drew nigh to the altar, and were filled with awe when they beheld and considered the acts of Friar John: and many of them wept through devotion. At the length, after a great space, to wit, when it pleased God, Friar John uttered, with a loud voice, *Enim corpus meum*; and straightway the form of the bread vanished, and Jesus Christ the blessed appeared, incarnate and glorified, in the Host, and showed forth to him the humility and charity that made Him become incarnate of the Virgin Mary, and that every day maketh Him to come into the hands of the priest, when he consecrateth the Host: for which thing he was the more exalted in sweetness and contemplation. And no sooner had he elevated the consecrated Host and cup than he was ravished out of himself, and his soul, being lifted up above all bodily senses, his body fell backwards; and had he not been held up by the warden that stood behind him, he had fallen supine on the ground. Whereat the friars hastened towards him, and the lay folk that were in the church, both men and women; and he was carried into the sacristy as one dead; for his body had grown cold, and the fingers of his hands were so tightly clenched that scarce could they be opened or moved. And in this manner he lay between life and death, or ravished, until the hour of tierce; for it was summer time. And since I, that was present at all these things, desired much to know what God had wrought in him, I went straightway to him when his senses had returned to him, and besought him, for love of God, that he would tell me all things. Wherefore, because he had great trust in me, he related all to me in order; and, among other things, he told me that while meditating on the body and blood of Jesus Christ before him, his heart was melted like heated wax, and his flesh seemed to be without bones, in such wise that scarce could he lift up arm or hand to make the sign of the cross over the Host, or over the cup. He likewise told me that before he was made a priest, God had revealed to him that he was to swoon away in the mass; but seeing that he had since said many masses, and this thing had not befallen him, he believed the revelation was not of God. And nevertheless, about fifty days before the Assumption of Our Lady, whereon the aforesaid case befell him, God had again revealed to him that this thing was to come to pass about the feast of the Assumption; but that thereafter he no longer remembered the said vision, or revelation, made to him by our Lord.

Here endeth the first part of the book of the venerable St. Francis, and of many of the holy friars his companions. Here followeth the second part concerning the sacred stigmas.

The Considerations of the Holy Stigmata

TOUCHING THE SACRED AND HOLY STIGMAS OF ST. FRANCIS AND SOME CONSIDERATIONS THEREON

In this part we will treat, with devout consideration, of the glorious, sacred, and hallowed stigmas of our blessed father, St. Francis, that he received from Christ on the holy mount of La Verna. And forasmuch as the said stigmas were five, according to the five wounds of our Lord Jesus Christ, this treatise shall be divided into five considerations.

The first consideration shall be touching the manner of the coming of St. Francis to the holy mount of La Verna.

The second consideration shall be touching the life he lived, and the discourse he held with his companions on the said holy mountain.

The third consideration shall be touching the seraphic vision and the impression of the most holy stigmas.

The fourth consideration shall be, how that St. Francis came down from the mount of La Verna after he had received the sacred stigmas and returned to St. Mary of the Angels.

The fifth consideration shall be touching certain divers visions and revelations of the said sacred and hallowed stigmas to holy friars and other devout persons after the death of St. Francis.

I. *Touching the first consideration of the sacred, hallowed stigmas.*

Be it known, touching the first consideration, that when St. Francis was forty-three years of age, in the year one thousand two hundred and twenty-four, he was inspired by God to set forth from the vale of Spoleto and journey into Romagna, with Friar Leo his companion; and as they went they passed by the foot of the town of Montefeltro, wherein a great banquet and a great procession were made by reason of the knighting of one of those counts of Montefeltro. And St. Francis, hearing of this solemn festival and that many noblemen of divers countries were assembled together there, said to Friar Leo, "Let us go up thither to this festival, for with God's help we shall gather some good spiritual fruit." Now among the other nobles that were come to that festival from the country round about was a certain rich and mighty nobleman of Tuscany, called Roland of Chiusi di Casentino, who, because of the wondrous things he had heard of the holiness and of the miracles of St. Francis, held him in great devotion, and had a very great desire to behold him and to hear him preach. And St. Francis came up to that town and entered within, and went to the market-place, where all the host of those nobles was gathered together, and in fervour of spirit climbed on to a low wall and began to preach, taking for the text of his sermon these words in the vulgar tongue—

"A joy to me is every pain,
For I await a greater gain."

And upon this text he preached so devoutly and so profoundly by inspiration of the Holy Spirit, proving it by divers pains and martyrdoms of the holy apostles and the holy martyrs, and by the hard penances of the holy confessors, and the many tribulations and temptations of the holy virgins and other saints, that all the people stood with eyes and minds lifted up towards him, and hearkened as if an angel of God were speaking. And among them was the said Roland, who, touched to the heart by God through the wondrous preaching of St. Francis, was minded to confer and take counsel with him, after the sermon, touching the state of his soul. Wherefore, the sermon ended, he drew St. Francis aside and said to him, "O father, fain would I take counsel with thee touching the salvation of my soul." St. Francis answered, "It pleaseth me well; but go this morning, honour thy friends that have bidden thee to this feast, and dine with them, and after thou hast dined, we will speak together as long as it shall please thee." Roland therefore went away to dine, and after he had dined, returned to St. Francis and thus conferred and discoursed with him fully, touching the state of his soul. And at last this Roland said to St. Francis, "I have a mountain in Tuscany most proper for devout contemplation that is called the mount of La Verna, and is very solitary and meet for those that desire to do penance in a place far away from the world, or to lead a solitary life; and if it so please thee, fain would I give it to thee and to thy companions for the salvation of my soul." St. Francis, hearing this bounteous offer of a thing he so much desired, rejoiced with exceeding great joy, and praising and giving thanks, first to God and then to Roland, spake to him thus, "Roland, when you are returned to your house I will send some of my companions to you, and you will show this mountain to them; and if it seem to them a proper place for prayer and penance, from this time forth I accept your charitable offer." This said, St. Francis departed, and when he had made an end of his journey he returned to St. Mary of the Angels; and Roland likewise, when he had celebrated the end of that festival, returned to his castle that was called Chiusi, and was distant a mile from La Verna. And St. Francis, being returned to St. Mary of the Angels, sent forth two of his companions to the said Roland, who, when they were come to him, received them with the greatest joy and charity. And being fain to show them the mount of La Verna, he sent with them full fifty men-at-arms to be their defence against the wild beasts; and these friars, thus escorted, ascended to the top of the mountain and sought diligently about, and at the last they came to a part of the mountain that was meet for a holy place and most proper for contemplation, in which place was an open plain: this spot they chose for the habitation of them and of St. Francis, and there, with the help of the men-at-arms that were in their escort, they made some little cells of the branches of trees. And thus in the name of God they accepted and took possession of the mount of La Verna, and of the friary on that mountain, and departed and returned to St. Francis. And when they were come to St. Francis they related to him how and in what manner they had taken a place on the mount of La Verna most meet for prayer and contemplation. Hearing these tidings, St. Francis rejoiced greatly, and praising and giving thanks to God, spake to these friars with a glad countenance, and said, "My sons, we are drawing nigh to our lent of St. Michael the Archangel, and I steadfastly believe that it is God's will we should keep this fast on the mount of La Verna, that by divine providences hath been prepared for us, in order that we may merit from Christ the joy of consecrating that blessed mount to the honour and glory of God and of His Mother, the glorious Virgin Mary, and the holy angels." This said, St. Francis took with him Friar Masseo of Marignano d'Assisi, that was a man of great wisdom and great eloquence; and Friar Angelo Tancredi of Rieti, that was a very noble gentleman, and in the world had been a knight; and Friar Leo, that was a man of great simplicity and purity, and therefore much beloved of St. Francis. And St. Francis with these three friars set himself to pray, and commended himself and the aforesaid companions to the prayers of the friars that were left behind; and then set forth, in the name of Jesus Christ crucified, with those three to go to the mount of La Verna. And as St. Francis went forth, he called one of those three companions, and he was Friar Masseo, and spake to him thus, "Thou, Friar Masseo, shalt be our warden and our superior on this journey, I say, while we go and remain together; and thus we will observe our Rule, for whether we say the office, or discourse of God, or keep silence, we will take no thought for the morrow, neither what we shall eat, nor what we shall drink, nor where we shall sleep; but when the hour of rest cometh we will beg a little bread, and then will stay our steps and rest ourselves in the place that God shall prepare for us." Then did these three companions bow their heads, and making the sign of the cross, journeyed on; and the first evening they came to a friary and there lodged. The second evening, by reason of the bad weather and of being so weary they were not able to come to a friary, nor to any town, nor to any hamlet, and night falling after the bad weather, they took refuge in a deserted and ruined church and there lay down to rest. And while his companions were sleeping, St. Francis betook himself to prayer, and lo, at the first watch of the night there came a great host of fiercest devils with a great noise and tumult and began to attack and annoy him mightily: for one plucked him here, another there; one pulled him down, another up; one threatened him with one thing, and one rebuked for another; and thus in divers ways they strove to disturb his prayers; but they could not, for God was with him. And when St. Francis had endured these assaults of the devils a long space, he began to cry with a loud voice, "O ye damned spirits, naught can ye avail except in so far as the hand of God suffereth you: therefore in the name of the omnipotent God I say unto you, do ye unto my body whatsoever is permitted you by God, for I suffer all willingly, since no greater enemy have I than my body; therefore, if ye avenge me of mine enemy, ye do me too great a service." Then the devils seized him and with great violence and fury began to drag him about the church and to wreak on him more grievous hurt and annoy than before. Whereat St. Francis began to cry aloud and say, "My Lord Jesus Christ, I thank Thee for the great love and charity Thou hast shown toward me; for 'tis a token of great love when the Lord well punisheth His servant for all his faults in this world, in order that he be not punished in the next. And I am prepared to endure joyfully every pain and every adversity that Thou, my God, art willing to send for my sins." Then the devils, confounded and vanquished by his constancy and patience, departed, and St. Francis came forth from the church in fervour of spirit and entered into a wood that was nigh and betook him to prayer, and with prayers and with tears, and with smitings of the breast, sought Jesus Christ, the beloved spouse of his soul.

And at last, finding Him in the secret places of his soul, now he spake with Him reverently as his Lord; now he gave answer to Him as his Judge; again he besought Him as a father, and yet again he reasoned with Him as a friend. On that night, and in that wood, his companions, after they awoke, stood hearkening and considering what he was doing, and they beheld and heard him with tears and cries devoutly entreat God's mercy for sinners. Then was he heard and seen to bewail, with a loud voice, the Passion of Christ, even as if he beheld it with corporeal eyes. And in that selfsame night they saw him praying with his arms held in the form of a cross, and lifted up from the ground and suspended for a great space, and surrounded by a bright and shining cloud. And thus he passed all that night in these holy exercises, without sleep; and in the morning his companions, knowing that St. Francis, by reason of the fatigues of that night passed without sleep, was very feeble in body, and would have ill borne to go afoot, went to a poor peasant of that country-side, and, for love of God, craved the loan of his ass for St. Francis, their father, that could not go afoot. This man, hearing the name of Friar Francis, asked of them, "Are ye of those friars of that friar of Assisi whereof so much good is told?" The friars answered, "Yea," and that in fact it was for him that they craved the animal. Then this honest fellow saddled the ass with great devotion and solicitude, and led him to St. Francis, and with great reverence bade him mount thereon; and so they went their way, the peasant with them, behind his ass. And after they had journeyed on a while, the peasant said to St. Francis, "Tell me, art thou that Friar Francis of Assisi?" And St. Francis answered, "Yea." "Now strive, then," said the peasant, "to be as good as thou art held to be by all folk, for many have great faith in thee; therefore I admonish thee that thou betray not the hopes men cherish of thee." St. Francis, hearing these words, disdained not to be admonished by a peasant, nor said within himself, "What beast is this that doth admonish me?" as many proud fellows that wear the cowl would say nowadays, but straightway flung himself off the ass and alighted on the ground and knelt down before him, and kissed his feet, and humbly thanked him for that he had deigned to admonish him thus charitably. Then the peasant, together with the companions of St. Francis, raised him up from the ground, with great devotion, and set him again on the ass and journeyed on. And when they had climbed about half-way up the mountain, a great thirst came upon this peasant, for the heat was very great, and toilsome the ascent; whereat he began to cry behind St. Francis, saying, "Ah me! I die of thirst, for if I have not water to drink I shall forthwith choke." Wherefore St. Francis got down from the ass and fell to prayer, and so long he knelt, with hands lifted up to heaven, until he knew by revelation that his prayer was heard of God. Then said St. Francis to the peasant, "Haste; hie thee quickly to that rock, there shalt thou find running water that Jesus Christ in this hour hath, in His mercy, made to issue from that rock." Now runs he to the place that St. Francis had shown to him, and there finds a fair spring which St. Francis, by virtue of his prayers, had made to gush forth from that hard rock; and he drank thereof abundantly, and was comforted. And well it appeareth that that spring was made to flow by God miraculously, at the prayers of St. Francis, for neither before nor after was ever a spring of water seen in that place, nor running water near that place for a great distance. This done, St. Francis, with his companions, and with the peasant, gave thanks to God for the miracle He had shown them, and then journeyed on. And when they were come nigh to the foot of the very rock of La Verna, it pleased St. Francis to rest a while under the oak tree that stood by the way, and there standeth to this day; and resting beneath it, St. Francis began to consider the lay of the place and of the country round about. And lo, while he was thus pondering there came a great multitude of birds from divers parts that, with singing and fluttering of their wings, showed forth great joy and gladness, and surrounded St. Francis, in such wise that some settled on his head, some on his shoulders, and some on his arms, some on his bosom, and some around his feet. His companions and the peasant, beholding this, marvelled greatly, and St. Francis rejoiced in spirit, and spake thus, "I do believe, dearest brothers, that it is pleasing to our Lord Jesus Christ that we abide on this solitary mountain, since our sisters and brothers, the birds, show forth such great joy at our coming." These words said, they rose up and journeyed on; and at last they came to the place that his companions had taken at first. And this is all that concerns the first consideration, to wit, how St. Francis came to the holy mount of La Verna.

II. *Touching the second consideration of the sacred, hallowed stigmas.*

The second consideration is touching the discourse of St. Francis with his companions on the said mount of La Verna. And as for this, be it known that when Roland heard that St. Francis, with his three companions, had gone up to dwell on the mount of La Verna, he rejoiced exceedingly, and the day following set forth with many of his friends, and came to visit St. Francis; and they brought with them bread and wine, and other necessaries of life for him and his companions. And when they came to the top of the mountain they found them at prayer, and drawing nigh, gave them salutation. Then St. Francis rose up and received Roland and his company with great joy and love; and this done, they began to discourse together. And after they had discoursed a while, and St. Francis had thanked Roland for the holy mountain he had given them, and for his coming, he besought him to have a poor little cell built at the foot of a very fair beech tree that stood about a stone's-throw from the friary; for that seemed to him a place most solemn and meet for prayer. And anon Roland had it made; and this done St. Francis, seeing that the evening was drawing nigh, and it was time to depart, preached to them a little ere they took leave; and after he had preached and had given them his blessing, it behoved Roland to depart; wherefore he called St. Francis and his companions aside, and said to them, "My dearest friars, I am not minded that ye should endure any bodily want on this wild mountain top, and so be less able to give heed to spiritual things. Therefore I desire, and this I say once for all, that ye send confidently to my house for all things needful to you, and if ye did not so I should take it very ill of you." This said, he set forth with his company and returned to his castle. Then St. Francis made his companions sit down, and instructed them touching the manner of the life that they, and whoso would desire to live like religious, in hermitages, should lead. And, among other things, he laid upon them the single-minded observance of holy poverty, saying, "Heed not overmuch Roland's charitable offer, lest ye in any way offend our lady, madonna holy Poverty. Be ye sure that the more we despise poverty, the more the world will despise us, and the greater need we shall suffer; but if we embrace holy poverty, immediately the world will follow after us and feed us abundantly. God hath called us to this holy Rule of life for the salvation of the world, and hath made this covenant between us and the world, that we give good example to the world and the world provide for our needs. Let us persevere, then, in holy poverty, because that is the way of perfection, and the earnest and pledge of everlasting riches." And after many fair and devout words, and admonitions of this sort, he made an end, saying, "This is the manner of life that I lay on myself and on you; and for that I see me drawing nigh unto death, I purpose to withdraw to a solitary place and make my peace with God, and weep for my sins before Him; and let Friar Leo, when it shall seem good to him, bring me a little bread and water, and on no account to suffer any lay folk to come to me: do ye answer them for me." These words said, he gave them his blessing, and went to the cell under the beech tree, and his companions remained in their habitation with the steadfast purpose to obey the commands of St. Francis. A few days thereafter, as St. Francis was standing beside the said cell, considering the form of the mountain, and marvelling at the exceeding great clefts and caverns in the mighty rocks, he betook himself to prayer; and then it was revealed to him by God that these clefts, so marvellous, had been miraculously made at the hour of the Passion of Christ, when, according to the gospel, the rocks were rent asunder. And this, God willed, should manifestly appear on the mount of La Verna, because there the Passion of our Lord Jesus Christ was to be renewed, through love and pity, in the soul of St. Francis, and in his body by the imprinting of the sacred, hallowed stigmas. No sooner had St. Francis received that revelation than he forthwith locked himself in his cell, and retired wholly into himself, and made him ready for the mystery of this revelation, and from that hour St. Francis, through his unceasing prayers, began to taste more often of the sweetness of divine contemplation; wherefore many times was he so rapt in God that he was seen of his companions to be lifted up bodily from the ground and ravished out of himself. And in these contemplative ecstasies, not only were things present and future revealed to him, but likewise the secret thoughts and longings of the friars, even as Friar Leo, his companion, made proof of that day. Now to this Friar Leo, while enduring a mighty temptation of the devil, and not a carnal one, but a spiritual one, there came a great desire to have some pious words written by the hand of St. Francis; for he thought within himself, that if he had them, that temptation would leave him, either wholly or in part; yet, through shame or reverence, he had not the heart to tell of this desire to St. Francis. But the desire that Friar Leo spake not of, was revealed by the Holy Spirit to St. Francis: whereat he called Friar Leo to him, and made him bring pen and ink and paper, and with his own very hand did write a praise of Christ, according to the friar's desire. And at the end thereof he made the letter Tau,[9] and he gave the writing to him, saying, "Dearest friar, take this paper and keep it diligently until thy death. God bless thee and keep thee from all temptation. Be not afraid that thou art tempted, for the more thou art assailed by temptations the greater friend and servant of God do I hold thee, and the greater love do I bear thee. Verily I say unto thee, let no man deem himself the perfect friend of God until he have passed through many temptations and tribulations." When Friar Leo received this writing, with exceeding devotion and faith, straightway every temptation departed, and returning to the friars, he related to them, with great joy, what grace God had bestowed upon him when he received that writing from St. Francis; and putting it away and keeping it diligently, the friars wrought many miracles by means thereof.[10] And from that hour the said Friar Leo began to watch closely and meditate with great purity and good intent on the life of St. Francis; and because of his purity it was vouchsafed to him many times and oft, to behold St. Francis rapt in God and lifted up from the earth: sometimes to the height of three cubits, sometimes four, sometimes as high as the top of the beech tree; and sometimes he saw him lifted up in the air so high, and surrounded by such dazzling splendour, that scarce could the eye behold him. Now what was this simple friar wont to do when St. Francis was lifted up but a little space from the earth so that he could reach him? He went softly and embraced his feet and kissed them, and said, in tears, "My God, have mercy on me, a sinner, and through the merits of this holy man give me to find grace with Thee." And one time, among others, while thus standing beneath the feet of St. Francis, when he was so far lifted up from the earth that he could not touch him, he saw a scroll descend from heaven, writ with letters of gold, and rest on the head of St. Francis; and on this scroll these words were writ, *Behold the Grace of God.* And after he had read it he saw it return to heaven. Through this gift of God's grace within him, St. Francis was not only rapt in God by ecstatic contemplation, but many times was likewise comforted by visits of angels. Wherefore, as St. Francis one day was meditating on his death, and on the state of his Order after his death, and saying, "Lord God, what will become of Thy poor little household, that Thou of Thy goodness hast committed to me, a sinner? Who shall comfort them? Who shall correct them? Who shall pray to Thee for them?" And while he was uttering such words, the angel sent of God appeared to him, and comforted him with these

---

[9] See Ezekiel ix. 4 (in the Vulgate). According to St. Jerome, Tau (T), which is the last letter of the Hebrew alphabet, was used in the Samaritan language to represent the cross, of which it had the form.

[10] This precious relic of St. Francis is still preserved in the sacristy of the great church of St. Francesco at Assisi.

words, "I say unto thee, in God's name, that the profession of thy Order shall not fail until the Judgment Day; and none shall be so great a sinner, but that if he love thy Order in his heart, the same shall find mercy in God's sight; and none that evilly persecuteth thy Order shall have length of life. Moreover, no wicked member of thy Order shall long continue therein, except he amend his life. Therefore be not cast down if thou seest some that are not good friars in thy Order, and that observe not the Rule as they ought; think not that for this thy Order shall perish; for ever shall there be of them—and they shall be many and many—that will observe perfectly the life of the gospel of Christ, and the purity of the Rule; and such as these shall go straightway to life everlasting after the death of the body, without passing through any purgatory. And some shall observe the Rule, but not perfectly; and they, ere they go to paradise, shall pass through purgatory, but the time of their purgation shall be committed to thee by God. But touching those that observe not the Rule at all—have no care of them, saith God, because He careth not." These words said, the angel departed, and St. Francis remained comforted and consoled. As the feast of the Assumption of Our Lady was now drawing nigh, St. Francis seeketh the opportunity of a more solitary and more secret place, wherein he may keep the fast of St. Michael the Archangel, that beginneth with the said feast of the Assumption. Wherefore he calls Friar Leo, and speaks to him thus, "Go and stand at the doorway of the oratory of the friary, and when I call thee do thou return to me." Friar Leo goes and stands at the doorway, and St. Francis withdrew a space and called loudly. Hearing himself called, Friar Leo returns to him, and St. Francis saith, "Son, let us seek a more secret place, whence thou canst not hear me when I call." And, in their search, they caught sight of a secret place on that side of the mountain that looketh to the south, and only too meet for his purpose; but they could not get there, because in front thereof was a horrible and fearful and very great chasm in the rock; wherefore, with great labour, they laid some logs across this chasm, after the manner of a bridge, and passed over. Then St. Francis sent for the other friars, and tells them how that he purposed to keep the lent of St. Michael in that solitary place, and therefore prays them to make a little cell there, so that no call of his might be heard by them. And the little cell of St. Francis being made, he saith to them, "Go ye to your dwelling, and leave me here alone, for with God's help I purpose to keep the fast here, with mind undistraught or unperturbed: therefore let none of you come to me, nor suffer any worldly folk to come to me. But thou only, Friar Leo, shalt come to me, once a day, with a little bread and water, and once again, by night, at the hour of matins: then shalt thou come to me in silence, and when thou art at the foot of the bridge thou shalt say to me, *Domine labia mea aperies*, and if I answer 'Come,' pass thou on to the cell, and we will say matins together; but if

I answer not, return thou straightway." And St. Francis said this because sometimes he was so rapt in God that he neither heard nor perceived aught with his bodily senses. This said, St. Francis gave them his blessing, and they returned to the friary. And the feast of the Assumption being come, St. Francis began the holy fast with great abstinence and severity, mortifying his body and comforting his spirit with fervent prayers, watchings, and scourgings; and ever waxing from virtue to virtue in these prayers, he made ready his soul to receive the divine mysteries and divine splendours, and his body to endure the cruel assaults of the devils, wherewith he was ofttimes smitten corporeally; and among other times, on a day during that fast, as St. Francis issued from his cell in fervour of spirit, and went to pray hard by in a hollow cave in the rock, at a great height from the ground and looking on a horrible and fearful abyss, suddenly the devil cometh in a terrible form, with tempest and mighty ruin, and smiteth him to thrust him down the abyss. Whereat St. Francis, having no whither to flee, and being unable to suffer the cruel aspect of the devil, anon turned with hands and face and all his body close to the rock, commending himself to God, and groping about with his hands, if haply he might find aught to cling to. But, as it pleased God, who never letteth His servants be tempted beyond what they can endure, straightway the rock, whereto he clung, was hollowed out by a miracle to the form of his body, and received him into itself, in such wise that the said rock was imprinted with the form of the face and the hands of St. Francis, as if he had pressed his hands and face against melted wax; and thus, with God's help, he escaped from the devil. But what the devil was unable to do then to St. Francis, to wit, thrust him down thence, was done a long time after the death of St. Francis to one, a dear and devoted friar, who was at that place, laying down some planks of wood, in order that he might go thither without peril, out of devotion to St. Francis, and in memory of the holy miracle there wrought; for on a day, as he was carrying a big log of wood on his head to lay across the chasm, he was pushed by the devil and thrust down and made to fall with that log on his head. But God, who had saved and preserved St. Francis from falling, saved and preserved that devout friar by his merits from the peril of his fall; for as the friar was falling he commended himself with a loud voice and with great devotion to St. Francis; and he straightway appeared to him, and grasping him, placed him down on the rocks, so that he felt neither shock nor wound. But the other friars, having heard the cry of this friar as he fell, and deeming him dead, and all dashed to pieces on the sharp rocks, by the great depth of his fall, took up the bier, and with great grief and many tears went to the other side of the mountain to seek the fragments of his body and bury them. And when they were come down to the foot of the rock, lo, that friar who had fallen met them, carrying the log on his head and singing *Te Deum laudamus* with a loud voice. And seeing the friars marvel greatly, he related to them, in order, all the manner of his fall, and how St. Francis had delivered him from all peril. Then all the friars came with him together to that place, singing most devoutly the aforesaid psalm, *Te Deum laudamus*, praising and giving thanks to God, and to St. Francis, for the miracle he had wrought for one of his friars.

St. Francis then, as hath been told, persevered in that fast, and albeit he endured many assaults of the devil, none the less did he receive many consolations from God, not only by visits of angels, but likewise of wild birds; for all the time of that lent, a falcon that had built her nest hard by his cell awoke him every night, a little before matins, by her singing and by beating her wings against his cell, and she departed not until he had risen up to say matins. And when St. Francis was more weary at one time than another, or more sick, or more feeble, this falcon, after the manner of a discreet and compassionate person, sang later. And so St. Francis had great pleasure of this clock; for the great solicitude of this falcon drove all sloth away from him and urged him to prayer, and beyond this, she ofttimes by day dwelt familiarly with him. Finally, as to this second consideration, St. Francis, being much weakened in body, in part by his great abstinence, and in part by the assaults of the devil, and being fain to comfort his body with the spiritual food of the soul, began to meditate on the ineffable glory and joy of the blessed in the life eternal; and he began to beseech God to grant him the grace of some foretaste of that joy. And while he remained thus meditating, anon an angel appeared to him with exceeding great splendour, that held a viol in his left hand and a bow in his right; and as St. Francis stood all dazed at this vision, the angel drew his bow once upwards across the viol; and straightway St. Francis heard such sweet melody that it ravished his soul and lifted him beyond all bodily sense, so that, as he afterwards related to his companions, he doubted lest his soul had wholly parted from his body, by reason of the unbearable sweetness, if the angel had drawn the bow downwards again. And this is all that concerneth the second consideration.

III. *Touching the third consideration of the sacred, hallowed stigmas.*

Coming to the third consideration, to wit, of the seraphic vision, and of the imprinting of the sacred, hallowed stigmas, be it known that the feast of the Most Holy Cross in the month of September drawing nigh, Friar Leo went one night at the wonted hour to the wonted place, in order to say matins with St. Francis, and having cried from the foot of the bridge, *Domine labia mia aperies*, as he was used to do, St. Francis did not answer. And Friar Leo turned not back, as St. Francis had bidden him, but passed over the bridge, with good and holy intent, and entered softly into his cell, and finding him not, thought he might be somewhere in the wood at prayer. Whereat he comes forth and goes about the wood in search of him by the light of the moon. And at last he heard the voice of St. Francis, and drawing nigh, beheld him on his knees in prayer with face and hands lifted up to heaven, saying in fervour of spirit, "Who art Thou, my God most sweet? What am I, Thy unprofitable servant and vilest of worms?" And these self-same words he again repeated and said naught besides. Whereat Friar Leo, marvelling greatly, lifted up his eyes and looked heavenward; and as he looked, he beheld a flaming torch coming down from heaven, most beautiful and resplendent, which descended and rested on the head of St. Francis; and from the said flame he heard a voice come forth which spake with St. Francis, but the words thereof this Friar Leo understood not. Hearing this, and deeming himself unworthy to remain so near the holy place where that wondrous vision was seen, and fearing likewise to offend St. Francis, or disturb him in his meditation if he were heard of him, he stole softly back, and standing afar off, waited to see the end. And as he gazed steadfastly, he beheld St. Francis stretch forth his hands thrice towards the flame; and at last, after a great space of time, he saw the flaming torch return to heaven. Whereupon he bestirred himself and returned secretly to his cell, glad in heart at the vision. And as he was going confidently away, St. Francis heard him by the rustling of the leaves under his feet, and bade him stay his steps and await him. Then Friar Leo, obedient, stood still and awaited him, with such great fear that, as he afterwards told his companions, at that moment he would rather the earth had swallowed him up than await St. Francis, who he thought would be displeased with him; for he guarded himself with the greatest diligence against offending his father, lest through his own fault St. Francis should deprive him of his companionship. Then St. Francis, as he came up to him, asked, "Who art thou?" And Friar Leo, all trembling, answered, "I am Friar Leo, my father." And St. Francis said to him, "Wherefore camest thou hither, friar, little sheep? Have I not told thee not to go spying on me? Tell me, by holy obedience, if thou didst see or hear aught?" Friar Leo answered, "Father, I heard thee speak and say many times, 'Who art Thou, my God most sweet? What am I, thy unprofitable servant and vilest of worms?'" And then Friar Leo knelt down before St. Francis and confessed his sin of disobedience, for that he had done contrary to his commands, craving forgiveness of him with many tears. And thereafter he entreated him devoutly to interpret to him those words he had heard, and tell him those he had not understood. Then St. Francis, seeing that God had revealed to this lowly Friar Leo, because of his purity and simplicity, or in sooth had suffered him to hear and behold certain things, deigned to reveal to him and interpret to him all those things he asked of him. And he spake thus, "Know thou, friar, little sheep of Jesus Christ, that when I was saying those words that thou didst hear, two lights were shown to me within my soul—one, the knowledge and understanding of myself; the other, the knowledge and understanding of the Creator. When I said, 'Who art Thou, my God most sweet?' then was I illumined by the light of contemplation, whereby I beheld the depths of the infinite goodness and wisdom and power of God. And when I said, 'What am I, etc.?' I was in the light of contemplation, whereby I beheld the deplorable depths of my own vileness and misery; and therefore I said, 'Who art Thou, Lord, infinite in goodness and wisdom, that deignest to visit me that am a vile and abominable worm?' And God was in that flame thou sawest, who spake to me in that vision even as of old He had spoken to Moses. And among other things He said, He asked of me to make Him three gifts; and I answered, 'My Lord, I am wholly Thine; well Thou knowest I have naught save tunic, cord, and breeches, and even these three things are Thine; what, then, can I offer or give unto Thy Majesty?' Then God said, 'Search in thy bosom and offer Me what thou findest there.' I sought there and found a ball of gold, and this I offered to God; and thus did I thrice, according as God had thrice bidden me. And then thrice knelt I down, and blessed and gave thanks to God that had given me wherewithal to offer to Him. And straightway it was given me to know that those three offers signified holy obedience, most exalted poverty, and most resplendent chastity, which God had vouchsafed to me by His grace to observe so perfectly that my conscience reproved me of naught. And even as thou sawest me place my hands in my bosom and offer to God those three virtues signified by the three balls of gold that God had placed in my bosom, even so hath God given me this virtue in my soul—that for all the good and for all the grace He hath bestowed upon me by His most holy goodness, I ever in my heart and with my lips do praise and magnify Him. These are the words thou didst hear when thou sawest me lift up my hands thrice. But beware, friar, little sheep; go thou not spying upon me, but return to thy cell with God's blessing, and have diligent care of me: for yet a few days and God shall work such great and wondrous things on this mountain that all the world shall marvel thereat; for He shall do things, new and strange, such as never hath He done to any creature in this world." These things said, St. Francis had the book of the gospels brought to him, for God had put it into his soul that by opening the book of the gospels thrice, those things that God was pleased to do with him should be shown forth. And when the book was brought, St. Francis betook himself to prayer, and the prayer ended, he had the book opened thrice by the hand of Friar Leo, and in the name of the most holy Trinity; and even as it pleased the divine providence, ever in those three openings the Passion of Christ was displayed to him. Through which thing it was given him to understand that even as he had followed Christ in the acts of his life, so was he to follow Him and conform himself unto Him in the afflictions and sorrows of the Passion, ere he passed from this life.

And from that time forth St. Francis began to taste and feel more bounteously the sweetness of divine contemplation and of divine visitations. Among which, he had one, immediate and preparatory to the imprinting of the divine stigmas, in this form. The day that goeth before the feast of the Most Holy Cross in the month of September, as St. Francis was praying in secret in his cell, the angel of God appeared to him and spake thus to him in God's name, "I am come to comfort and admonish thee that thou humbly prepare thee and make thee ready, with all patience, to receive that which God willeth to give thee and to work in thee." St. Francis answered, "I am ready to endure patiently all things that my Lord would do with me." This said, the angel departed. The day following, to wit, the day of the Most Holy Cross, St. Francis, on the morn before daybreak, knelt down betimes in prayer before the door of his cell; and turning his face eastwards, prayed in this wise, "O my Lord Jesus Christ, two graces do I pray Thee to grant unto me ere I die: the first, that while I live I may feel in my body and in my soul, so far as is possible, that sorrow, sweet Lord, that Thou didst suffer in the hour of Thy bitterest Passion; the second is, that I may feel in my heart, so far as may be possible, that exceeding love wherewith, O Son of God, Thou wast enkindled to endure willingly for us sinners agony so great." And remaining a long time thus praying, he knew that God would hear him; and that, so far as might be possible to a mere creature, thus far would it be vouchsafed to him to suffer the aforesaid things. St. Francis, having this promise, began to contemplate most devoutly the Passion of Christ and His infinite love; and the fervour of devotion waxed so within him that through love and through compassion he was wholly changed into Jesus. And being thus inflamed by this contemplation, he beheld, that same morning, a seraph with six resplendent and flaming wings come down from heaven; which seraph, with swift flight, drew nigh to St. Francis so that he could discern him, and he knew clearly that he had the form of a man crucified; and thus were his wings disposed: two wings were extended over his head; two were spread out in flight; and the other two covered the whole of the body. St. Francis, beholding this, was sore afraid, and yet was he filled with sweetness and sorrow mingled with wonder. Joy had he, exceeding great, at the gracious aspect of Christ that appeared to him thus familiarly and looked on him so graciously; but, on the other hand, seeing him nailed upon the cross, he suffered unspeakable grief and compassion. Thereafter, he marvelled greatly at so stupendous and unwonted a vision, well knowing that the infirmity of the Passion doth not accord with the immortality of the seraphic spirit. And being in this wonderment, it was revealed by the seraph who appeared to him, that that vision had been shown to him in such form, by divine providence, in order that he might understand he was to be changed into the express similitude of the crucified Christ in this wondrous vision, not by bodily martyrdom but by spiritual fire. Then the whole mount of La Verna seemed to flame forth with dazzling splendour, that shone and illumined all the mountains and the valleys round about, as were the sun shining on the earth. Wherefore when the shepherds that were watching in that country saw the mountain aflame and so much brightness round about, they were sore afraid, according as they afterwards told the friars, and affirmed that that flame had endured over the mount of La Verna for the space of an hour and more. Likewise, certain muleteers that were going to Romagna, arose up at the brightness of this light which shone through the windows of the inns of that country, and thinking the sun had risen, saddled and loaded their beasts. And as they went their way, they saw the said light wane and the real sun rise. Now Christ appeared in that same seraphic vision, and revealed to St. Francis certain secret and high things that St. Francis would never, during his life, disclose to any man; but, after his death, he revealed them, according as is set forth hereafter. And the words were these, "Knowest thou," said Christ, "what I have done to thee? I have given thee the stigmas that are the marks of my Passion, in order that thou be My standard-bearer. And even as I, on the day of my death, descended into limbo and delivered all the souls I found there by virtue of these My stigmas, so do I grant to thee that every year, on the day of thy death, thou mayst go to purgatory and deliver all the souls that shalt find there of thy three orders—Minors, Sisters, and Penitents—and others likewise that shall have had great devotion to thee, and thou shalt lead them up to the glory of paradise in order that thou be conformed to Me in thy death, even as thou art in thy life." This wondrous vision having vanished, after a great space, this secret converse left in the heart of St. Francis a burning flame of divine love, exceeding great, and in his flesh, a marvellous image and imprint of the Passion of Christ. For the marks of the nails began anon to be seen on the hands and on the feet of St. Francis, in the same manner as he had then seen them in the body of Jesus Christ crucified that had appeared to him in the form of a seraph: and thus his hands and feet seemed nailed through the middle with nails, the heads whereof were in the palms of his hands and in the soles of his feet, outside the flesh; and the points came out through the backs of the hands and the feet, so far, that they were bent back and clinched in such wise that one might easily have put a finger of the hand through the bent and clinched ends outside the flesh, even as through a ring: and the heads of the nails were round and black. In like fashion, the image of a lance-wound, unhealed, inflamed, and bleeding, was seen in his right side, whence thereafter blood came out many times from the holy breast of St. Francis and stained his tunic and his under garments with blood. Wherefore his companions, before they learned these things from him, perceiving nevertheless that he never uncovered his hands or his feet, and that he could not put the soles of his feet to the ground, and finding thereafter that his tunic and under garments were all bloody when they washed them, knew of a surety that he had the image and similitude of our Lord Jesus Christ crucified, expressly imprinted on his hands and feet, and likewise on his side. And albeit he strove much to conceal and to hide those glorious, sacred, and hallowed stigmas, thus clearly marked on his flesh; yet on the other hand, seeing that he could ill conceal them from his familiar companions, and fearing to publish abroad the secrets of God, he remained in great doubt whether he ought to reveal the seraphic vision and the imprint of the sacred, hallowed stigmas. At last, pricked by conscience, he called to him certain of his most familiar friars and propounded his doubts to them in general terms, without giving expression to the fact and asked counsel of them. Now among these friars was one of great holiness called Friar Illuminatus, and he, verily illumined by God, understood that St. Francis must have beheld wondrous things, and answered him thus, "Friar Francis, know that not for thee alone, but also for others, God showeth to thee at divers times his holy mysteries; therefore hast thou reason to fear lest thou be worthy of reproof if thou keep this thing hidden that God hath shown to thee for profit of others." Then St. Francis, moved by these words, laid before them, with exceeding great fear, all the manner and form of the aforesaid vision, and added that Christ when He appeared to him, had said certain things that he would never tell while he lived. And albeit those most holy wounds, in so far as they were imprinted by Christ, gave him great joy in his heart, nevertheless to his flesh and to his bodily senses they gave unbearable pain. Wherefore, being constrained by necessity, he chose Friar Leo, simplest and purest among the friars, and to him revealed all things; and he suffered him to see and touch those holy wounds and bind them with bandages to ease the pain and staunch the blood that issued and ran therefrom: which dressings, at the time of his sickness, he suffered often to be changed, yea, even every day, save from Thursday evening to Saturday morning; for he would not that the pains of the Passion of Christ, that he bore in his body, should be eased in any way by human remedies and medicines during the time our Saviour Jesus Christ had been taken and, for our sakes, crucified and slain and buried. It befell on a time when Friar Leo was changing the swathings of the wound in his side, that St. Francis, by reason of the pain he felt in the loosing of the blood-stained bandage, laid his hand on Friar Leo's breast; and at the touch of those holy hands, Friar Leo felt such great sweetness of devotion in his heart that, a little more, and he had fallen swooning on the ground. And finally, as to this third consideration: St. Francis having completed the forty days' fast of St. Michael the Archangel, made ready by divine revelation to return to St. Mary of the Angels. Wherefore he called Friar Masseo and Friar Angelo to him, and after many words and many holy admonitions, commended the holy mountain to them with all the zeal in his power, saying that it behoved him, together with Friar Leo, to return to St. Mary of the Angels. This said, he took leave of them and blessed them in the name of the crucified Jesus; and deigned, in answer to their prayers, to stretch forth to them his most holy hands, adorned with those glorious and sacred and hallowed stigmas, that they might see them and touch them and kiss them, and leaving the friars thus comforted he departed from them and descended the holy mountain.

IV. *Touching the fourth consideration of the sacred, hallowed stigmas.*

Touching the fourth consideration, be it known, that after the true love of Christ had perfectly transformed St. Francis into God and into the true image of Christ crucified, that angelic man, having completed the fast of forty days in honour of St. Michael the Archangel on the holy mount of La Verna, came down from the mountain with Friar Leo and a devout peasant on whose ass he rode, because, by reason of the nails in his feet, he could not well go a-foot. And when he was come down from the mountain, forasmuch as the fame of his sanctity was noised abroad throughout the land (because the shepherds that had seen the mount of La Verna all aflame had said it was a sign of some great miracle God had wrought on St. Francis), the folk of that country-side all flocked to behold him as he passed by: men and women, small and great, all with great devotion and desire, strove to touch him and to kiss his hands. And St. Francis, being unable to deny his hands to the devotion of the people, albeit he had bound up the palms, nevertheless bound them over again, and covered them with his sleeves, and only held forth his uncovered fingers for them to kiss. But albeit he sought to conceal and hide the sacred mystery of the holy stigmas, that he might flee all occasion of worldly glory, it pleased God to show forth many miracles for His own glory, by virtue of the said sacred, hallowed stigmas, and notably on that journey from La Verna to St. Mary of the Angels. And very many other miracles thereafter were wrought in divers parts of the world, both during his life and after his glorious death; and this to the end that their hidden and wondrous virtue, and the exceeding love and mercy of Christ, so wondrously vouchsafed to him, might be made manifest to the world through clear and evident miracles, whereof we here set down a few.

When St. Francis was drawing nigh to a village which was on the confines of the district of Arezzo, a woman came before him, weeping greatly, and bearing her son in her arms, that was eight years of age; and this child for four years had been sick of the dropsy; and his belly was so swollen and so deformed that when he stood up he could not see his feet; and placing this child before him, this woman besought St. Francis to pray to God for him. And St. Francis first betook himself to prayer, and then, the prayer ended, laid his holy hands on the child's belly, and straightway all the swelling was down, and he was wholly healed; and St. Francis gave him back to his mother, who received him with the greatest joy, and led him home, giving thanks to God and to St. Francis; and willingly she showed her son healed to all those of the country-side that came to her house to behold him. The same day, St. Francis passed by Borgo di San Sepolcro, and before he came nigh to the town, the crowds therefrom and from the villages made towards him; and many of them went before him, bearing olive branches in their hands, crying with a loud voice, "Behold the saint! Behold the saint!" And by reason of the devotion and desire that the folk had to touch him, they made a great throng and press about him; but he went on with mind uplifted and rapt in God, through contemplation; and albeit he was touched and held and dragged about, yet as one insensible he felt naught that was done or said to him; nay, he perceived not even that he was passing by that town or through that land. Wherefore, having passed through the town, and the crowds being gone to their homes, he came to a leper house, a good mile beyond, and this celestial contemplative then returned to himself, as if he were come back from another world; and he asked his companions, "When shall we be nigh the town?" For of a truth his soul, fixed and rapt in contemplation of celestial things, had been sensible of no earthly thing; neither variety of place, nor change of time, nor of persons he passed. And this befell many other times, even as his companions proved by clear experience. On that evening, St. Francis came to the friary of Monte Casale, wherein a friar lay so cruelly sick and so horribly tormented by his sickness that his ill seemed rather a tribulation and torment of the devil than a natural sickness; for sometimes he flung himself on the ground in a mighty trembling and foaming at the mouth; now he contracted all the limbs of his body, now he thrust them forth; now he bent his body, now he writhed; now bending back his heels to the nape of his neck, he sprang high up into the air, and straightway fell again on his back. And St. Francis, hearing from the other friars, as he sat at table, of this miserably sick and incurable friar, had compassion on him; and taking a slice of the bread he was eating, he made thereon the sign of the most holy cross with his holy wounded hands, and sent it to the sick friar; and no sooner had he eaten thereof than he was perfectly healed, and never more felt that sickness. The next morning being come, St. Francis sent two of the friars that were in that house to dwell at La Verna, and sent back with them the peasant that had followed behind the ass he had lent him, desiring that he should return home with them. St. Francis, after he had sojourned some days in that friary, departed and went to Città di Castello. And behold, many of the townsfolk brought before him a woman that for a long time had been possessed by a devil, and besought him humbly to deliver her, for that she, now with grievous howlings, now with cruel shrieks, now with barks like a dog, disturbed the whole country-side. Then St. Francis, having first prayed and made the sign of the most holy cross over her, commanded the devil to depart from her, and straightway he departed, leaving her whole in body and mind. And this miracle being noised abroad among the people, another woman, with great faith, brought to him her child, that was grievously sick of a cruel wound, and devoutly besought him that he would be pleased to make the sign over him with his hands. Then St. Francis, granting her prayer, takes this child and unbinds the wound and blesses him, making thrice the sign of the most holy cross over the wound; then with his own hand he binds the wound up again, and restores him to his mother. And because it was evening, she straightway laid him in his bed to sleep. In the morning she goes to take her child from the bed and finds the wound unbound, and looks and finds him perfectly healed, as if he had never had any ill, save that the flesh had grown over the place where the wound was, in the form of a red rose; and this was to bear witness to the miracle rather than in token of the wound; for the said rose remaining there all the days of his life, did oft move him to a special devotion for St. Francis, who had made him whole. In that same city St. Francis, at the prayers of the devout townsfolk, abode a month, in which time he wrought very many other miracles, and departed thence, to go to St. Mary of the Angels with Friar Leo and an honest fellow that lent him his ass whereon he rode. Now it befell, that what with the bad roads and what with the great cold, they could not, even by journeying the whole day, come to any place where they might lodge. Wherefore, constrained by the darkness and by the bad weather, they took shelter under the hollow cliff of a rock, to escape the snow and the darkness that had overtaken them. And being thus in sorry plight, and but ill sheltered, the man that had lent the ass was unable to sleep, and having no means of kindling a fire, he began to complain softly within himself and to weep, murmuring at St. Francis that had brought him to such a pass. Then St. Francis, hearing this, had compassion on him, and in fervour of spirit, stretched forth his hand and laid it upon him and touched him. Marvellous to tell! no sooner had he touched him with his hand, pierced and enkindled by the fire of the seraph, than all the cold vanished, and so much heat warmed him from within and without, that himseemed to be nigh to a fiery furnace; wherefore, comforted in body and soul, anon he fell asleep; and, according as he was wont to say, he slept all that night till morn, amid rocks and snow, better than he had ever slept in his own bed. On the morrow, they journeyed on and came to St. Mary of the Angels; and when they were nigh thereto Friar Leo lifted up his eyes and looked towards the said friary of St. Mary of the Angels; and he beheld a cross, exceeding beautiful, whereon was the figure of the Crucified, going before St. Francis, who was riding in front of him; and so closely did that cross conform to the movements of St. Francis, that when he stopped, it stopped; and when he went on, it went on: and that cross shone with such exceeding brightness that not only did the face of St. Francis shine resplendent, but likewise the whole way around him was illumined. And that brightness endured even up to the time that St. Francis entered the friary of St. Mary of the Angels. St. Francis then being come with Friar Leo, they were received with the greatest joy and charity, and from that hour St. Francis abode the most of his time in the friary of St. Mary of the Angels, even until his death. And ever more the fame of his holiness and of his miracles was spread abroad throughout the Order and throughout the world, albeit he, of his deep humility, concealed, so far as he could, the gifts and the graces of God, and called himself the greatest of sinners. Whereat Friar Leo marvelled, and on a time thought within himself thus foolishly, "Lo, this man calleth himself in public places the greatest of sinners; he is grown great in the Order, and is much honoured of God; nevertheless, in secret he never confessed any carnal sin: could he be a virgin?" And a very great desire came upon him to know the truth of this thing; but he had not dared to ask St. Francis. Wherefore, having recourse to God, and beseeching with great insistence that He would certify to him, through the many prayers and the merits of St. Francis, that which he desired to know, his prayer was heard, and he was certified by a vision that St. Francis was verily a virgin in body: for in a dream he beheld St. Francis standing on a high and exalted place, whereunto none could go nor attain; and it was revealed to him in spirit that that place, so high and exalted, betokened in St. Francis the high excellence of virginal chastity, that rightly was in accord with the flesh that was to be adorned with the sacred, hallowed stigmas of Christ. Now St. Francis, seeing that by reason of the stigmas of Christ his bodily strength was little by little ebbing away, and that he could no longer have care for the government of the Order, hastened to summon the Chapter-General; and when all were assembled he humbly excused himself to the friars for his waning strength, whereby he was no longer able to give heed to the cares of the Order, nor fill the office of General; albeit he might not lay down the generalship, for he could not, since he was made general by the pope; therefore, he could not leave the office nor appoint another in his place without the express licence of the pope; but he instituted Friar Peter of Catana his vicar, and commended the Order to him and to the ministers of the provinces with all the affection he could. This done, St. Francis was comforted in spirit, and lifting up his eyes and hands to heaven, spake thus, "To Thee, my Lord God, to Thee I commend Thy household, that until this hour Thou hast committed to my charge, and now, because of my infirmities, whereof Thou knowest, my sweetest Lord, no more can I have the care thereof. Likewise I commend it to the ministers of the provinces; let them answer to Thee for it, on the Day of Judgment, if any friar perish through their negligence, or through their evil example, or through their too harsh correction." And with these words, as it pleased God, all the friars at the Chapter understood that he spake of the sacred, hallowed stigmas, in that he excused himself because of his infirmities; and of their devotion none could henceforth keep back his tears. And, from that time forth, he left the care and government of the Order in the hands of his vicar and of the ministers of the provinces, and then he said, "Now since I have laid aside the cares of the Order, because of my infirmities, I am henceforth held to naught save to pray to God for our Order, and to give a good example to the friars. And well I know, and truly, that if my sickness left me, the greatest aid I could give to the Order would be to pray unceasingly to God for it, and that He would defend it and guide it and preserve it." Now, as hath been said above, albeit St. Francis strove with all his might to conceal the sacred, hallowed stigmas, and, after he had received them, ever went about or remained with his hands swathed and his feet shod, it availed not but that many friars, in divers ways, saw and felt them; and especially the wound in his side, that he strove to conceal with the greatest diligence. Wherefore, a friar that served him, craftily contrived on a time to induce him to take off his tunic, that the dust might be shaken therefrom; and it being taken off in his presence, that friar saw clearly the wound in the side; and, putting forth his hand quickly, he touched his breast with three fingers, and felt the width and depth thereof; and in like manner his vicar saw it at that time. But Friar Ruffino, a man of very great contemplation, was most clearly certified thereof—he of whom St. Francis said on a time that there was no saintlier man in the world, and whom, for his holiness, he loved tenderly and granted to him all he desired. This Friar Ruffino certified himself and others in three ways of the sacred, hallowed stigmas, and especially of the wound in the side. The first way was this: The said Friar Ruffino, when he was about to wash the hose (which St. Francis wore so large that by drawing them well up he could cover the wound in his right side), was wont to look at them and consider them diligently; and every time he did so he found them stained with blood on the right side; wherefore he perceived, of a surety, that blood issued from the said wound: and St. Francis chid him, when he saw him unfold the clothes he took away from him, in order to see the said stains. The second way was, that the said Friar Ruffino on a time purposely put his fingers in the wound in the side, whereat St. Francis, for the pain he felt, cried out loudly, "God forgive thee, O Friar Ruffino, for that thou hast done this thing." The third way was, that on a time he craved with great earnestness that St. Francis would give him his cloak, as an exceeding great favour, and take his in exchange, for love of charity; which petition the charitable father designed to grant, albeit unwillingly, and took off his cloak and gave it to him, receiving his in return: and then, as he took it off and put on the other, Friar

Ruffino clearly saw the wound. Friar Leo, likewise, and many other friars, saw the sacred, hallowed stigmas of St. Francis while he yet lived: which friars, albeit they were by their holiness worthy of faith, and to be believed on their simple word, nevertheless, to remove all doubt from men's hearts, did swear upon the sacred Book that they had clearly seen them. Certain cardinals likewise saw them that were very familiar with him, and composed and made fair and devout hymns and antiphones and rhymes[11] out of reverence for the said sacred and hallowed stigmas of St. Francis. The high pontiff, Pope Alexander, preaching to the people in the presence of the cardinals, and among them the saintly Friar Bonaventure, that was a cardinal, said and affirmed that he had seen with his own eyes the sacred and hallowed stigmas of St. Francis while he was alive. And the lady Jacqueline of Settesoli, that in her day was the greatest lady in Rome, and had a very great devotion to St. Francis, beheld them and kissed them many times with great reverence, both before he died and after his death; for she came from Rome to Assisi, by divine revelation, at the death of St. Francis, and it was in this wise: St. Francis, some days before his death, lay sick in the bishop's palace at Assisi with some of his companions; and notwithstanding his sickness, he ofttimes sang certain lauds of Christ. On a day, one of his companions said to him, "Father, thou knowest the men of this city have great faith in thee, and deem thee a holy man; and therefore they may think, that if thou art such as they believe thee to be, thou oughtest in this thy sickness to meditate on thy death, and weep rather than sing, since thou art so grievously sick; and know that this singing of thine, and ours that thou biddest, is heard of many, both within and without, since this palace is guarded by many men-at-arms by reason of thy presence, who haply may have evil example thereof. Wherefore," said the friar, "methinks thou wouldst do well to depart hence and all we return to St. Mary of the Angels, because it is not well with us here among worldly men." St. Francis answered, "Dearest brother, thou knowest that two years now agone, when we were at Foligno, God revealed to thee the term of my life; and even so hath He revealed again to me that, yet a few days and the said term shall end during this sickness; and in this revelation God hath certified me that all my sins are remitted, and that I shall go to paradise. Until that revelation I bewailed my death and my sins; but since I had that revelation I am so filled with joy that I can weep no more; therefore do I sing, and will sing, to God, that hath given me the joy of His grace, and hath made me certain of the joys of the glory of paradise. Touching our departure hence, it pleaseth me well, and I

---

[11] *Prose.* See Purg. xxvi. 118. The *Anonimo fiorentino*, commenting on this passage, says *far prosa di romanzi* means to compose in rhyme. The interpretation is, however, disputed.

consent thereto; but find ye some means to carry me, for by reason of my sickness I cannot walk." Then the friars took him in their arms, and so carried him, accompanied by many citizens. And when they came to an hospice that was on the way, St. Francis said to them that bore him, "Lay me down on the ground, and turn me towards the city." And when he was laid with his face towards Assisi, he blessed the city with many blessings, saying, "Blessed be thou of God, holy city, for many souls shall be saved because of thee, and in thee shall dwell many of God's servants; and from thee many shall be chosen to the kingdom of life everlasting." These words said, he had himself borne towards St. Mary of the Angels. And when they were come to St. Mary of the Angels they carried him to the infirmary, and there laid him down to rest. Then St. Francis called one of his companions to him, and spake to him thus, "Dearest friar, God hath revealed to me that on such a day in this sickness I shall pass from this life: and thou knowest that if the Lady Jacqueline of Settesoli, the dearest friend of our Order, came to hear of my death, and were not present, she would sorrow overmuch; therefore signify to her that she must straightway come hither, if she would see me alive." The friar answered, "Thou sayst but too true, father, for verily of the great devotion she hath for thee, it would be most unseemly if she were not present at thy death." "Go then," said St. Francis, "and fetch me ink and paper and pen, and write what I shall tell thee." And when he had brought them, St. Francis dictated the letter in this wise, "To the Lady Jacqueline, servant of God, greeting and fellowship of the Holy Ghost in our Lord Jesus Christ, from Friar Francis, Christ's poor little one. Know, dearest lady, that the blessed Christ hath revealed to me by His grace that the end of my life is at hand. Therefore, if thou wouldst find me yet alive, set forth when thou hast seen this letter, and come to St. Mary of the Angels; for if by such a day thou art not come, thou shalt not find me alive; and bring sackcloth, wherein my body may be shrouded, and wax needful for my burial. Prithee, also, bring me of those meats to eat that thou wast wont to give me when I lay sick at Rome." And while this letter was writing, it was revealed by God to St. Francis that the Lady Jacqueline was coming to him, and was near by, and had brought with her all those things he was sending to ask for in the letter. Whereupon, having had this revelation, St. Francis told the friar that was writing the letter to write no further, since there was no need, but lay the letter aside: whereat the friars marvelled greatly, because the letter was not finished, nor would he have it despatched. Then a little while, and a loud knocking was heard at the door, and St. Francis sent the doorkeeper to open it; and the door being opened, there was the Lady Jacqueline, the noblest lady of Rome, with her two sons, that were Roman senators, and with a great company of horsemen, and they entered in; and the Lady Jacqueline goes straight to the infirmary and comes to St. Francis.

And at her coming St. Francis had great joy and consolation, and she likewise, when she beheld him living, and was able to speak with him. Then she recounted how that God had revealed to her at Rome, while she was at prayer, that the term of his life was at hand, and that he was to send for her and to ask of her all those things she had brought; and she bade them be carried in to St. Francis, and gave him to eat thereof. And when he had eaten, and was much comforted, the Lady Jacqueline knelt at the feet of St. Francis, and took those most holy feet, marked and adorned with the wounds of Christ, and kissed them, and bathed his feet with her tears, and this with such exceeding great devotion that the friars that stood around seemed to behold the Magdalen herself at the feet of Jesus Christ, and in no wise could they draw her away. Finally, after a great space, they led her thence and drew her aside; and they asked her how she had come thus in due time and provided with all those things that were necessary for the comfort and burial of St. Francis. The Lady Jacqueline answered, that one night, when she was praying at Rome, she heard a voice from heaven, saying, "If thou wouldst find St. Francis living, delay not, but haste to Assisi, and bear with thee those things thou art wont to give him when he is sick, and the things needful for his burial"; "And," said she, "thus have I done." The said Lady Jacqueline abode there until such time as St. Francis passed from this life and was buried, and she and all her company did very great honour to his burial, and paid the cost of all that was needed. And then, being returned to Rome, this noble lady, in a short time, died a holy death; and, through devotion to St. Francis, she appointed St. Mary of the Angels to be her burial-place: thither was she borne, and even there was buried.

    V. *How Jerome, that believed not therein, touched and saw the sacred and hallowed stigmas.*

    Not only did the said Lady Jacqueline and her sons and her company see and kiss the glorious and sacred stigmas of St. Francis at his death, but likewise many men of the city of Assisi; and among them a knight of much renown and a mighty man, called Jerome, that was incredulous and doubted much, even as St. Thomas the Apostle doubted of the wounds of Christ; and to certify himself and others thereof, he boldly moved the nails in the hands and feet, and openly felt the wound in the side in the presence of the friars and of lay folk. Wherefore he was ever after a constant witness of the truth, and sware on the gospel that thus it was and thus he had seen and touched. St. Clare also, with her nuns that were present at the burial, saw and kissed the glorious and hallowed stigmas of St. Francis.

    VI. *Touching the day and the year of the death of St. Francis.*

    St. Francis, glorious confessor of Christ, passed from this life in the year of our Lord one thousand two hundred and twenty-six, on Saturday, the fourth day of October, and was buried on the Sunday.

And that year was the twentieth year of his conversion, to wit, when he had begun to do penance; and it was the second year after the imprinting of the sacred and hallowed stigmas, and the forty-fifth year of his life.

VII. *Of the canonisation of St. Francis.*

St. Francis was thereafter canonised by Pope Gregory IX., in the year one thousand two hundred and twenty-eight, and he came in person to Assisi to canonise him. And let this suffice for the fourth consideration.

VIII. *Touching the fifth and last consideration of the sacred and hallowed stigmas.*

The fifth and last consideration is of certain visions and revelations and miracles that God wrought and showed forth after the death of St. Francis, in confirmation of his sacred and hallowed stigmas, and in certification of the day and the hour when Christ gave them to him. And touching this be it remembered that in the year of our Lord one thousand two hundred and eighty-two, on the . . . day of October, Friar Philip, minister of Tuscany, by command of Friar John Buonagrazia, the minister-general, bade by holy obedience Friar Matthew of Castiglione Aretino, a man of great devotion and sanctity, tell him what he knew touching the day and the hour whereon the sacred and hallowed stigmas were imprinted by Christ on the body of St. Francis: for he had heard that of this he had a divine revelation. This Friar Matthew, constrained by holy obedience, answered him thus, "When I was sojourning at La Verna, this past year, in the month of May, I betook me one day to prayer in my cell, which is on the spot where it is believed that the vision of the seraph was seen. And in my prayers I besought God, most devoutly, that it would please Him to reveal to some person the day and the hour whereon the sacred and hallowed stigmas were imprinted on the body of St. Francis. And I, persevering in prayer and in this petition beyond the first sleep, St. Francis appeared to me in a great light and spake to me thus, 'Son, wherefore prayest thou to God?' And I said to him, 'Father, I pray for such a thing.' And he to me, 'I am thy father, Francis, knowest thou me well?' 'Father,' said I, 'yea!' Then he showed to me the sacred and hallowed stigmas in his hands and feet and in his side, and said, 'The time is come when God willeth that to His glory those things shall be made manifest that the friars in the past have not cared to know. Know that He who appeared to me was no angel, but Jesus Christ in the form of a seraph, that with His hands imprinted these wounds on my body, even as He received them in His body on the cross; and it was in this manner—the day before the exaltation of the holy cross, an angel came to me and in God's name bade me make ready to suffer and receive that which God willed to send me. And I answered that I was ready to receive and endure all things at God's pleasure. Then on the morrow, to wit, the morning of Holy Cross day, which in that year fell on a Friday, I came forth from my cell at the dawn in exceeding great fervour of spirit, and I went to pray in this place where thou now art, in which place I was ofttimes wont to pray. And while I was at prayer, lo, there came down through the air from heaven a youth crucified, in the form of a seraph, with six wings; and he came with great swiftness; at whose wondrous aspect I knelt me down humbly and began to meditate devoutly on the ineffable love of Jesus Christ crucified, and on the unspeakable pain of His Passion. And His aspect begat in me compassion so great that meseemed verily to feel this passion in mine own body; and at His presence all the mountain shone, bright as the sun: and thus descending from heaven He came nigh to me. And standing before me He spake to me certain secret words that I have not yet revealed to any man; but the time is at hand when they shall be revealed. Then after some space Christ departed and went back to heaven, and I found me thus marked with these wounds.' 'Go then,' said St. Francis, 'and tell these things confidently to thy minister, for this is the work of God and not of man.' These words said, St. Francis blessed me and returned to heaven with a great multitude of youths in shining raiment." All these things Friar Matthew said he had seen and heard, not sleeping, but waking. And even so he sware that he had said really and truly to the minister in his cell at Florence when he required him thereof by obedience.

IX. *How a holy friar was reading in the legend about the secret words that the seraph said when he appeared to St. Francis as set forth in the chapter touching the sacred and hallowed stigmas, and how the said friar prayed to God so fervently that St. Francis revealed them to him.*

Another time, when a devout and holy friar was reading the chapter of the sacred and hallowed stigmas in the Legend of St. Francis, he began to think with great anxiety of mind what those words, so secret, might have been that St. Francis said he would reveal to no man while he lived, and that the seraph had spoken when he appeared to him. And this friar said within himself, "St. Francis would never tell those words to any man while he lived, but now after his bodily death haply he might tell them if he were devoutly entreated." And thenceforth the devout friar began to pray to God and to St. Francis that they would be pleased to reveal those words; and this friar, persevering for eight years in this prayer, on the eighth year, by his merits, his prayer was answered in this wise: One day after he had eaten and had returned thanks in church, he was at prayer in another part of the church, beseeching God and St. Francis to grant his prayer more devoutly than he was wont to do, and with many tears, when he was called by another friar and bidden by order of the warden to bear him company to the city on the business of the Order. Wherefore, doubting not that obedience was more meritorious than prayer, on hearing the command of the prelate, he forthwith ceased to pray and humbly went forth with that friar who had called him. And, as it pleased God, in that act of ready obedience he merited what by long years of prayer he had failed to merit. Wherefore no sooner were they outside the friary door than they encountered two stranger friars that seemed to have come from a far country; and one of them seemed young in years, the other aged and lean; and by reason of the bad weather, they were all bemired and wet. And this obedient friar, having great compassion on them, said to the companion with whom he went, "O my dearest brother, if the business wherefore we go may be delayed a while, forasmuch as these stranger friars have great need of being charitably received, prithee let me first go and wash their feet, and especially the feet of that aged friar that hath the greater need thereof, and you can wash the feet of this younger one: and then we will go our way on the affairs of the Order." This friar then consenting to the charity of his companion, they returned within, and receiving these stranger friars very charitably, they led them to the kitchen fire to warm and dry themselves; and at this fire eight other friars were warming themselves. And after they had stood a while at the fire, they drew them aside to wash their feet, according as they had agreed together. And as that obedient and devout friar was washing the feet of the aged stranger, and cleansing them from the mire, he looked, and beheld his feet marked with the sacred and hallowed stigmas; and straightway embracing them tenderly, for very joy and amazement, he began to cry, "Either thou art Christ, or thou art St. Francis." At this cry and at these words the friars that were by the fire rose up and with great trembling and reverence drew nigh to behold those glorious stigmas. And at their entreaties this aged friar suffered them to see them clearly and to touch them and kiss them. And as they marvelled yet more for very joy, he said to them, "Doubt not, nor fear, dearest friars, my children; I am your father, Friar Francis, who, according to God's will, established three Orders. And forasmuch as I have been entreated, these eight years past, by this friar that washeth my feet, and this day more fervently than ever, that I would reveal to him those secret words the seraph said to me, when he gave me the stigmas, which words I would never reveal during my life, this day, by commandment of God, and because of his perseverance and his ready obedience, when he renounced the sweetness of contemplation, I am sent by God to reveal to him, in your sight, what he asked of me." And St. Francis, turning towards that friar, spake thus, "Know, dearest friar, that when I was on the mount of La Verna, all rapt in the contemplation of the Passion of Christ, in this seraphic vision I was by Christ thus stigmatised in my body; and then Christ said to me, 'Knowest thou what I have done to thee? I have given thee the marks of my Passion in order that thou mayst be My standard-bearer. And even as I, on the day of My death, descended into limbo and drew thence all the souls I found therein, by virtue of my stigmas, and led them up to paradise, so do I grant to thee from this hour (that thou mayst be conformed to Me in thy death as thou hast been in thy life) that after thou hast passed from this life thou shalt go every year, on the day of thy death, to purgatory, and shalt deliver all the souls thou shalt find there of thy three Orders, to wit, Minors, Sisters, and Penitents, and likewise the souls of thy devoted followers, and this, in virtue of thy stigmas that I have given thee; and thou shalt lead them to paradise.' And those words I told not while I lived in the world." This said, St. Francis and his companion vanished; and many friars thereafter heard this from those eight friars that were present at the vision and heard the words of St. Francis.

X. *How St. Francis appeared after his death to Friar John of La Verna while he was at prayer.*

On the mount of La Verna, St. Francis appeared on a time to Friar John of La Verna, a man of great sanctity, while he was at prayer, and remained and held converse with him a very long space; and at last being willed to depart, he spake thus, "Ask of me what thou wilt." Said Friar John, "Father, I pray thee, tell me that which for a long time I have desired to know, to wit, what you[12] were doing, and where you were, when the seraph appeared to you." St. Francis answers, "I was praying in that place where the chapel of Count Simon of Battifolle now stands, and I was craving two graces of my Lord Jesus Christ. The first was, that he would vouchsafe to me, during my life, to feel in my soul and in my body, so far as might be, all that pain He had felt in Himself at the time of His bitterest Passion. The second grace I asked of Him was that I should likewise feel in my heart that exceeding love wherewith he was enkindled to endure that Passion so great, for us sinners. And then God put in my heart that He would grant me to feel the one and the other, so far as might be possible to a mere creature: which thing was well fulfilled in me by the imprinting of the stigmas." Then Friar John asks of him if those secret words that the seraph said to him were after the manner that the aforesaid holy friar had recited, who had affirmed he had heard them from St. Francis in the presence of eight friars. St. Francis answered that the truth was even as that friar had said. Then Friar John takes heart from the freedom of his condescension and says thus, "O father, thee I pray most earnestly, suffer me to behold and kiss thy sacred and glorious stigmas; not because I doubt aught thereof, but only for my consolation, for this have I ever desired." And St. Francis, freely showing them and holding them forth to him, Friar John beheld them clearly, and touched them, and kissed them. And finally he asked of him, "Father, what consolation did your soul feel on beholding the blessed Christ coming

---

[12] *See* note, p. 5.

to give you the signs of His most holy Passion? Would to God that I now might feel a little of that sweetness!" Then St. Francis answers, "Seest thou these nails?" Saith Friar John, "Yea, father." "Touch yet again," saith St. Francis, "this nail in my hand." Then Friar John with great reverence and fear touched that nail, and anon, as he touched it, a great fragrance issued forth like to a column of incense, and, entering the nostrils of Friar John, filled his soul and his body with such sweetness that straightway he was rapt in God and became senseless in ecstasy, and he remained thus ravished from that hour, which was the hour of tierce, until vespers. And this vision and familiar converse with St. Francis, Friar John told to no man save to his confessor, until he came to die; but, being nigh unto death, he revealed it to many friars.

XI. *Of a holy friar who beheld a wondrous vision of one of his companions that was dead.*

A most devout and holy friar saw this wondrous vision in the province of Rome. A very dear friar, his companion, having died one night, was buried on the morrow before the entrance to the chapter-room; and on that same day this friar withdrew, after dinner, into a corner of the chapter-room to pray devoutly to God and to St. Francis for the soul of the dead friar, his companion. And as he persevered in prayer with supplication and tears, lo, at noon, when all the other friars were gone to sleep, he heard a great moving about in the cloister. Whereat, greatly afeard, anon he turned his eyes towards the grave of this his companion, and beheld St. Francis at the entrance of the chapter, and behind him a great multitude of friars all standing round the said grave; and he saw a fire with great tongues of flame in the middle of the cloister, and in the midst of the flames stood the soul of his dead companion. He looks around the cloister and sees Jesus Christ going around the cloister with a great company of angels and saints. And gazing at these things with great amaze he sees that when Christ passes before the chapter, St. Francis and all those friars kneel down; and St. Francis saith these words, "I pray Thee, my dearest Father and Lord, by that inestimable love Thou didst show forth to the generations of men when Thou didst die on the wood of the cross, have mercy on the soul of this my friar that burneth in this fire." And Christ answered naught but passed on. And He returns a second time, and passing before the chapter-room, St. Francis again kneels down with his friars as before and entreats Him in this wise, "I pray Thee, pitying Father and Lord, by the ineffable love Thou didst show to the generations of men when Thou didst die on the wood of the cross, have mercy on the soul of this my friar." And Christ, in like manner, passed on and heard him not. And going round the cloister He returned a third time and passed before the chapter-room; and then St. Francis, kneeling down as before, showed Him his hands and feet and breast, and spake thus, "I pray Thee, pitying Father and Lord, by that great pain and great consolation I felt when Thou didst imprint these stigmas on my flesh, have mercy on the soul of this my friar that is in this purgatorial fire." Marvellous to tell! Christ, being entreated this third time by St. Francis, in the name of his stigmas, straightway stays His steps and looks on the stigmas and answers his prayer and saith these words, "To thee, Francis, I grant the soul of thy friar." And thereby of a surety He willed to confirm and honour the glorious stigmas of St. Francis and openly signify that the souls of his friars that go to purgatory are delivered from their pains in no other way more readily than by virtue of his stigmas, and led to the glories of paradise; according to the words that Christ said to St. Francis when He imprinted them upon him. Wherefore, these words said, straightway that fire in the cloister vanished, and the dead friar came to St. Francis, and all that company of the blessed ascended to heaven with him, and with Christ their glorious King. Whereat this friar, his companion, that had prayed for him, had exceeding great joy when he beheld him delivered from the pains of purgatory and taken up to heaven; and thereafter he related this vision in due order to the other friars, and together with them gave praise and thanks to God.

XII. *How a noble knight, that had devotion to St. Francis, was certified of his death and of the sacred and hallowed stigmas.*

A noble knight of Massa di San Pietro, named Rudolph, that had a great devotion to St. Francis, and who at length had received the habit of the third Order at his hands, was thuswise certified of the death of St. Francis and of his sacred and hallowed stigmas: When St. Francis was nigh unto death, the devil at that time entered into a woman of the said town and tormented her cruelly, and withal made her speak with such subtle learning that she overcame all the wise men and learned doctors that came to dispute with her. And it fell out that the devil departed from her and left her free two days: and the third day he returned to her and afflicted he more cruelly than before. Rudolph, hearing this, goes to this woman, and asks of the devil that possessed her, for what cause he had departed from her two days, and then returned and tormented her more harshly than before. The devil answers, "When I left her, it was because I, with all my companions that are in these parts, assembled together and went in mighty force to the death-bed of the beggar Francis, to dispute with him and capture his soul; but his soul being surrounded and defended by a multitude of angels, greater than we were, was carried by them straight to heaven, and we went away confounded; so I restore and make up to this miserable woman what I let pass by during those two days." Then Rudolph conjured him in God's name to tell the whole truth of the holiness of St. Francis, who he said was dead, and of St. Clare that was alive. The devil answers, "Willy-nilly, I will tell thee what there is of truth in this. God the Father was so wroth against the sinners of this world that it seemed He would, in brief time, give His last judgment against men and women, and, if they did not amend, destroy them from the face of the earth. But Christ, His Son, praying for sinners, promised to renew His life and His Passion in a man, to wit, in Francis, the poor little one and a beggar, through whose life and teaching He would bring back many from all over the world to the way of truth, and many also to repentance. And now, to show forth to the world what He had wrought in St. Francis, He hath willed that the stigmas of His Passion that He had imprinted on St. Francis's body during his life, might, at his death, be seen and touched by many. Likewise, the Mother of Christ promised to renew her virginal purity and her humility in a woman, to wit, in Sister Clare, in such wise that by her example she would deliver many thousands of women from our hands. And thus God the Father, being softened, did delay His final sentence." Then Rudolph, desiring to know of a surety if the devil, that is the abode and father of lies, spake truth in these things, and especially as to the death of St. Francis, sent one, his trusty squire, to St. Mary of the Angels at Assisi, to learn if St. Francis were alive or dead; which squire, coming thither, found of a surety it was so, and returning to his lord, reported that on the very day and at the very hour that the devil had said, St. Francis had passed from this life.

XIII. *How Pope Gregory IX., doubting of the stigmas of St. Francis, was certified thereof.*

Setting aside all the miracles of the sacred and hallowed stigmas of St. Francis, which may be read in his legend, be it known, in conclusion of this fifth consideration, that St. Francis appeared one night to Pope Gregory IX., as he afterwards told, when he was in some doubt touching the wound in the side of St. Francis, and lifting up a little his right arm, discovered the wound in his side, and asked for a vase, and he had it brought to him; and St. Francis had it held under the wound in his side, and verily it seemed to the pope that he saw the vase filled to the brim with blood mingled with water, that issued from the wound: and thenceforth all doubt departed from him. Then, in council with all the cardinals, he approved the sacred and hallowed stigmas of St. Francis, and thereof gave special privilege to the friars by a sealed Bull; and this he did at Viterbo, in the eleventh year of his pontificate; and then, in the twelfth year, he issued another Bull yet more fully indited. Pope Nicholas III. likewise, and Pope Alexander, gave abundant privileges whereby whosoever denied the sacred and hallowed stigmas of St. Francis should be proceeded against as a heretic. And let this suffice as to the fifth consideration of the glorious, sacred, and hallowed stigmas of St. Francis our father. And may God give us the grace to follow after his life, in this world, so that, through the virtue of his glorious stigmas, we may merit salvation, and be with him in paradise. To the praise of Jesus Christ and of the poor little one, St. Francis. Amen.

The Life of Friar Juniper

I. How Friar Juniper cut the foot off a pig only to give it to a sick man.

Friar Juniper was one of the most chosen disciples and first companions of St. Francis. He was a man of deep humility and of great zeal and charity; and of him St. Francis said, speaking on a time with those holy companions of his, "He were a good friar that had so overcome himself and the world as Friar Juniper hath." One day, as he was visiting a sick friar at St. Mary of the Angels, all aflame with charity, he asked with great compassion, "Can I serve thee in aught?" The sick man answers, "Much comfort and great solace would it be to me if I might have a pig's foot." And Friar Juniper said, "Trust to me, for I will get one forthwith." And off he goes and snatches up a knife (I believe 'twas a kitchen knife) and goes in fervour of spirit about the wood, where certain pigs were feeding, and falling on one of them, cuts off a foot and runs away with it, leaving the pig maimed; he returns, washes and dresses and cooks this foot, and having well dished it up, carries the said foot to the sick man with much charity. And the sick friar ate thereof greedily, to the great consolation and joy of Friar Juniper, who told the story of the assaults he had made on the pig with great glee, to rejoice the heart of the sick man. Meanwhile the swineherd, that saw this friar cut the foot off, told over the whole story with much bitterness to his master. And he, being informed of this deed, comes to the friary and calls the friars hypocrites, thieves, false knaves, and wicked rogues, exclaiming, "Wherefore have ye cut off my pig's foot?" Hearing the great uproar he made, St. Francis and all the friars hurried along, and St. Francis made excuse for his friars, saying, with all humility, that they knew naught of the deed; and to pacify the man, promised to make amends for every wrong done to him. But for all this he was not to be appeased, but departed from the friary in great wrath, uttering many insults and threats, repeating over and over again how that they had wickedly cut off his pig's foot, and accepting neither excuses nor promises, he hastened away greatly scandalised. But St. Francis, full of prudence, bethought him the while the other friars stood all stupefied, and said in his heart, "Can Friar Juniper have done this thing out of indiscreet zeal?" So he bade call Friar Juniper secretly to him, and asked him, saying, "Hast thou cut off that pig's foot in the wood?" To whom Friar Juniper answered, right gleefully, and not as one having committed a fault, but as one that believed he had done a deed of great charity, and spake thus, "My sweet father, true it is I have cut off a foot from that said pig; and the cause thereof, my father, hear, if thou wilt, compassionately. I went out of charity to visit a certain friar that was sick"; and then he related the whole story in order, and added, "I tell thee this much, that considering the consolation this friar of ours felt, and the comfort he took from the said foot, had I cut off the feet of a hundred pigs as I did this one, I believe of a surety God would have looked on it as a good deed." Whereupon St. Francis, with righteous zeal, and with great bitterness, said, "O Friar Juniper, wherefore hast thou wrought this great scandal? Not without cause doth that man grieve, and thus rail against us; and perchance even now, as I speak, he is going about the city defaming us of evil, and good cause hath he. Wherefore I command thee, by holy obedience, run after him until thou overtake him, and cast thyself on the ground prostrate before him and confess thy fault, and promise to make him such full amends as that he shall have no cause to complain of us: for of a surety this hath been too monstrous an offence." Friar Juniper marvelled much at the aforesaid words, and was filled with amaze, being astonished that there should be any disturbance over such an act of charity; for these temporal things seemed to him naught, save in so far as they were charitably shared with one's neighbour. And Friar Juniper answered, "Fear not, father mine, for anon will I repay him and make him content. And wherefore should he be so troubled, seeing that this pig, whose foot I have cut off, was God's rather than his own, and a very charitable use hath been made thereof?" And so he sets forth at a run, and cometh up with this man that was raging beyond all measure and past all patience; and he told him how, and for what cause, he had cut off the said pig's foot, and withal in such great fervour and exultation and joy, even as one that had done him a great service for which he ought to be well rewarded. But the man, boiling with anger, and overcome with fury, heaped many insults on Friar Juniper, calling him a mad fellow and a fool, a big thief, and the worst of scoundrels. But Friar Juniper cared naught for these abusive words, and marvelled within himself, for he rejoiced in being reviled, and believed that he had not heard aright; for it seemed to him matter for rejoicing, and not for spite: and he told the story anew, and fell on the man's neck and embraced him and kissed him, and told him how that this thing had been done for charity's sake alone, inviting him and entreating him to give likewise what was left of the pig; and all with such charity and simplicity and humility that the man, being come to himself, fell on the ground before him, not without many tears; and asking pardon for the wrong he had said and done to these friars, he goes and takes this pig and kills it, and having cooked it, he carries it, with much devotion and many tears, to St. Mary of the Angels, and gives it to these holy friars to eat, out of compassion for the said wrong he had done them. And St. Francis, considering the simplicity and the patience under adversity of this said holy friar, said to his companions and to the others that stood by, "Would to God, my brethren, that I had a whole forest of such junipers!"

II. *An example of Friar Juniper's great power against the devil.*

That the devil was unable to endure the purity of the innocence of Friar Juniper and his deep humility appeareth in this. On a time, a man possessed with a devil, flung out of the way he was going, and, beyond his wont and with much fury, all of a sudden fled full seven miles by divers paths. And being overtaken and questioned by his kinsfolk who followed after him with bitter grief, wherefore in his flight he had taken such devious ways, he answered, "The reason is this: forasmuch as that fool Juniper was passing by that way, being unable to endure his presence, nor to encounter him, I fled through these woods." And certifying themselves of this truth, they found that Friar Juniper had passed along at that hour even as the devil had said. Wherefore St. Francis, when the possessed were brought to him that they might be healed, was wont to say, if the devils departed not straightway at his command, "If thou depart not forthwith from this creature I will bring Friar Juniper up against thee." And then the devil, fearing the presence of Friar Juniper and unable to endure the virtue and humility of St. Francis, would straightway depart.

III. *How at the instigation of the devil Friar Juniper was condemned to the gallows.*

On a time, the devil, desiring to affright Friar Juniper and to vex and trouble him, went to a most cruel tyrant named Nicholas that was then at war with the city of Viterbo, and said, "My lord, guard this your castle well, for anon a false traitor is to come hither, sent by the men of Viterbo, that he may slay you and set fire to your castle. And, in token of the truth of this, I give you these signs. He goeth about after the fashion of a poor simpleton, with garments tattered and patched, and with a ragged cowl falling on his shoulders; and with him he beareth an awl wherewith he is to kill you, and he hath a flint and steel with him to set fire to this castle. And if you find I speak not sooth, deal with me as you will." At these words Nicholas was filled with amaze and grew sore afraid, because he that spake these words seemed an honest fellow. And he commanded diligent watch and ward to be kept, and that if this man, with the aforesaid tokens came, he should be straightway brought into his presence. Meanwhile Friar Juniper comes alone, for because of his perfection he had licence to go forth and stay alone, even as it pleased him. Now Friar Juniper happened on certain evil youths that began to mock and abuse him shamefully; and at all these things he was not troubled, but rather led them to deride him the more. And when he came up to the door of the castle, the guards seeing him thus ill favoured and in a scant habit all in rags (for he had given part thereof to the poor by the way), and seeing he had no semblance of a friar minor, and that the tokens given them were manifestly apparent, dragged him, with great fury, before this tyrant Nicholas. And being searched by his servants for hidden weapons, they found an awl in his sleeve wherewith he was wont to mend his sandals; likewise they found a flint and steel, which he carried with him to kindle fire; for his time was his own, and oft he abode in woods and desert places. Nicholas, beholding these signs on him, in accord with the testimony of the accusing devil, commanded his servants to bind a rope about his neck, and this they did, with such great cruelty that the rope entered into his flesh; and then they put him on the rack and stretched his arms and racked his whole body without any mercy. And being asked who he was, he answered, "I am the greatest of sinners." And when asked if he had purposed to betray the castle and give it over to the men of Viterbo, he answered, "I am the greatest of traitors, and unworthy of any good thing." And asked if he purposed to kill Nicholas the tyrant with that awl and set fire to the castle, he answered that he would do even worse things and more monstrous, if God permitted. This Nicholas, maddened with rage, would suffer no more questioning of him, but, without any term or delay, condemned Friar Juniper, in his fury, as a traitor and manslayer, to be tied to the tail of a horse and dragged along the ground to the gallows and there straightway hanged by the neck. And Friar Juniper made no defence, but, as one that was content to suffer tribulation for love of God, was all joyous and glad. And the sentence of the tyrant being put in execution, Friar Juniper was bound by his feet to the tail of a horse and dragged along the ground; and he complained not, nor lamented, but as a gentle lamb led to the slaughter, went with all humility. At this spectacle and swift justice all the people ran to behold him executed thus hastily and thus cruelly: and they knew him not. But, as God willed, a good man that had seen Friar Juniper taken and thus quickly dragged to execution, runs to the house of the friars minor, and saith, "For love of God, I pray you, come quickly, for a poor wretch hath been taken and straightway condemned and led forth to die: come that at least he may give his soul into your hands; for he seemeth to me an honest fellow, and hath had no time wherein he may confess; lo, he is led forth to the gallows and seemeth to have no care for death, nor for the salvation of his soul: ah! I beseech you, deign to come quickly." The warden, that was a compassionate man, goes forthwith to provide for the salvation of his soul, and coming up to the place of execution, finds that the multitudes who had come to see were so increased that he could not pass through: and he stood and watched for an opening. And as he waited, he heard a voice in the midst of the crowd that cried, "Don't, don't, ye bad men; ye hurt my legs." At this voice a suspicion took the warden that this might be Friar Juniper, and in fervour of spirit he flung himself among them and tore aside the wrappings from the face of him; and there truly was Friar Juniper. Wherefore the compassionate warden was minded to take off his cloak to clothe Friar Juniper withal; but he, with joyous countenance and half laughing, said, "O warden, thou art fat, and it were an ill sight to see thy nakedness. I will not have it." Then the warden, with many tears, besought the hangmen and all the people for pity's sake to wait a while until he should go and entreat the tyrant for Friar Juniper, that he might grant him pardon. The hangmen and certain bystanders consenting thereto (for they truly believed he was a kinsman), the devout and compassionate warden goes to Nicholas the tyrant, and with bitter tears saith, "My lord, I am in such great bitterness and wonderment of soul that tongue cannot tell thereof, for it seems that the greatest sin and the greatest wickedness ever wrought in the days of our forefathers is this day being done in this city: and I believe it is done in ignorance." Nicholas hears the warden patiently, and asks of him, "What is the great wrong and evil deed committed this day in our city?" The warden answers, "My lord, you have condemned one of the holiest friars in the Order of St. Francis, for whom you have singular devotion, to a cruel death, and, as I verily believe, without cause." Saith Nicholas, "Now tell me, warden, who is this? for perchance knowing him not I have committed a great wrong." Saith the warden, "He that you have doomed to death is Friar Juniper, the companion of St. Francis." Nicholas the tyrant, stupefied, for he had heard of the fame and of the holy life of Friar Juniper, runs, astonished and all pale, together with the warden, and coming up to Friar Juniper looseth him from the tail of the horse and sets him free; then, in the presence of all the people, flings himself prostrate on the ground before Friar Juniper, and with many tears confesses his guilt, and bewails the wrong and the villainy he had done to this holy friar, and cried, "Verily I believe that the days of my evil life are numbered, since I have thus tortured the holiest of men without cause. God will appoint an end to my wicked life, and in brief time I shall die an evil death, albeit I have done this thing in ignorance." Friar Juniper freely forgave Nicholas the tyrant; but God suffered, ere a few days were passed, that this Nicholas the tyrant should end his life and die a very cruel death. And Friar Juniper departed, leaving all the people edified.

IV. *How Friar Juniper gave to the poor all he could lay hands on for love of God.*

So much pity and compassion had Friar Juniper for the poor that when he saw any one ill clad or naked, anon he would take off his tunic, and the cowl from his cloak, and give them to poor souls such as these. Therefore the warden commanded him, by obedience, not to give away the whole of his tunic, nor any part of his habit. Now it fell out that Friar Juniper, ere a few days had passed, happened on a poor creature, well-nigh naked, who asked alms of him for love of God, to whom he said with great compassion, "Naught have I, save my tunic, to give thee; and this my superior hath laid on me, by obedience, to give to no one; nay, nor even part of my habit; but if thou wilt take it off my back, I will not gainsay thee." He spake not to deaf ears, for straightway this poor man stripped him of his tunic and went his way with it, leaving Friar Juniper naked. And when he was back at the friary, he was asked where his tunic was, and he answered, "An honest fellow took it from my back and made off with it." And the virtue of pity increasing within him, he was not content with giving away his tunic, but likewise gave books and church ornaments and cloaks, or anything he could lay hands on, to the poor. And for this reason the friars never left things lying about the friary, because Friar Juniper gave all away for love of God and in praise if Him.

V. *How Friar Juniper stripped certain little bells from the altar, and gave them away for love of God.*

Friar Juniper, being on a time in Assisi, at the Nativity of Christ, engaged in deep meditation at the altar of the friary, which was richly decked and adorned, was asked by the sacristan to guard the said altar while he went to eat. And while he was in devout meditation, a poor little woman begged alms of him for love of God: to whom Friar Juniper thus answered, "Tarry a while and I will see if I can give thee aught from this altar so rich." Now there was on that altar a hanging of gold, richly and sumptuously adorned with little silver bells of great worth. Saith Friar Juniper, "These bells are a superfluity." So he takes a knife and cuts them all from the hanging, and gives them, out of compassion, to this poor little woman. No sooner had the sacristan eaten three or four mouthfuls than he remembered the ways of Friar Juniper, and was sore afeard lest out of his zealous charity he might work some mischief to the rich altar he had left in his charge. And straightway he rose from the table, in much dread, and went to the church and looked to see if any of the ornaments of the altar had been removed or taken away; and lo, he beheld the hanging hacked about and the bells cut off: whereat he was beyond all measure perturbed and scandalised. And Friar Juniper, beholding him thus agitated, saith, "Be not troubled about those bells, for I have given them to a poor woman that had very great need of them, and here they were of no use, save that they made a show of wordly pomp." Hearing this, the sacristan ran straightway through the church and about the whole city, in great affliction, to see if haply he might find her. But so far from finding her, he could not even find any one that had seen her. Returning to the friary, he took the hanging from the altar, in a great rage, and carried it to the general that was at Assisi, and said, "Father-general, I demand of you justice on Friar Juniper, who hath spoiled this hanging for me, that was the most precious thing in our sacristy; look now how he hath destroyed it and stripped off all the little silver bells, and he saith he hath given them away to a poor woman." The general answered, "Friar Juniper hath not done this, rather hath thy folly done it, for thou oughtest by this time to know his ways well; and I say unto thee, I marvel that he hath not given away all the rest; but none the less will I correct him for this fault." And having called all the friars together in

Chapter, he bade call Friar Juniper, and in the presence of the whole house rebuked him very harshly because of the aforesaid little bells; and he waxed so furious in his wrath, that by raising his voice so high he grew quite hoarse. Friar Juniper heeded those words little or naught, for he rejoiced in contumely and when he was well abased; but returning good for evil, he began to think only how he might find a remedy for his general's hoarseness. So having endured the general's scolding, Friar Juniper goes to the city and orders a good dish of porridge and butter; and a good part of the night being spent, he goes and lights a candle and comes back with this mess of porridge and takes it to the general's cell and knocks. The general opens to him, and, beholding him with a lighted candle in one hand and the dish of porridge in the other, asks softly, "What is this?" Friar Juniper answered, "My father, to-day, when you chid me for my faults, I perceived that your voice was growing hoarse, and, as I ween, from over-fatigue; therefore I bethought me of a remedy, and I had this porridge made for thee; pray eat thereof, for I tell thee it will ease thy chest and throat." Said the general, "What hour is this for thee to go disturbing folk?" Friar Juniper answered, "Look now, for thee 'tis made; prithee make no more ado, but eat thereof, for 'twill do thee much good." And the general, angry at the late hour and at his importunity, bade him begone, for at such an hour he had no desire to eat, and called him a base fellow and a rogue. Friar Juniper, seeing that neither prayer nor coaxing was of any avail, spake thus, "My father, since thou wilt not eat of this porridge that was made for thee, at least do me this favour: hold the candle for me, and I will eat it." And the pious and devout general, bearing in mind Friar Juniper's compassion and simplicity, and knowing that all this was done by him out of devotion, answered, "Look now, since thou wilt have it so, let us eat, thou and I, together." And both ate of this dish of porridge, because of his importunate charity. And much more were they refreshed by their devotion than by the food.

VI. *How Friar Juniper kept silence for six months.*

Friar Juniper, on a time, made a vow to keep silence for six months, in this manner. The first day, for love of the Heavenly Father. The second day, for love of His Son, Jesus Christ. The third day, for love of the Holy Ghost. The fourth day, for reverence of the most holy Virgin Mary; and so in this order, every day, for six months, he observed silence for love of some saint.

VII. *How to resist temptations of the flesh.*

Friar Giles and Friar Simon of Assisi, and Friar Ruffino and Friar Juniper, being on a time gathered together to discourse of God and of the salvation of the soul, Friar Giles said to the others, "How do ye with temptations to carnal sin?" Said Friar Simon, "I consider the baseness and turpitude of the sin, and then ariseth within me a great horror thereof, and thus I escape." Saith Friar Ruffino, "I cast me prostrate on the ground, and so fervently do I continue in prayer, beseeching God's mercy and the Mother of Jesus Christ, until I feel me wholly delivered therefrom." Friar Juniper answers, "When I feel the tumult of this devilish suggestion, straightway I run and close the door of my heart, and for defence of the fortress of my heart I occupy me in holy meditations and in holy desires; so that when the temptation cometh and knocketh at the door of my heart, I, as it were from within, answer, 'Begone! for the hostel is already full, and herein no more guests can enter;' and thus I suffer no thought to enter within my heart: whereat the devil, seeing himself vanquished, departeth as one discomfited, not only from me, but from the whole country." Friar Giles answers, "Friar Juniper, I hold with thee: against the enemy of the flesh one cannot fight, but only flee; for within, through the traitorous appetite, and without, through the senses of the body, the enemy feeleth himself so mighty that one cannot overcome him save by flight. And, therefore, he that would fight otherwise seldom hath the victory after the toil of battle. Flee, then, from vice, and thou shalt be victorious."

VIII. *How Friar Juniper abased himself to the glory of God.*

On a time Friar Juniper, desiring truly to abase himself, stripped him of all save his breeches; and having made a bundle of his habit, placed his clothes on his head, and entering Viterbo, went to the market-place to be derided. And standing there, the children and youths of the city, deeming him bereft of his senses, reviled him sorely, casting much mire at him, and pelting him with stones. Hither and thither they rushed him, with many mocking words; and thus persecuted and scorned, he remained for the greater part of the day: then he went to the friary. And when the friars beheld him they were full of wrath, most of all for that he had come through the whole city with his bundle on his head; and they rebuked him very severely, uttering great threats. And one said, "Let us cast him into prison." And another said, "Let us hang him." And the others said, "We cannot inflict too great a punishment for so evil an example as this friar hath made of himself this day and of all the Order." And Friar Juniper, right glad, answered with great humility, "Ye say well, for I am worthy of all these pains and many more."

IX. *How Friar Juniper, to abase himself, played at see-saw.*

On a time as Friar Juniper was journeying to Rome, where the fame of his holiness was already noised abroad, many Romans, of their great devotion, went out to meet him; and Friar Juniper, beholding so many people coming, imagined how he might turn their devotion into sport and mockery. Now there were two children playing at see-saw, to wit, they had placed one log of wood across another, and each of them sat at his end of the log and see-sawed up and down. Away goes Friar Juniper and takes off one of these children from the log, and mounting thereon he begins to play see-saw. Meanwhile the people came up and marvelled to see Friar Juniper see-sawing, yet, with great devotion, they greeted him and waited for him to end the game of see-saw, in order to accompany him honourably as far as the friary. And Friar Juniper heeded little their greetings, their reverence, and their waiting, but held very diligently to his see-sawing. And waiting thus a long space, certain of them began to weary thereof, and said, "What a blockhead!" Others, knowing his ways, waxed in great devotion. Nevertheless all departed and left Friar Juniper on his see-saw. And when they were all gone, Friar Juniper was left wholly comforted, because he saw that certain of them had mocked at him. He then set forth and entered Rome, and with all meekness and humility came to the house of the friars minor.

X. *How Friar Juniper once cooked enough food to last the friars a fortnight.*

Friar Juniper, being on a time left alone in a small friary, inasmuch as all the friars, for a certain reasonable cause, had to go out from the friary, the warden saith to him, "Friar Juniper, all we have to go abroad; look to it, therefore, that when we return thou have some dish ready cooked for the refreshment of the friars." Friar Juniper answers, "Right gladly, leave it to me!" And all the friars being gone forth, as hath been told, Friar Juniper saith, "What unprofitable care is this, for one friar to be lost in the kitchen and far away from all prayer! Truly, if I am left here to cook, this time will I cook so much that all the friars, and even more, shall have enough to eat for a fortnight." And so he goes very diligently to the city and begs several great cooking pots and pans, and procures fresh meat and salt, fowls and eggs and pot herbs, and begs much firewood, and puts everything on the fire, to wit, the fowls with their feathers on, and eggs in their shells, and all the other things one after the other. When the friars came home, one that was ware of Friar Juniper's simplicity entered the kitchen and beheld many great pots and pans on a raging fire. And he sat him down and looked on with wonderment and said no word, but watched with what great diligence Friar Juniper went about his cooking. Now the fire was very fierce, and since he could not get very close to his pots to skim them, he took a wooden board and bound it closely to his body with his cord, and then leapt from one pot to another, so that it was a joy to behold. Thinking over these things, with great delight, this friar comes from the kitchen and seeks the other friars, and saith, "Friar Juniper is making a wedding feast, I can tell you!" But the friars took this for a jest. And Friar Juniper lifted his pots from the fire and bade ring the bell for supper. And the friars, having taken their places at table, Friar Juniper comes into the refectory, all ruddy with his toil and the heat of the fire, with that meal of his, and saith to the friars, "Eat well, and then let us all to prayers; and let no one have any care about cooking for days to come, because I have cooked so much to-day that I shall have enough for more than a fortnight." And he served up this hotch-potch to the friars at table, and there is no hog in the whole of Rome hungry enough to have eaten thereof. Friar Juniper, to push his wares, cries up his cooking, but seeing that the other friars eat naught thereof, saith, "Now look you, fowls such as these are comforting to the brain, and this mess will keep the body moist, for 'tis right good." And while the friars were lost in wonderment and devotion at the simplicity and devotion of Friar Juniper, lo, the warden, angry at such folly and at the waste of so much good food, rebuked Friar Juniper very harshly. Then Friar Juniper dropped straightway on his knees before the warden and humbly confessed his fault to him and to all the friars, saying, "I am the worst of men: such a one committed such a crime, and therefore his eyes were plucked out, but I was more worthy thereof than he: such a one was hanged for his sins, but I deserve it far more for my wicked deeds: and now have I wasted so much of God's bounty and of the good things of the Order." And thus he departed, all sorrowing, and all that day was not seen of any friar. And then the warden said, "My dearest friars, I would that every day this friar should spoil, even as he hath now, as many more of our good things, if we had them, solely for our edification; for he hath done this thing out of his great simplicity and charity."

XI. *How Friar Juniper went on a time to Assisi for his confusion.*

On a time, when Friar Juniper was dwelling in the vale of Spoleto, seeing that there was a solemn festival at Assisi, and that much people were going thither with great devotion, a desire took him to go to that festival: and hear how he went. Friar Juniper stripped himself to his breeches, and thus fared forth, passing through the midst of the city of Spoleto and comes to the friary. The friars, much perturbed and scandalised, rebuked him very harshly, calling him a mad fellow and a fool that brought confusion to the Order of St. Francis; and they would have put him in chains as a madman. And the general, that was then in the house, bade call Friar Juniper and all the friars, and in the presence of the whole community gave him a hard and bitter reproof. And after many words of vigorous condemnation, he spake thus to Friar Juniper, "Thy fault is such, and so heavy, that I know not what penance to lay upon thee." Friar Juniper answers, even as one that rejoiced in his own confusion, "Father, I will tell thee: for penance bid me return, in the same guise as I came hither, to the place whence I set forth to come to this festival."

XII. *How Friar Juniper was rapt in God as he was attending mass.*

Friar Juniper, on a time, while hearing mass with great devotion, was rapt in God through the elevation of his mind, and for a long space. And being left in the room, far away from the other friars, he began, when he came to himself, to say with great devotion, "O my brethren, who is there in this life so noble that would not fain carry a bushel of dung through the whole earth, if a house filled with gold were given to him?" And he said, "Ah me! wherefore are we not willing to endure a little shame, in order that we may win the blessed life?"

XIII. *Of the grief that Friar Juniper felt at the death of his companion, Friar Amazialbene.*

Friar Juniper had a companion friar that he dearly loved, whose name was Amazialbene. And truly had this friar the virtue of highest patience and obedience; for if he were beaten the whole day long never did he utter one single world of lamentation or complaint. Often was he sent to friaries where the whole community was ill to get on with, and from whom he suffered much persecution; and this he endured very patiently and without murmuring. He, at the bidding of Friar Juniper, was wont to laugh and to weep. Now, as it pleased God, this Friar Amazialbene died in the highest repute; and Friar Juniper, hearing of his death, felt such great sadness of spirit as he never in his life had felt for the loss of any material thing. And he showed forth outwardly the great bitterness that was within him, and said, "Woe is me! poor wretch! now no good thing is left to me, and all the world is out of joint at the death of my sweet and most beloved brother Amazialbene. Were it not that I should have no peace with the other friars, I would go to his grave and take away his head, and with the skull I would make me two bowls: and from one I would ever eat for devout memory of him; and from the other would I drink whenever I were athirst or had desire to drink."

XIV. *Of the hand that Friar Juniper saw in the air.*

Friar Juniper, being on a time at prayer, and haply thinking on the great works he would do, himseemed to behold a hand in the air, and he heard with his bodily ears a voice that spake to him thus, "O Friar Juniper, without this hand thou canst do naught." Whereat he straightway arose and lifted up his eyes to heaven and ran through the friary crying with a loud voice, "True indeed! True indeed!" And this he repeated for a good space.

XV. *How St. Francis bade Friar Leo wash the stone.*

When St. Francis was speaking with Friar Leo on the mount of La Verna, St. Francis said, "Friar, little sheep, wash this stone with water." And Friar Leo was quick to wash the stone with water. Saith St. Francis with great joy and gladness, "Wash it with wine." And 'twas done. Saith St. Francis, "Wash it with oil." And this was done. Saith St. Francis, "Friar, little sheep, wash that stone with balm." Friar Leo answers, "O sweet Father, how shall I obtain balm in this wilderness?" St. Francis answered, "Know, friar, thou little sheep of Christ, that this is the stone whereon Christ sat when He appeared to me here: therefore have I bidden thee four times; wash it, and hold thy peace, for Christ hath promised me four singular graces for my Order. The first is, that all those who shall love my Order with all their hearts, and all steadfast friars, shall, by grace divine, make a good end. The second is, that the persecutors of this holy Order shall be notably punished. The third is, that no evil-doer who remaineth in his perversity can endure long in this Order. The fourth is, that this Order shall endure until the last judgment."

The Life of the Blessed Friar Giles

The Companion of St. Francis

I. *How Friar Giles and three companions were received into the Order of the friars minor.*

Forasmuch as the example of holy men on the minds of devout hearers, is to make them despise fleeting pleasures and to beget a desire for eternal salvation, I will recite, to the honour of God and of His most reverend Mother, Madonna St. Mary, and for the profit of all hearers, certain words touching the work that the Holy Ghost wrought in our holy Friar Giles, who, while yet wearing the secular habit, was touched by the Holy Ghost, and began to ponder in his heart how in all his works he might please God alone. In those days St. Francis, a new herald of God, sent as an exemplar of the life of humility and of holy penitence, drew and led, two years after his conversion, Master Bernard, a man adorned with wondrous prudence and very rich in worldly goods, and likewise Peter Cattani, to the observance of the gospel and of holy poverty. And they, by the counsel of St. Francis, gave away all their worldly treasures to the poor, for love of God, and put on the glory of meekness and of gospel perfection with the habit of the friars minor; and they, with the greatest fervour, promised to keep their vows all the days of their life: and even so did they with great perfection. A week after their conversion and the distribution of their goods, Friar Giles, while yet in the secular habit, beholding such contempt of earthly things in these two noble knights of Assisi that the whole city was in amaze thereat, went betimes on the day following (that was the feast of St. George in the year one thousand two hundred and nine) to the church of St. Gregory, where the convent of St. Clare was, all enkindled with divine love and careful for his salvation. And having prayed, he had a great desire to behold St. Francis, and went towards the lazar-house, where he was dwelling apart in a hovel, in great humility, with Friar Bernard and Friar Cattani. And being come to a crossway, and knowing not whither to turn, he directed his prayer to Christ, our precious Guide, who led him to the said hovel by the straight way. And while he was pondering on the reason of this his coming, St. Francis met him as he was returning from the wood wherein he had gone to pray; whereupon, anon, he fell on his knees on the ground before St. Francis, and humbly besought him to receive him into his company, for love of God. St. Francis, gazing on the devout aspect of Friar Giles, answered and said, "Dearest brother, God hath wrought in thee a very great grace. If the emperor came to Assisi, and would make one of the men of this city his knight, or private chamberlain, ought he not to rejoice greatly? How much greater joy oughtest thou to receive in that God hath chosen thee for His knight and most beloved servant, to observe the perfect way of the holy gospel? Therefore, be steadfast and constant in the vocation whereto God hath called thee." And he takes him by the hand and raises him up, and leads him into the aforesaid hovel; and he calls Friar Bernard and saith, "Our Lord and Master hath sent us a good friar, wherefore rejoice we all in the Lord and eat together in charity." And after they had eaten, St. Francis went with this Giles to Assisi, to get cloth to make Friar Giles's habit. And they found a poor woman by the way, that begged alms of them for love of God; and knowing not how to minister to the poor little woman's needs, St. Francis turned to Friar Giles with an angelic countenance and said, "For love of God, dearest brother, let us give this cloak to the poor creature." And Friar Giles obeyed the holy father with so ready a heart, that himseemed to behold that alms fly forthwith to heaven; and Friar Giles flew with it straightway to heaven, whereat he felt unspeakable joy, and a renewed heart within him. And St. Francis, having procured the cloth and made the habit, received Friar Giles into the Order; and he was one of the most glorious religious in the contemplative life the world had ever seen in those days. After the reception of Friar Giles, anon St. Francis went with him into the Marches of Ancona, singing with him and magnifying with praise the Lord of heaven and earth; and he said to Friar Giles, "Son, our Order shall be like unto the fisher that casteth his net into the water and taketh a multitude of fishes: and the big fish he holds, and puts the little ones back into the waters." Friar Giles marvelled at this prophecy, because there were not yet in the Order more than St. Francis and three friars; and albeit St. Francis had not preached to the people in public places, yet as he went by the way he admonished and corrected both men and women, saying, with loving simplicity, "Love and fear God, and do fitting penance for your sins." And Friar Giles said, "Do that which my spiritual father telleth you, for he speaketh excellently well."

II. *How Friar Giles went to St. James the Great.*

Once in the course of time, Friar Giles went, by leave of St. Francis, to St. James the Great in Galicia; and in the whole of that way only once did he satisfy his hunger, by reason of the great poverty of all that land. Wherefore, asking alms and finding none that would give him charity, he happened by chance that evening on a threshing floor, where some few grains of beans were left: these he gathered up, and these were his supper. And here he slept that night, for he was ever fain to abide in solitary places, far from the haunts of men, that he might the better give himself up to prayer and to vigils. And in that supper he was so greatly comforted by God, that if he had eaten of divers viands he deemed he would not have eaten so full a meal. And journeying on, he finds by the way a poor man that craves alms, for love of God; and Friar Giles, most charitable of men, having naught save his habit to cover his body, cut off the cowl from his cloak, and gave it to that poor man for love of God; and thus, sans cowl, he journeyed for twenty days together. And returning by way of Lombardy, he was hailed by a man, to whom he went right gladly, thinking to receive some alms of him: and stretching forth his hand, this man put a pair of dice therein, and invited him to play a game. Friar Giles answered, very humbly, "God forgive thee this, my son." And so journeying through the world, he was much mocked at, and endured all these things meekly.

III. *Of Friar Giles's way of life when he went to the Holy Sepulchre.*

Friar Giles went, by leave of St. Francis, to visit the Holy Sepulchre of Christ, and came to the port of Brindisi, and there stayed over many days, for there was no ship ready. And Friar Giles, desiring to live by his labour, begged a pitcher, and filling it with water, went about the city crying, "Who lacks water?" And for his toil he received bread and things needful for the life of the body, both for himself and for his companion. And then he crossed the seas, and visited the Holy Sepulchre of Christ, and the other holy places, with great devotion. And journeying back, he abode many days in the city of Ancona; and forasmuch as he was wont to live by the labour of his hands, he made baskets of rushes and sold them, not for money, but for bread for himself and for his companion; and he carried the dead to burial for the aforesaid price. And when these things failed him, he returned to the table of Jesus Christ, asking alms from door to door. And thus, with much toil and poverty, he came back to St. Mary of the Angels.

IV. *How Friar Giles praised obedience more than prayer.*

A friar on a time was at prayer in his cell, and his warden bade tell him, by obedience, to go questing for alms. Whereupon he straightway went to Friar Giles and said, "Father mine, I was at prayer, and the warden hath bidden me go for bread, and meseems 'twere better to remain at prayer." Friar Giles answered, "My son, hast thou not yet learned or known what prayer is? True prayer is to do the will of our superior; and it is a token of great pride in him who, having put his neck under the yoke of holy obedience, refuseth it for any cause, in order to work his own will, even though it may seem to him that he is working more perfectly. The perfectly obedient religious is like unto a knight mounted on a mighty steed, by whose power he passeth fearlessly through the midst of the fray; and contrariwise, the disobedient and complaining and unwilling religious is like unto one that is mounted on a lean and infirm and vicious horse, because with a little striving he is slain or taken by the enemy. I say unto thee, were there a man of such devotion and exaltation of mind that he spake with angels, and while thus speaking he were called by his superior, straightway he ought to leave his converse with the angels and obey his superior."

V. *How Friar Giles lived by the labour of his hands.*

Friar Giles, being on a time in the friary at Rome, was minded to live by bodily toil, even as he was ever wont to do since he entered the Order, and he wrought in this wise: Betimes, in the morning, he heard mass with much devotion, then he went to the wood that was eight miles distant from Rome and carried a faggot of wood back on his shoulders, and sold it for bread, or aught else to eat. One time, among others, when he was returning with a load of wood, a woman asked to buy it; and being agreed on the price, he carried it to her house. The woman, notwithstanding the bargain, gave him much more than she had promised, for she saw he was a religious. Saith Friar Giles, "Good woman, I would not that the sin of avarice overcame me, therefore I will not take a greater price than I bargain with thee." And not only would he take no more, but he took only the half of the price agreed upon, and went his way; wherefore that woman conceived a very great devotion for him. Friar Giles did any honest work for hire, and always gave heed to holy honesty; he gave a hand to gather olives and to tread the wine-press for the peasants. Standing on a day in the market-place, a certain man sought hands to beat down his walnuts, and begged one to beat them down for him, at a price; but he made excuse, saying it was very far away, and the trees were very hard to climb. Saith Friar Giles, "Friend, if thou wilt give me part of the walnuts I will come with thee and beat them down." The bargain made, he went his way, and, first making the sign of the holy cross, he climbed up to beat a tall walnut tree with great fear. And after he had beaten the branches thereof so many walnuts were due to him for his share that he could not carry them away in his lap. Wherefore he took off his habit and bound up the sleeves and the cowl, and made a sack thereof, and having filled this his habit with walnuts, he lifted it on to his shoulder and carried the walnuts to Rome; and he gave all to the poor, with great joy, for love of God. When the corn was cut, Friar Giles went with the other poor folk to glean some ears; and if any one offered him a handful of corn he answered, "Brother, I have no granary wherein to store it." And the ears of wheat he gleaned he gave away, more often than not, for love of God. Seldom did Friar Giles work the whole day through, for he always bargained to have some space of time to say the canonical hours and not fail in his mental prayers. Once on a time Friar Giles went to the fountain of San Sisto to draw water for the monks, and a man asked him for a drink. Friar Giles answers, "And how shall I carry this vessel half filled to the monks?" And this man angrily spake many words of contumely and abuse to Friar Giles: and Friar Giles returned to the monks grieving much. Begging a large vessel anon he returned to the said fountain for water, and finding that man again, said to him, "My friend, take and drink as much as thy soul desireth, and be not angry, for methinks 'tis a base thing to take water that hath been drunk of, to those holy monks." He, pricked and constrained by the charity and humility of Friar Giles, confessed his fault, and from that hour forth held him in great veneration.

VI. *How Friar Giles was miraculously provided for in a dire need when, because of the heavy snow, he could not quest for alms.*

Friar Giles, when dwelling with a cardinal at Rome, forasmuch as he had not the peace of mind he desired, said to the cardinal, as the time of the greater lent drew nigh, "My father, with your leave I would go, for my peace, with this my companion, to keep this lent in some solitary place." The cardinal answers, "Prithee, my dearest friar, whither wouldst thou go? There is a sore famine in these parts, and ye are strangers. Ah! be pleased to remain at my court, for to me 'twill be a singular grace to have you given whatsoever ye may need for love of God." But Friar Giles was minded to go forth, and he went out of Rome to the top of a high mountain where in days of old stood a town, and he found there a deserted church that was called St. Lawrence, and therein he and his companion entered, and remained in prayer and in many meditations; and for that they were not known, small reverence or devotion was shown to them. Wherefore they suffered great want; and moreover there fell a great snowstorm that endured many days. They could not issue from the church, and naught was sent them to live upon, and of themselves they had no store; and so they remained, shut in for three mortal days. Friar Giles, seeing he could not live by his labour, and for alms could not go forth, said to his companion, "My dearest brother, let us call on our Lord Jesus Christ with a loud voice, that of His pity He may provide for us in this sore extremity and need; for certain monks, being in dire need, have called on God, and divine providence did provide for them in their needs." And after the example of these, they betook them to prayer, and besought God, with all affection, that He would provide a remedy in so sore a need. God, that is all-pitiful, had regard to their faith and devotion and simplicity and fervour in this wise: A certain man was looking towards the church where Friar Giles and his companion were, and being inspired by God, said within himself, "Haply in that church there be some good souls doing penance and, in this season of heavy snows, have naught for their needs, and by reason thereof may die of hunger." And urged by the Holy Ghost he said, "Certes, I will go and learn if my foreboding be true or not." And he took some loaves and a vessel of wine and set forth on his journey, and with very great difficulty he won his way to the aforesaid church, where he found Friar Giles and his companion devoutly engaged in prayer; and they were so ravaged by hunger that in their aspect they had the semblance of dead rather than of living men. He had great compassion on them, and having refreshed and comforted them, he returned and told his neighbours of the extreme poverty and need of these friars, and besought them, for love of God, to provide for them; whereupon many, after the example of this man, brought them bread and wine and other necessaries to eat, for love of God; and through all that lent they ordered among themselves that the needs of these friars should be provided for. And Friar Giles, considering the great mercy of God and the charity of these folk, said to his companion, "My dearest brother, but now have we prayed to God to provide for us in our need, and we have been heard; therefore it is meet that we return thanks and glory to Him and pray for those that have fed us with their alms, and for all Christian folk." And by his great fervour and devotion, so much grace was given by God to Friar Giles that many, by his example, forsook this blind world, and many others that were not called to take up the religious life did very great penance in their homes.

VII. *Touching the day of the holy Friar Giles's death.*

On St. George's eve, at the hour of matins, these fifty-two years past, the soul of Friar Giles, for that he had received the habit of St. Francis in the first days of the month, was received by God into the glory of paradise, to wit, on the feast of St. George.

VIII. *How a holy man being at prayer saw the soul of Friar Giles go to life everlasting.*

A good man being at prayer when Friar Giles passed from this life, saw his soul, together with a multitude of souls, come out of purgatory and ascend to heaven; and he beheld Jesus Christ come forth to meet the soul of Friar Giles, and with a multitude of angels, and with all those souls ascend with sweet melody into the glory of paradise.

IX. *How the soul of a friar preacher's friend was delivered from the pains of purgatory through the merits of Friar Giles.*

When Friar Giles lay sick so that in a few days he died, a Dominican friar fell sick unto death. And he had a friend that was also a friar, who, seeing him draw nigh unto death, said to the sick man, "My brother, I desire, if it be God's will, that after thy death thou return to me and tell me in what state thou mayst be." The sick friar promised to return whensoever it might be possible. The sick man died on the self-same day as Friar Giles, and after his death he appeared to the living friar preacher, and said, "'Twas God's will that I should keep my promise to thee." Saith the living friar to the dead, "How fares it with thee?" The dead friar answered, "'Tis well with me, for I died on a day whereon a holy friar minor passed from this life whose name was Friar Giles, and to him for his great holiness Christ granted that he should lead all the souls that were in purgatory to holy paradise, among which souls was I, in great torments; and through the merits of the holy Friar Giles I am delivered therefrom." This said, he forthwith vanished; and the friar revealed that vision to no man. This said friar fell sick; and anon deeming that God had smitten him because he had not revealed the virtue and the glory of Friar Giles, he sent for the friars minor, and there came to him five couples of them; and having called them, together with the preaching friars, he declared the aforesaid vision to them with great devotion, and seeking very diligently they found that on that self-same day these twain had passed from this life.

X. *How God had given certain graces to Friar Giles and of the day of his death.*

Friar Bonaventure of Bagnoreggio was wont to say of Friar Giles that God had given and vouchsafed singular grace to him for all those that commended themselves to him, with devout intent, in the things that appertained to the soul. He wrought many miracles during his life and after his death, as appeareth from his legend; and he passed from this life to supernal glory, in the year of our Lord one thousand two hundred and fifty-two, on the day of the feast of St. George; and he is buried at Perugia in the house of the friars minor.

The Sayings of Friar Giles

HERE BEGINNETH THE CHAPTERS OF CERTAIN DOCTRINES AND
NOTABLE SAYINGS OF FRIAR GILES

I. *Chapter of vices and virtues.*

The grace of God and the virtues are the way and the ladder whereby we ascend to heaven; but the vices and the sins are the way and the ladder whereby we descend to the depths of hell. Vices and sins are poison and deadly venom; but virtues and good works are healing treacle.[13] One grace bringeth and draweth after it another. Grace desireth not to be praised, and vice cannot endure to be despised. The mind is at peace and resteth in humility: patience is her daughter. Holy purity of heart seeth God; but true devotion savoureth him. If thou lovest, thou shalt be loved. If thou servest, thou shalt be served. If thou fearest, thou shalt be feared. If thou bearest thyself well towards others, it behoves that others bear themselves well towards thee. But blessed is he that truly loveth and desireth not to be loved. Blessed is he that serveth and desireth not to be served. Blessed is he that feareth and desireth not to be feared. Blessed is he that beareth himself well towards others, and desireth not that others bear themselves well

---

[13] Compare Chaucer, "Christ which that is to every harm treacle." The Venetians were famed for their skilful preparation of this medicinal compound, which was universally regarded in the Middle Ages as an antidote against snake bites and other poisons.

towards him. But forasmuch as these things are exceeding high, and of great perfection, the fool can neither know them nor attain to them. Three things are exceeding high and useful, and he that shall have attained to them shall never fall. The first is, if thou endure willingly, and with gladness, every tribulation that shall befall thee, for love of Jesus Christ. The second is, if thou humble thyself every day in all things thou doest, and in all things thou seest. The third is, if thou love steadfastly, and with all thy heart, that highest celestial and invisible good, which cannot be seen with mortal eyes. Those things that are most despised and most reviled by worldly men are verily most acceptable and pleasing to God and to His saints; and those things that are most honoured and most loved and are most pleasing to worldly men, those are most despised and scorned and most hated by God and by His saints. This foul unseemliness proceedeth from the ignorance and the wickedness of men, for the wretched man loveth most those things he should hate, and hateth those things he should love. Once on a time, Friar Giles asked another friar, saying, "Tell me, dearest, is thine a good soul?" That friar answered, "This I know not." Then said Friar Giles, "My brother, I would have thee to know that holy contrition and holy humility and holy charity and holy devotion and holy joy make the good and blessed soul."

II. *Chapter of faith.*

All things whatsoever that can be thought in the heart or told with the tongue, or seen with the eyes, or touched with the hands—all are as naught in respect of, and in comparison with, those things that cannot be thought, nor seen, nor touched. All the saints and all the sages that have passed away, and all those that are in this present life, and all that shall come after us, that spake or wrote, or that shall speak or write, of God, ne'er told nor e'er can tell of God so much as a grain of millet would be in respect of, or in comparison with, the heavens and the earth, nay, even a thousand thousandfold less. For all scripture that speaketh of God, speaketh of Him with stammering voice, as the mother doth who prattles with her child, that could not understand her words if she spoke in other fashion. Friar Giles said, on a time, to a worldly judge, "Believest thou that the gifts of God are great?" The judge answered, "Yea, I believe." Whereat Friar Giles said, "I will show thee how that thou believest not faithfully." And then he said to him, "What price is all thou possessest in this world worth?" The judge answered, "'Tis worth, perchance, a thousand pounds." Then said Friar Giles, "Wouldst thou give those thy possessions for ten thousand pounds?" The judge answered, without delay, "Verily, that would I." And Friar Giles said, "Certain it is that all the possessions of this world are as naught in respect to heavenly things; therefore, why givest thou not these thy possessions to Christ, that thou mayst buy those possessions that are celestial and eternal?" Then that judge, wise with the foolish wisdom of the world, made answer to the pure and simple Friar Giles, "God hath filled thee with wise and divine foolishness. Thinkest thou, Friar Giles, that there lives a man whose outward works accord with all he believes in his inmost heart?" Friar Giles answered, "Look now, my dearest, it is very truth that all the saints have striven to fulfil by their works those things they were able to comprehend or to know were the will of God, according to their power. And all those things they were not able to fulfil by their works, these they fulfilled by the holy desire of their will; in such wise, that what was lacking in their works by reason of their defect of power, this they fulfilled by the desire of their soul: and they were not found wanting." Yet again Friar Giles said, "If any man could be found of perfect faith, in short time he would attain to the perfect state, whereby full assurance of his salvation would be given to him. What hurt or what ill could any temporal adversity in this present life do to that man who, with steadfast faith, awaiteth this eternal and supreme and highest good? And the miserable man, that awaiteth everlasting torment, what could any prosperity, or temporal possession, in this world avail him? Yet how grievous a sinner soever a man may be, let him not despair, while he yet liveth, of the infinite mercy of God; for there is no tree in this world so full of thorns, nor so knotted nor so gnarled, but that men cannot plane it and polish it and adorn it, and make it fair to look upon. Even so, there is no man in this world so sunk in iniquity, nor so great a sinner, but that God can convert him and adorn him with peculiar grace, and with many virtuous gifts."

III. *Chapter of holy humility.*

No man can attain to any knowledge or understanding of God, save by the virtue of holy humility: for the straight way upward is the straight way downward. All the perils and the great falls that have come to pass in this world have come about for no cause save the lifting up of the head, to wit, of the mind, in pride; and this is proven by the fall of the devil, that was cast out of heaven; and by the fall of our first parent, Adam, that was driven out of paradise through the exaltation of the head, to wit, through disobedience; and again by the Pharisee, whereof Christ speaketh in the gospel, and by many other examples. And so contrariwise: for all the great and good things that have e'er come to pass in this world, have come to pass through the abasement of the head, to wit, through the humility of the mind, even as is proven by the blessed and most humble Virgin Mary, and by the publican, and by the holy thief on the cross, and by many other examples in the scriptures. And, therefore, it were well if we could find some great and heavy weight that we might ever hang about our necks, in order that it might ever bear us down, to wit, that it might ever make us humble ourselves. A friar asked Friar Giles, "Tell me, father, how shall we flee from this sin of pride?" To whom Friar Giles answered, "My brother, be persuaded of this: never hope to be able to flee from pride, except thou first place thy mouth where thou hast set thy feet; but if thou wilt consider well the blessings of God, then shalt thou know that of thy duty thou art held to bow thy head. And, again, if thou wilt think much on thy faults and on thy manifold offences against God, most of all wilt thou have cause to humble thyself. But woe unto those that would be honoured for their wickedness! One degree in humility hath he risen that knoweth himself to be the enemy of his own good; another degree in humility is to render to others those things that are theirs, and not to appropriate them to ourselves, to wit, that every good thing and every virtue a man findeth in himself, he ought not to own it to himself, but to God alone, from whom proceedeth every grace and every virtue and every good thing; but all sin or passion of the soul, or whatsoever vice a man find in himself, this should he own to himself, since it proceedeth from himself and from his own wickedness, and not from others. Blessed is that man that knoweth himself, and deemeth himself vile in the sight of God, and even so in the sight of men. Blessed is he that ever judgeth himself and condemneth himself, and not others, for he shall not be judged at that dread and last judgment eternal. Blessed is he that shall bend diligently under the yoke of obedience and under the judgment of others, even as the holy apostles did before and after they received the Holy Spirit." Likewise said Friar Giles, "He that would gain and possess perfect peace and rest must needs account every man his superior; he must ever hold himself the subject and inferior of others. Blessed is that man who in his deeds and in his words desireth not to be seen or known, save only in that unalloyed being, and in that simple adornment which God created and adorned him with. Blessed is the man that knoweth how to treasure up and hide divine revelations and consolations, for there is nothing so hidden but that God shall reveal it, when it pleaseth Him. If a man were the most perfect and the holiest man in the world, and yet deemed and believed himself the most miserable of sinners and the vilest wretch on the earth—therein is true humility. Holy humility knoweth not how to prate, and the blessed fear of God knoweth not how to speak." Said Friar Giles, "Methinks humility is like unto a thunderbolt; for even as the bolt maketh a terrible crash, breaking, crushing, and burning all that it findeth in its path, and then naught of that bolt is found, so, in like manner, humility smiteth and scattereth and burneth and con-sumeth every wickedness and every vice and every sin; and yet is found to be naught in itself. The man that possesseth humility findeth grace in the sight of God, through that humility, and perfect peace with his neighbour."

IV. *Chapter of the holy fear of God.*

He that feareth naught showeth that he hath naught to lose. The holy fear of God ordaineth, governeth, and ruleth the soul and maketh it to come to a state of grace. If any man possess any grace or divine virtue, holy fear is that which preserveth it. And he that hath not yet gained virtue or grace, holy fear maketh him to gain it. The holy fear of God is the bringer of divine graces, for it maketh the soul, wheresoever she abideth, to attain quickly to holy virtue and divine graces. All creatures that have fallen into sin would never have fallen if they had had the holy fear of God. But this holy gift of fear is given only to the perfect; for the more perfect a man is, the more godfearing and humble he is. Blessed is he that knoweth he is in a dungeon in this world, and ever remembereth how grievously he hath offended his Lord. A man ought ever to fear pride with a great fear, lest it thrust against him and make him fall from the state of grace wherein he standeth; for a man can never stand secure being girt about with enemies; and our enemies are the seductions of this miserable world and our own flesh that, together with the devil, is ever the enemy of the soul. A man hath need of greater fear lest his own wickedness overcome him and beguile him than of any other of his enemies. It is impossible that a man can rise and ascend to any divine grace, or virtue, or persevere therein, without holy fear. He that feareth not God goeth in danger of perishing, and in yet greater peril of everlasting perdition. The fear of God maketh a man to obey humbly, and maketh him bow down his head under the yoke of obedience; and the greater the fear a man hath, the more fervently doth he worship. Not a little gift is prayer to whosoever it is given. The virtuous words of men, however great they may appear to me, are not therefore accounted nor rewarded according to our measure, but according to the measure and good pleasure of God; for God regardeth not the sum of our toils, but the sum of our love and humility. Therefore, the better part for us is to love always, and fear with great humility, and never put trust in ourselves for any good thing; ever having suspicion of those thoughts that are begotten in the mind under the semblance of good.

V. *Chapter of holy patience.*

He that with steadfast humility and patience suffereth and endureth tribulation, through fervent love of God, soon shall attain to great grace and virtues, and shall be lord of this world, and shall have a foretaste of the next and glorious world. Everything that a man doeth, good or evil, he doeth it unto himself; therefore, be not offended with him that doeth thee an injury, for rather oughtest thou to have humble patience with him, and only grieve within thee for his sin, taking compassion on him and praying God earnestly for him. The stronger a man is to endure and suffer patiently injuries and tribulations, for love of God, the greater is he in the sight of God, and no more; and the weaker a man is to endure pain and adversity, for love of God, the less is he in the sight of God. If any man praise thee, speaking well of thee, render thou that praise to God alone; and if any man speak evil of thee, or revile thee, aid thou him, speaking evil of thyself, and worse. If thou wilt make good thine own cause, strive ever to make it appear ill, and uphold thy fellow's cause, ever imputing guilt to thyself, and ever praising and truly excusing thy neighbour. When any man would contend or have the law of thee, if thou wouldst win, lose; and then shalt thou win; but if thou wouldst go to law to win, when thou thinkest to win, then shalt thou find thou hast lost heavily. Therefore, my brother, believe of a surety, the straight way of salvation is the way to perdition. But when we are not good bearers of tribulation, then we cannot be seekers after everlasting consolations. Much greater consolation and a more worthy thing it is to suffer injuries and revilings patiently, without murmuring, for love of God, than to feed a hundred poor folk and fast continually every day. But how shall it profit a man, or what shall it avail him, to despise himself and afflict his body with great fastings and vigils and scourgings, if he be unable to endure a small injury from his neighbour? For which thing, a man shall receive a much greater reward and greater merit than for all the afflictions a man can give to himself of his own will; because to endure the revilings and injuries of one's neighbour, and humble patience and without murmuring, purgeth sin away much more quickly than doth a fount of many tears. Blessed is the man that ever holdeth before the eyes of the mind the memory of his sins and the good gifts of God; for he will endure with patience every tribulation and adversity, whereby he looketh for great consolations. The truly humble man looketh for no reward nor merit from God, but striveth ever only how he can give satisfaction in all things, owning himself God's debtor: and every good thing he hath, that, he knoweth he hath through the goodness of God, and not through any merit of his own; and every adversity he endureth, he knoweth it to be truly because of his sins. A certain friar asked Friar Giles, saying, "If in our time any great adversity, or tribulation, should befall, what should we do in that case?" To whom Friar Giles answered, saying, "My brother, I would have thee know that if the Lord rained down stones and arrows from heaven, they could not injure nor do any hurt to us, if we were such men as we ought to be; for if a man were verily what he ought to be, he would transmute every evil and every tribulation into good; for we know what the apostle said, that all things work together for good to them that love God: even so all things work together for ill and to the condemnation of him that hath an evil will. If thou wilt save thyself and go to celestial glory, thou shalt desire no vengeance nor punishment of any creature; for the heritage of the saints is ever to do good and ever to suffer evil. If thou knewest in very truth how grievously thou hast offended thy Creator, thou wouldst know that it is a worthy and just thing that all creatures should persecute thee and give thee pain and tribulation, in order that these creatures might take vengeance for the offences thou hast done to their Creator. A high and great virtue it is for a man to overcome himself; for he that overcometh himself shall overcome all his enemies, and attain to all good. And yet a greater virtue would it be if a man suffered himself to be overcome by all men; for he would be lord over all his enemies, to wit, his vices, the devil, the world, and his own flesh. If thou wilt save thyself, renounce and despise all consolation that the things of this world and all mortal creatures can give thee; for greater and more frequent are the falls that come through prosperity and through consolation than are those that come through adversity and tribulation." Once on a time a religious was murmuring against his superior, in the presence of Friar Giles, by reason of a harsh obedience he had laid upon him; to whom Friar Giles said, "My dearest, the more thou murmurest the heavier is the weight of thy burden, and the harder shall it be to thee to bear; and the more humbly and devoutly thou shalt place thy neck under the yoke of holy obedience, the lighter and easier will that obedience be to bear. But methinks thou wouldst not be rebuked in this world, for love of Christ, and yet wouldst be with Christ in the next world; thou wouldst not be persecuted or cursed for Christ's sake in this world, and in the next, wouldst be blessed and received by Christ; thou wouldst not labour in this world, and in the next, wouldst rest and be at peace. I tell thee, friar, friar, thou art sorely beguiled; for by the way of poverty and of shame and of reviling a man cometh to true celestial honour; and by enduring patiently mocking and cursing, for love of Christ, a man shall come to the glory of Christ. Therefore, well saith a wordly proverb,

> He whose gifts cost him no woe,
> Good gifts from others must forgoe.

How useful is the nature of the horse! for how swiftly soever the horse runneth, he yet letteth himself be ruled and guided, and leapeth hither and thither, and forward and backward, according to the will of his rider: and so, likewise, ought the servant of God to do, to wit, he should let himself be ruled, guided, turned aside, and bent, according to the will of his superior, or of any other man, for love of Christ. If thou wouldst be perfect, strive diligently to be full of grace and virtue, and fight valiantly against vice, enduring patiently every adversity for the love of thy Lord, that was mocked and afflicted and reviled and scourged and crucified and slain for love of thee, and not for His own sin, nor for His glory, nor for His profit, but only for thy salvation. And to do all this that I have told thee, above all things it is necessary that thou overcome thyself; for little shall it profit a man to lead and draw souls to God, if first he overcome not himself, and lead and draw himself to God."

VI. *Chapter of sloth.*

The slothful man loseth both this world and the next; for himself beareth no fruit and he profiteth not another. It is impossible for a man to gain virtue without diligence and great toil. When thou canst abide in a safe place stand not in a perilous place: he abideth in a safe place who striveth and suffereth and worketh and toileth through God, and for the Lord God; and not through fear of punishment, or for a price, but for love of God. The man that refuseth to suffer and labour for love of Christ, verily he refuseth the glory of Christ; and even as diligence is useful and profitable to us, so is negligence ever against us. Even as sloth is the way that leads to hell, so is holy diligence the way that leads to heaven. A man ought to be very diligent to gain and keep virtue and the grace of God, ever labouring faithfully with this grace and virtue; for many times it befalleth that the man who laboureth not faithfully loseth the fruit for the leaves, or the grain for the straw. To some God giveth of His grace good fruit with few leaves; to others He giveth fruit and leaves together; and there are others that have neither fruit nor leaves. Methinks 'tis a greater thing to know how to guard and keep well the good gifts and graces given to us by the Lord, than to know how to gain them. For albeit a man may know well how to gain, yet if he know not how to save and treasure up, he shall never be rich; but some there be that make their gains little by little, and are grown rich because they save well their gains and their treasure. Oh, how much water would the Tiber have stored up if it flowed not away to the sea! Man asketh of God an infinite gift, that is without measure and without bounds, and yet will not love God, save with measure and with bounds. He that would be loved of God and have infinite reward from Him, beyond all bounds and beyond all measure, let him love God beyond all bounds and beyond all measure, and ever serve Him infinitely. Blessed is he that loveth God with all his heart and with all his mind, and ever afflicteth his body and his mind for love of God, seeking no reward under heaven, but accounting himself only a debtor. If a man were in sore poverty and need, and another man said to him, "I will lend thee a very precious thing for the space of three days: know that if thou use well this thing within this term of three days thou shalt gain an infinite treasure, and be rich evermore," is it not a sure thing that this poor man would be very careful to use well and diligently this thing so precious, and would strive much to make it fruitful and profit him well: so do I say likewise that this thing lent unto us by the hand of God is our body, which the good God hath lent us for three days; for all our times and years are but as three days in the sight of God. Therefore if thou wouldst be rich and enjoy the divine sweetness ever-lastingly, strive to labour well and make this thing, lent by the hand of God, bear good fruit; to wit, thy body, in this space of three days; to wit, in the brief time of thy life: for if thou art not careful of gain in this present life, while thou hast yet time, thou shalt not enjoy that everlasting riches nor find holy rest in that celestial peace everlastingly. But if all the possessions of the world were in the hands of one person that never turned them to account himself, nor put them out for others to use, what fruit or what profit would he have of those things? Of a surety, neither profit nor fruit would he have. But it might well be that a man, having few possessions and using them well, should have much profit and a great abundance of fruit for himself and for others. A worldly proverb saith, "Never set an empty pot on the fire hoping thy neighbour will come and fill it." And so likewise God willeth that no grace be left empty; for the good God never giveth a grace to any man that it be kept empty, rather doth he give it that a man may use it and bring forth fruit of good works; for good-will sufficeth not except a man strive to pursue it and use it to a profit of holy words. On a time a wayfarer said to Friar Giles, "Father, I pray thee give me some consolation." Whereto Friar Giles answered, "My brother, strive to stand well with God and straightway shalt thou have the consolation thou needest; for if a man make not a pure dwelling-place ready in his soul, wherein God may abide and rest, never shall he find an abiding place nor rest nor true consolation in any creature. When a man would work evil he never asketh much counsel for the doing thereof; but, ere they do good, many folk seek much counsel and make long delay." Once Friar Giles said to his companions, "My brethren, methinks, in these days, one findeth no man that would do those things that he seeth are most profitable, and not only for the soul but also for the body. Believe me, my brethren, I can swear, of a truth, that the more a man flees and shuns the burden and the yoke of Christ the more grievous he maketh it to himself and the more heavily it weigheth upon him, and the greater is the burden; but the more ardently a man taketh up his burden, ever heaping up more weight of his own will, the lighter and the more pleasant he feeleth it to bear. Would to God that men would labour to win the good things of the body, since they would win also those of the soul; forasmuch as the body and the soul, without any doubt, must ever be joined together, either to suffer or to enjoy; to wit, either ever to suffer together in hell everlasting pains and boundless torments, or, through the merits of good works, to enjoy perpetual joys and ineffable consolations with the saints and angels in paradise. Because, if a man laboured well, or forgave well, yet lacked humility, his good deeds would be turned to evil; for many have there been that have wrought many works that seemed good and praiseworthy, but since they lacked humility they were discovered and known to be done through pride; and their deeds have shown this, for things done through humility are never corrupted." A friar said to Friar Giles, "Father, methinks we know not yet how to understand our own good." To whom Friar Giles answered, "My brother, of a surety each man worketh the art he hath learned, for no man can work well except he have first learned: wherefore I would have thee know, my brother, that the noblest art in this world is the art of working well; and who could know that art except first he learn it? Blessed is that man in whom no created thing can beget evil; but yet more blessed is he that receiveth in himself good edification from all things he sees or hears."

VII. *Chapter of the contempt of temporal things.*

Many sorrows and many woes will the miserable man suffer that putteth his desire and his heart and his hope in earthly things, whereby he forsaketh and loseth heavenly things, and at last shall even lose also these earthly things. The eagle soareth very high, but if she had tied a weight to her wings she would not be able to fly very high: and even so for the weight of earthly things a man cannot fly on high, to wit, he cannot attain to perfection; but the wise man that bindeth the weight of the remembrance of death and judgment to the wings of his heart, could not for the great fear thereof go astray nor fly at the vanities nor riches of this world, which are a cause of damnation. Every day we see worldly men toil and moil much and encounter great bodily perils to gain these false riches; and after they have toiled and gained much, in a moment they die and leave behind all that they gained in their lives; therefore put not thy trust in this false world that beguileth every man that believeth therein, for it is a liar. But whoso desireth and would be great and truly rich, let him seek after and love everlasting riches, and good things that ever savour sweetly and never satiate and never grow less. If we would not go astray, let us take pattern from the beasts and the birds, for these, when they are fed, are content and seek not their living save from hour to hour when their need cometh: even so should a man be content with satisfying his needs temperately, and not seek after superfluities. Friar Giles said that the ant was not so pleasing to St. Francis as other living things because of the great diligence she hath in gathering together and storing up, in the time of summer, a treasure of grain for the winter; but he was wont to say that the birds pleased him much more, because they laid not up one day for the next. But yet the ant tea-cheth us that we ought not to be slothful in the summer of this present life, so that we be not found empty and barren in the winter of the last day and judgment.

VIII. *Chapter of holy chastity.*

Our miserable and frail human flesh is like unto the swine that ever rejoiceth to wallow and bemire himself in filth, choosing the mire for his own delight. Our flesh is the devil's knight-errant, for it fighteth and resisteth all those things that pertain to God and to our salvation. A friar asked Friar Giles, saying unto him, "Father, teach me in what manner we may guard ourselves from carnal sin." To whom Friar Giles answered, "My brother, he that would move any great weight or any great stone from one place to another, it behoveth him to strive to move it by skill rather than by force. And so likewise, if we will overcome carnal sin and gain the virtue of chastity, we shall rather gain it by humility and by good and discreet spiritual guidance, than by our presumptuous austerities and by the violence of penance. Every sin cloudeth and darkens holy and shining chastity, for chastity is like unto a bright mirror that is clouded and darkened, not only by the touch of foul things, but also by the breath of man. It is impossible for a man to attain to any spiritual grace so long as he findeth him inclined to carnal lust; therefore, thou mayst turn and turn again, as it please thee, and thou shalt find no other remedy, nor be able to attain to spiritual grace, except thou trample under foot every carnal sin. Therefore, fight valiantly against thy sensual and frail flesh, thy proper enemy, that ever striveth against thee, day and night; let him that overcometh this flesh our mortal foe, know of a surety that he hath overcome and routed all his enemies, and soon shall attain to spiritual grace and to every good state of virtue and of perfection." Said Friar Giles, "Among all the other virtues I most do prize the virtue of chastity; for sweetest chastity hath in itself alone some perfection; but no other virtue can be perfect without chastity." A friar asked Friar Giles, saying, "Father, is not charity a greater and more excellent virtue than chastity?" And Friar Giles said, "Tell me, brother, what thing in this world is found more chaste than holy charity?" Many a time did Friar Giles chant this little song—

> O holy chastity,
> How great a good thou holdest!
> How precious to possess!
> For such sweet fragrance issueth forth from thee,
> The taste thereof the wise alone can know:
> Therefore the foolish never learn thy worth.

A friar asked Friar Giles, saying, "Father, thou that commendest so the virtue of chastity, prithee make plain to me what chastity is." Whereto Friar Giles answered, "My brother, I tell thee that the diligent custody and continual watching of our bodily and spiritual senses, keeping them pure and spotless before God—that is truly called chastity."

IX. *Chapter of temptations.*

The greater graces that a man receiveth from God cannot be possessed in peace and quietness, for many contrary things and many tribulations and many adversities rise up against these graces, because the more acceptable a man is in the sight of God, the more mightily is he assailed and warred against by the devil. Therefore it behoveth a man never to cease from fighting, that he may pursue that grace he hath received from God; for the fiercer the battle the more precious shall be the crown, if he conquers in the fight. But we have not many battles, nor many hindrances, nor many temptations; for we are not such as we ought to be in the spiritual life. But, nevertheless, true it is that if a man walk warily and well in the way of God, he shall have neither toil nor weariness on his journey; but the man that walketh in the way of the world shall ne'er be able to flee from the many toils, the weariness, the anguish, the tribulations, and sorrows, even to the day of his death. Said a friar to Friar Giles, "My father, methinks thou sayest two things, one contrary to the other; for thou didst first say that the more acceptable and the more virtuous a man is in the sight of God, the more hindrances and the more battles he hath in the spiritual life, and then thou saidst the contrary; to wit, that the man who walked warily and well in the way of God would feel neither toil nor weariness on his journey." Whereto Friar Giles made plain the contrariness of these two sayings, and answered thus, "My brother, of a surety the devils assail men of good will with mightier temptations than they do others that have not good will, I mean, in the sight of God. But the man that walketh warily and fervently in the way of God, what toil, what weariness, and what hurt can the devils and all the adversities of the world bring on him? Doth he not know and see that he selleth his wares for a price a thousandfold higher than they are worth? But I tell thee more: of a surety he that were kindled with the fire of divine love, the more mightily he were assailed by sins, the more would he hate and abominate them. The worst devils are wont to pursue and tempt a man when he is weighed down by some infirmity or bodily weakness, or by great cold, or anguish, or when he is ahungered or athirst, or when he hath suffered some injury, or shame, or temporal or spiritual hurt; for these evil spirits know that it is in hours and moments such as these that a man is more apt to receive temptations. But I say unto thee that for every temptation and for every sin thou overcomest thou shalt gain in virtue; and that if thou conquer that sin that warreth against thee, thou shalt receive therefore the greater grace and a greater crown of victory." A friar asked counsel of Friar Giles, saying, "Father, ofttimes am I tempted by a sore temptation, and oft have I prayed to God to be delivered therefrom, and yet the Lord taketh it not away from me. Give me thy counsel, father, what ought I to do?" Whereto Friar Giles answered, "My brother, the more richly a king harnesseth his knights with noble armour and strong, the more valiantly he desireth they should fight against his enemies, for love of him." A friar asked Friar Giles, saying, "Father, what remedy can I find that I may go more willingly to prayer and with a more fervent desire? for when I go to pray, I am hard, slothful, withered, and slack." Whereto Friar Giles answered, saying, "A king hath two servants, and the one is armed for battle, but the other hath no arms wherewith to fight; and both would go forth to battle and fight against the enemies of the king. He that is armed goeth forth to battle and fighteth valiantly; but the other that is unarmed saith thus to his lord, 'My lord, thou seest I am naked and without arms, but for love of thee fain would I join the battle and fight thus unarmed as I am.' And then the good king, beholding the love of his trusty servant, saith to his ministers, 'Go with this my servant, clothe him with all those arms that are needful for the fight, in order that he may hie securely forth to battle; and mark ye all his arms with my royal scutcheon, that he be known as my trusty knight.' And even so, ofttimes it befalleth a man, when he goeth forth to pray and findeth himself naked, indevout, slothful, and hardened in spirit; but, nevertheless, let him gird himself, for love of the Lord, and go forth to the battle of prayer; and then our good King and Lord, beholding the wrestling of his knight, giveth him fervent devotion and good will by the hands of his ministering angels. Some time this befalleth: a man setteth about some great work of heavy labour, as to clear and till the ground, or a vineyard, that in due season he may be able to gather the fruit thereof. And many men, because of the great labour and the many toils, grow a-weary and repent them of the work they have begun; but if a man sweat and toil till the time of harvest, then he forgetteth all his heaviness; he is consoled and glad, beholding the fruit he shall enjoy. Even so, a man that is strong under temptations shall attain to many consolations; for after tribulation, saith St. Paul, cometh consolation and the crown of eternal life: and not only in heaven shall the reward be given to them that resist temptation, but also in this life, even as the psalmist saith, 'Lord, in the multitude of my temptations and my sorrows thy comforts delight my soul'; so that the greater the temptation and the fight, the more glorious shall be the crown." A friar asked counsel of Friar Giles touching a temptation, saying, "O father, I am tempted by two sore temptations: one is, that when I do some good thing, anon I am tempted by vainglory; the other is, when I work any evil I fall into such sadness and such dejection that I well-nigh sink into despair." Whereto Friar Giles answered, "My brother, well dost thou and wisely to grieve for thy sin, but I counsel thee to grieve temperately and discreetly, and ever shouldst thou remember that God's mercy is greater than thy sin. But if, in His infinite mercy, God accepteth the repentance of a man that is a great sinner and one that sinneth wilfully, when he repents, thinkest thou this good God will forsake the good sinner that sinneth against his will, when he is contrite and repentant? I counsel thee, also, faint not in well-doing through fear of vainglory; for if a man said, when he should sow his seed, 'I will not sow, for if I were to sow, haply the birds would come and eat thereof'; and, if saying thus, he sowed not his seed, of a surety he would gather no corn that year. But if he sowed his seed, albeit the birds did eat of that seed, yet the labourer would reap the greater part; even so a man, assailed by vainglory, if he do good not for the sake of vainglory, but ever fighteth against it, I say he shall not lose the merit of the good he hath done, because he is tempted." A friar said to Friar Giles, "It is told that St. Bernard once recited the seven penitential psalms with such peace of mind and such devotion that he thought of naught save the proper meaning of the aforesaid psalms." Whereto Friar Giles thus made answer, "My brother, I deem there is much more prowess in a lord that holdeth his castle when it is besieged and assaulted by his enemies, defending it so valiantly that he letteth not one of his enemies enter therein, than there is in one that liveth in peace and hath no enemy."

X. *Chapter of holy penitence.*

A man ought ever to afflict himself much and mortify his body, and suffer willingly every injury, tribulation, anguish, sorrow, shame, contempt, reproach, adversity, and persecution, for love of our good Lord and Master, Jesus Christ, who gave us the example in Himself; for from the first day of His glorious Nativity, until His most holy Passion, He ever endured anguish, tribulation, sorrow, contempt, pain, and persecution, solely for our salvation. Therefore, if we would attain to a state of grace, above all things it is necessary that we walk, as far as lieth in us, in the paths and in the footsteps of our good Master, Jesus Christ. A secular once asked of Friar Giles, saying, "Father, in what way can we men in the world attain to a state of grace?" Whereto Friar Giles answered, "My brother, a man ought first to grieve for his sins, with great contrition of heart, and then he should confess to the priest with bitterness and sorrow of heart, accusing himself sincerely, without concealment and without excuse: then he must fulfil the penance perfectly that is given and laid upon him by his confessor. Likewise, he must guard himself against every vice and every sin, and against every occasion of sin; and also he must exercise himself in good and virtuous works before God and towards his neighbour; and, doing these things, a man shall attain to a state of grace and of virtue. Blessed is that man that hath continual sorrow for his sins, bewailing them ever, day and night, in bitterness of heart, solely for the offences he hath done to God! Blessed is the man that hath ever before the eyes of his mind the afflictions and the pains and the sorrows of Jesus Christ, and that for love of Him neither desireth nor receiveth any temporal consolation in this bitter and stormy world, until he attain to that heavenly consolation of life eternal, where all his desires shall be fully satisfied with gladness."

XI. *Chapter of holy prayer.*

Prayer is the beginning, middle, and end of all good: prayer illumines the soul, and through prayer the soul distinguishes good from evil. Every sinful man ought to make this prayer with a fervent heart, every day unceasingly; to wit, let him pray humbly to God to give him a perfect knowledge of his own misery and of his sins and of the blessings he hath received, and doth receive, from this good God. But the man that knoweth not how to pray, how shall he know God? All those that would be saved, if they are persons of true understanding, above all things it is necessary that they be at last converted to holy prayer. Friar Giles said, "If a man had a son, guilty of so many offences that he was condemned to death, or to be banished from the city, of a surety this man would be very diligent, and strive with all his might, both day and night, and at every hour, to obtain pardon for this his son, and save him from death or banishment, making earnest prayers and supplications, and giving presents or paying fines, to the uttermost of his means, both of himself or through his friends and kinsfolk. Therefore, if a man do this for his son that is mortal, how much more diligent ought a man to be in beseeching God, by his own prayers and through the prayers of good men in this world, and through His saints in the other world, for his own soul that is immortal, when she is banished from the celestial city, or doomed to everlasting death for sin and wickedness." A friar said to Friar Giles, "Father, methinks a man ought to grieve much, and be exceeding sorrowful, when he cannot have the grace of devotion in his prayers." Whereto Friar Giles answered, "My brother, I counsel thee, go very gently about thy business; for if thou hadst a little good wine in a cask, and in that cask the lees were still below this good wine, of a surety thou wouldst not shake or move that cask about, lest thou mingle the good wine with the lees. And so I say: as long as prayer is not free from all carnal and sinful lust it shall receive no divine consolation; for that prayer which is mingled with the lees of fleshly lusts is not clear in the sight of God. Therefore, a man ought to strive, with all his might, to free himself from all lees of vicious lusts, in order that his prayers be pure in the sight of God, and that he receive devotion and divine consolation therefrom." A friar asked Friar Giles, saying, "Father, wherefore doth this thing come to pass: that when a man is worshipping God he is more sorely tempted, assailed, and troubled in his mind than at any other time?" Whereto Friar Giles thus answered, "When any man hath a suit to further before a judge, and he goeth to plead his own cause, as 'twere asking counsel and aid, and his adversary heareth this, doth he not straightway appear before the judge and oppose and gainsay the petition of that man, and so give him great hindrance, as 'twere disproving all he said? Even so it befalleth when a man goeth forth to pray; forasmuch as he asketh God's help in his cause, straightway his adversary, the devil, appeareth with his temptations and maketh great resistance and opposition, and striveth, with all his might and cunning and devices, to hinder this prayer, so that it be not acceptable in God's sight, and that the man may have neither merit nor consolation from his prayers. And this we can see clearly, for when we speak of worldly things, then do we suffer no temptation nor distraction of mind, but if we go to prayer to delight and comfort the soul with God, anon we feel our soul smitten with divers arrows, to wit, divers temptations, which the devils put in our way to warp our minds, in order that the soul have neither joy nor consolation from those things that the said soul hath uttered to God." Friar Giles said that a prayerful man was like unto a good knight at battle, who, albeit he were pierced or smitten by his enemy, departeth not straightway from the battle, but rather resisteth manfully to gain the victory over his enemy, in order that the victory won, he may be comforted and rejoice in that victory; but if he departed from the battle when he was smitten or wounded, of a surety he would suffer confusion and shame and dishonour. And so should we do likewise; to wit, never depart from prayer for any temptation, but rather resist stoutly; for blessed is the man that endureth temptations, as the Apostle saith, for by overcoming them he shall receive the crown of eternal life; but if a man cease from prayer because of temptations, of a surety he shall suffer confusion, defeat, and discomfiture at the hands of his enemy, the devil." A friar said to Friar Giles, "Father, I have seen certain men that have received from God the grace of devotion and tears in their prayers, and none of these graces can I feel when I pray unto God." Whereto Friar Giles answered, "My brother, I counsel thee, labour faithfully and humbly in thy prayers, for the fruits of the earth are not to be had without much toil and labour beforehand; and even after this labour the desired fruit followeth not straightway, before the time and season are come: even so God giveth not this grace forthwith to a prayerful man until the convenient time be come, and the mind be purged from every carnal affection and sin. Therefore, my brother, labour humbly in thy prayer; for God, who is all-good and all-gracious, knoweth all things and discerneth the better way: when the time and the season are come, He, of His loving-kindness, will give much fruit of consolation." Another friar said to Friar Giles, "What art thou doing, Friar Giles? What art thou doing?" He answered, "I am doing ill." And that friar said, "What ill art thou doing?" Then Friar Giles turned to another friar and bespake him thus, "Tell me, my friar, who thinkest thou is the readier, our God to grant us His grace, or we to receive it?" And that friar answered, "Of a surety, God is more ready to give us His grace than we are to receive it." And then Friar Giles said, "Then do we well?" And that friar said, "Nay, we do ill." And then Friar Giles turned to the first friar and said, "Behold, friar, it is clearly shown that we do ill; and what I answered was true, to wit, that I am doing ill." Said Friar Giles, "Many works are commended and praised by Holy Scripture, to wit, the works of mercy and other holy works; but when the Lord spake of prayer, He spake thus, 'Your heavenly Father seeketh and desireth of men that they worship Him on earth in spirit and in truth.'" Friar Giles said likewise that the true religious are like unto wolves; for they seldom issue forth in public places save for hard necessity, and incontinently do strive to return to their hiding-place without much converse or dwelling with men. Good works adorn the soul, but, above all other works, prayer adorns and illumines the soul. A friar, the companion and familiar of Friar Giles, said, "Father, wherefore goest thou not sometimes to discourse of the things of God, and teach and win the salvation of Christian souls?" Whereto Friar Giles answered, "My brother, I desire to fulfil my duty to my neighbour with humility and without hurt to my soul, I mean by prayer." And that friar said to him, "At least if thou went sometimes to visit thy kinsfolk!" And Friar Giles answered, "Knowest thou not that Christ saith in the gospel, 'Every one that hath forsaken father or mother, or brethren or sisters, or possessions, for My name's sake, shall receive a hundredfold.'" Again he said, "A man of noble birth entered the Order, whose riches were worth perchance sixty thousand pounds: therefore, great rewards await them that forsake great riches, for love of God; since God giveth them a hundredfold more. But blind are we that when we behold any man virtuous and gracious in the sight of God, we cannot understand his perfection because of our own imperfection and blindness. But if a man were truly spiritual, hardly would he desire to behold or to hear any man save for great necessity; for the truly spiritual man desireth ever to dwell apart from men, and to be one with God through contemplation." Then said Friar Giles to another friar, "Father, fain would I know, what is contemplation?" And that friar said, "Father, that truly know not I." And then Friar Giles said, "Methinks the high grace of contemplation is a divine flame and a sweet emanation of the Holy Ghost, and a rapture and an exaltation of the mind, which is inebriated in the contemplation of that ineffable savour of divine sweetness; 'tis a sweet and peaceful and gentle delight of the soul that is lifted up and rapt in great marvel at the glory of supernal and celestial things—a burning inward sense of celestial and unspeakable glory."

XII. *Chapter of holy spiritual prudence.*

O servant of the King of heaven, thou that wouldst learn the mysteries and the profitable and virtuous lessons of holy spiritual doctrine, open well the ears of the understanding of thy soul, and receive with thy heart's desire, and carefully keep in the chamber of thy memory, the precious treasure of these doctrines and precepts and spiritual admonitions which I declare to thee: thereby shalt thou be illumined and guided on thy journey—the journey of the spiritual life— and shalt be defended from the wicked and cunning assaults of thine enemies, real and shadowy, and shalt walk securely, with humble boldness, voyaging on this stormy sea, to wit, of this present life, until thou come to the longed-for haven of salvation. Therefore, my son, hearken and mark well what I say unto thee. If thou wouldst see well, pluck out thine eyes and be blind; if thou wouldst hear well, be deaf; if thou wouldst speak well, be dumb; if thou wouldst walk well, stand still and walk with thy mind; if thou wouldst work well, cut off thy hands and work with thy heart; if thou wouldst love well, hate thyself; if thou wouldst live well, mortify thyself; if thou wouldst gain well and grow rich, lose and be poor; if thou wouldst enjoy well and take thine ease, afflict thyself and be ever sorrowful; if thou wouldst dwell secure, be ever afeard and in dread of thyself; if thou wouldst be exalted and have great honour, abase and decry thyself; if thou wouldst be held in great reverence, despise thyself and do reverence unto them that revile thee and spitefully use thee; if thou wouldst have good always, suffer ill always; if thou wouldst be blessed, desire that all men curse thee and speak evil of thee; if thou wouldst have true and everlasting peace, labour and afflict thyself, and desire every temporal affliction. O, how great is the wisdom that knoweth and doeth these things! But because these things are great and very lofty, therefore are they vouchsafed by God to few men. But, verily, whoso striveth well after all the aforesaid things, and doeth them, I say he will need to go neither to Bologna nor to Paris to learn other theology; for if a man lived a thousand years, and had naught to do with outward things and naught to say with his tongue, I say he would have enough to do with the inward discipline of his heart, labouring within him for the purgation and ruling and justification of his mind and of his soul. A man should neither desire, nor behold, nor hear, nor discourse of aught save in so far as it may be profitable to his soul. The man that knoweth not himself is not known; therefore, woe unto us that receive gifts and graces from the Lord and understand them not; but woe, and greater woe, unto those that neither receive them nor know them, nor even care to gain them or possess them! Man that is made in the image of God changeth even as he willeth, but the good God never changeth.

XIII. *Chapter of profitable and unprofitable knowledge.*

The man that would know much, should work much and humble himself much, abasing himself and bowing down his head, so that his belly goeth on the ground: then the Lord will give him much knowledge and wisdom. The highest wisdom is to be steadfast in well-doing, working virtuously and well, guarding oneself against every sin and every occasion of sin, ever meditating on the judgments of God. Friar Giles said, on a time, to one that would go to the schools to get knowledge, "My brother, wherefore wouldst thou go to the schools? I would have thee know that the sum of all knowledge is to fear and to love: let these two things suffice thee. For sufficient for a man's works shall his knowledge be, and no more. Vex thee not overmuch for the profit of others, but ever strive and further and do those things that are profitable to thyself; for ofttimes this befalleth: we would gain much knowledge to help others and little to help ourselves. I say unto thee, the word of God is not in the speaker, nor in the hearer, but in the true worker. Men there have been that knew not how to swim and entered the water to help those that were drowning; and it came to pass that they were all drowned together. If thou canst not save thine own soul, how shalt thou save the souls of thy neighbours? If thou canst not profit thyself, how shalt thou profit another? For it cannot be that thou lovest another's soul more than thine own. The preacher of God's word ought to be the standard-bearer, the torch and the mirror of the people. Blessed is the man that in such wise guideth others in the way of salvation and himself ceaseth not to walk in that way of salvation! Blessed is the man that in such wise inviteth others to run and himself ceaseth not to run! But more blessed is he that in such wise aideth others to gain and be rich, and himself ceaseth not to gain riches. I believe the good preacher admonishes and preaches more unto himself than to others. Methinks, the man that would convert and draw sinners to the paths of God should ever fear lest he be evilly perverted by them and drawn astray to the paths of sin and of the devil and of hell."

XIV. *Chapter of good and of evil speaking.*

The man that uttereth good words and profitable to souls is verily as 'twere the mouth of the Holy Spirit; and likewise the man that uttereth evil and unprofitable words is, of a surety, the mouth of the devil. Whenever good and spiritual men are assembled to discourse together they ought ever to speak of the beauty of virtue, in order that virtue be more pleasing to them, and that they may delight the more therein; for by delighting and taking more pleasure in virtue, the more they will be disciplined therein, and by exercising themselves therein they will be kindled to greater love thereof; and by that unceasing love and exercise of virtue, and by pleasure therein, they will ever rise to more fervent love of God and to a higher state of the soul; for which cause more gifts and more divine graces shall be vouchsafed to them by the Lord. The more a man is tempted the greater need hath he to discourse of the holy virtues; for even as a man ofttimes falleth lightly into sinful deeds through evil and sinful talk, so ofttimes through discoursing of virtue a man is lightly led and disposed to the holy works of virtue. But how shall we tell of the good that cometh from virtue? For it is so exceeding great that we cannot speak worthily of its marvellous and infinite excellence. And also, what shall we say of the evil and everlasting torments that proceed from sin? For it is an evil so great, and an abyss so deep, that it is impossible for us to comprehend or to fathom it, or, in sooth, to speak thereof. I deem it no lesser virtue to know how to keep silence well than to know how to speak well: therefore methinks a man hath need of a neck as long as the crane's, so that when he would speak, his words should pass through many joints before they came to his mouth, I mean that when a man would speak, it were needful that he should think and think again, and examine and discern right well, the how and the why, the time and the manner, and the condition of his hearers and the effect on his own self and his purpose and motives.

XV. *Chapter of good perseverance.*

What doth it profit a man to fast much and pray and give alms and afflict himself with the overpowering sense of heavenly things if he come not to the blessed haven of the salvation he desireth; to wit, the haven of good and steadfast perseverance? Some time this cometh to pass: a certain ship, very fair and mighty and strong and new, and filled with great riches, is seen on the seas; and it befalleth that through some tempest, or through the fault of the helmsman, this ship perisheth and is wrecked, and miserably sunk, and cometh not to the desired haven. What then availed all her beauty and goodness and riches since she perished thus miserably in the great waters of the sea? And, likewise, on a time, some little ship and old appeareth on the sea, with small merchandise; but having a good and skilful helmsman, she weathers the storm and escapeth from the deep waters of the sea and cometh to the desired haven: and so it befalleth men in this stormy sea of the world. Therefore, said Friar Giles, a man ought ever to fear; and albeit he abide in great prosperity, or in high estate, or in great dignity, or in great perfection, if he have not a good helmsman, to wit, a wise rule over himself, he may miserably perish in the deep waters of sin. Therefore, above all things, perseverance is needful for well-doing, as the Apostle saith, "Not he that beginneth, but he that persevereth to the end shall win the crown." When a tree springeth up, it doth not straightway wax great; and after it hath become great, it doth not forthwith yield fruit; and when it beareth fruit, not all that fruit cometh to the mouth of the lord of that tree; for much of that fruit falleth on the ground, or rots, or is spoiled; and such as this is eaten by the beasts: but yet, persevering until the proper season, the lord of that tree gathereth the greater part of the fruit thereof. Again, Friar Giles said, "What would it profit me if I tasted full a hundred years of the kingdom of heaven, if thereafter I came not to a good end?" And also he said, "I deem that these are the two greatest graces and gifts of God to him that can gain them in this life, to wit, to persevere with love in the service of God and ever guard himself from falling into sin."

XVI. *Of the true religious life.*

Friar Giles was wont to say, speaking of himself, "I would rather, as a religious in the Order, have a little of the grace of God than I would, as a secular, living in the world, have many graces of God; for many more are the perils and hindrances in the world, and much less the healing and the help than in the religious life." Friar Giles also said, "Methinks the sinful man is more afraid of his good than he is of his hurt and his evil; for he fears to enter the religious life and do penance, but fears not to offend God and injure his own soul by remaining in the hard and stubborn world and in the filthy mire of his own sins, awaiting his eternal doom at last." A secular asked Friar Giles, saying, "Father, what dost thou counsel me to do? Shall I enter the religious life, or shall I remain in the world and do good works?" Whereto Friar Giles answered, "My brother, if any needy man knew that a great treasure lay hidden in the common field, of a surety he would not ask counsel of any man to know whether it were good to dig it out and carry it to his own house; how much the more ought a man to strive and make haste, with all care and diligence, to search out that heavenly treasure which is found in the holy orders of religion, and in spiritual communities, without so much asking of counsel?" And that secular, when he heard this answer, anon gave away all he possessed to the poor, and thus, stripped of everything, entered the Order. Friar Giles was wont to say that many men entered the religious life and yet put not those things into practice and into operation that pertain to the perfect state of the holy religious life; but that such as these are like unto that ploughman that armed himself with the arms of Roland, and knew not how to fight or wield them. Not every man knoweth how to ride a restive and vicious horse, and if he yet bestrode it, perchance he would know not how to save himself from falling when the horse ran or reared. Again, Friar Giles said, "I deem it no great thing that a man may know how to enter the court of the king, nor do I esteem it a great thing that a man may know how to win some of the king's graces or favours; but the great thing is, that he know how to stand well, and abide in, and frequent the king's court, while persevering in prudence according to that is meet and fitting. The state of the court of that great King of heaven, is the holy religious life, wherein is no great labour to enter and receive some gifts and graces from God; but the great thing is that a man shall know how to live well and persevere therein discreetly, even unto death." Yet again, Friar Giles said, "I would rather live in the world, and hope and desire unceasingly and devoutly to enter the religious life, than be clothed in the habit of the holy religious life without the practice of virtuous works, and continue in sloth and negligence. Therefore, the religious ought ever to strive to live well and virtuously, knowing that he cannot live in any other state than in his professed vows." Once Friar Giles said, "Methinks the Order of the friars minor was truly sent of God for the profit and the edification of the people; but woe unto us friars if we be not such men as we ought to be. Of a surety, in this life no more blessed men than we could be found; for he is holy that followeth holiness, and he is truly good that walketh in the way of the good, and he is rich that goeth the way of the rich; for the Order of the friars minor, more than any other Order, followeth the footsteps and the ways of the best, the richest, and the holiest that ever was or ever shall be, to wit, our Lord Jesus Christ.

XVII. *Chapter of holy obedience.*

The more bound under the yoke of holy obedience the religious is, for love of God, the greater fruit of himself he will yield unto God; and the more he is subject to his superior, for God's honour, the more free and more cleansed shall he be from his sins. The truly obedient religious is like unto a knight well armed and well horsed that breaks fearlessly through the ranks of his enemies and scatters them, because none of them can do him hurt. But he that obeys with murmurings, and as one driven, is like unto an unarmed and ill-horsed knight, that when he joineth battle shall be dragged to the ground by his enemies and wounded and taken by them and sometimes cast into prison and slain. The religious that would live according to the determination of his own will, showeth that he would build a perpetual habitation in the abyss of hell. When the ox putteth his neck under the yoke, then he plougheth the earth well, so that it bringeth forth good fruit in due season; but when the ox goeth wandering around, the ground is left untilled and wild, and giveth not fruit in its season. Even so the religious that bendeth his neck under the yoke of obedience yieldeth much fruit to the Lord God in its time; but he that is not obedient with a good heart to his superior, is barren and wild and without any fruit from his vows. Wise and great-hearted men bend their necks readily, without fear and without doubt, under the yoke of holy obedience; but foolish and fainthearted men strive to wrest their necks from under the yoke of holy obedience, and then would obey no creature. I deem it a greater perfection in the servant of God to obey his superior with a pure heart, for reverence and love of God, than it would be to obey God in person if He commanded him: for he that is obedient to the Lord's vicar would surely obey sooner the Lord Himself if He commanded him. Methinks also that if any man having the grace of speaking with angels had promised obedience to another, and it befell that while he was standing and discoursing with these angels this other man to whom he had promised obedience called him, I say, that straightway he ought to leave his converse with the angels and run to do that obedience, for honour of God. He that hath put his neck under the yoke of holy obedience, and then would draw back his neck from under that obedience, that he might follow a life of greater perfection, I say, that if he be not first perfect in the state of obedience, it is a sign of great pride that lieth hidden in his soul. Obedience is the way that leadeth to every good and every virtue, and disobedience is the way to every evil and every vice.

XVIII. *Chapter of the remembrance of death.*

If a man had the remembrance of his death and of the last eternal judgment and of the pains and the torments of damned souls ever before the eyes of his mind, of a surety, nevermore would the desire come upon him to sin or to offend God. But if it were possible that any man had lived from the beginning of the world, even to the time that now is, and during all this time had endured every adversity, tribulation, pain, affliction, and sorrow, and if he were to die, and his soul should go to receive everlasting reward in heaven, what hurt would all that ill he had endured, in past times, do him? And so, likewise, if a man during all the aforesaid time had had every good thing and every joy and pleasure and consolation the world could give, and then when he died his soul should receive the everlasting pains of hell, what would all the good things he had received, during that past time, profit him? An unstable man said to Friar Giles, "I tell thee, fain would I live much time in this world and have great riches and abundance of all things, and I would be greatly honoured." Whereto Friar Giles answered, "My brother, but if thou wert lord of all the world, and shouldst live therein for a thousand years in every joy and delight and pleasure and temporal consolation, ah, tell me, what reward or what merit wouldst thou expect to have from this thy miserable flesh which thou hadst served and pleased so greatly! I say unto thee, that the man who liveth well in the sight of God, and guardeth him well from offending God, he shall surely receive from God the highest good and an infinite and everlasting reward, and great bounty and great riches, and great honour and long life eternal in that perpetual glory of heaven, whereunto may the good God, our Lord and King Jesus Christ, bring us, to the praise of Jesus Christ and of His poor little one, Francis."

THE END

www.ingramcontent.com/pod-product-compliance
Lightning Source LLC
Chambersburg PA
CBHW031549040426
42452CB00006B/255